Magna Carta
and the England
of King John

Magna Carta
and the England
of King John

Edited by Janet S. Loengard

THE BOYDELL PRESS

First published 2010
The Boydell Press, Woodbridge
Paperback edition 2015

ISBN 978 1 84383 548 6 hardback
ISBN 978 1 78327 054 5 paperback

The Boydell Press is an imprint of Boydell & Brewer Ltd
PO Box 9, Woodbridge, Suffolk IP12 3DF, UK
and of Boydell & Brewer Inc.
668 Mt Hope Avenue, Rochester, NY 14620–2731, USA
website: www.boydellandbrewer.com

A CIP catalogue record for this book is
available from the British Library

The publisher has no responsibility for the continued existence
or accuracy of URLs for external or third-party internet websites
referred to in this book, and does not guarantee that any content
on such websites is, or will remain, accurate or appropriate

Designed and typeset in Adobe Jenson Pro by
David Roberts, Pershore, Worcestershire

This publication is printed on acid-free paper

Contents

Contributors

James A. Brundage, Ahmanson-Murphy Distinguished Professor of History Emeritus at the University of Kansas, specializes in the history of medieval law, particularly canon law. His books in the field include *Medieval Canon Law* (1995), *The Profession and Practice of Medieval Canon Law* (2004) and, most recently, *Medieval Origins of the Legal Profession: Canonists, Civilians, and Courts* (2008).

David Crook was formerly an Assistant Keeper of the Public Records, The National Archives, before retiring in 2007. He published a PRO Handbook, *Records of the General Eyre*, in 1982 and has also published widely on various aspects of the general eyre and texts of some thirteenth-century plea rolls; his most recent article is 'A Petition from the prisoners in Nottingham Jail', in *Medieval Petitions: Grace and Grievance*, ed. W. M. Ormrod, G. Dodd, and A. Musson (2009).

David Crouch is Professor of Medieval History at the University of Hull. He has published widely on English, Welsh, and French political, cultural, and social history, working particularly on the medieval aristocracy. His recent books include *William Marshal* (2nd edn 2002), *Tournaments* (2005), *The Birth of Nobility* (2005), and *The English Aristocracy, 1070–1272* (forthcoming). He is currently co-editing a collection of formulary letters from the first half of the thirteenth century.

John Gillingham is a Fellow of the British Academy and Emeritus Professor of History at the London School of Economics and Political Science. He is the author of numerous articles on medieval warfare and historical writing, and has edited *Anglo-Norman Studies* vols 23–7 (2000–4). His books include *Richard I* (1999), *The English in the Twelfth Century: Imperialism, National Identity and Political Values* (2000), and with Danny Danziger *1215: The Year of Magna Carta* (2003).

Barbara A. Hanawalt is the King George III Professor of History Emerita at Ohio State University. Her most recent books include *Growing Up in Medieval London: The Experience of Childhood in History* (1993), *Of Good and Ill Repute: Gender and Social Control in Medieval England* (1999) and *The Wealth of Wives: Women, Law, and the Economy in Late Medieval London* (2007). She has also edited eight volumes of essays on medieval topics and has published a number of articles.

John Hudson is Professor of Legal History at the University of St Andrews. His books include *The Formation of the English Common Law* (1996) and an edition and translation of *The History of the Church of Abingdon* (2002, 2007). He co-edited *Law and Government in Medieval England and Normandy: Essays in Honour of Sir James Holt* (1994) and is currently completing a volume of the *Oxford History of the Laws of England*, covering the period from Alfred the Great to Magna Carta.

Janet S. Loengard is Professor of History Emerita at Moravian College. She works in legal history, with especial interest in women and property. Her most recent article is '"Which may be said to be her own": widows and goods in late medieval England', in *Medieval Domesticity*, ed. Maryanne Kowaleski and P. J. P. Goldberg (2008). She edited *London Viewers and Their Certificates, 1508–1558* (1989) and is working on the right to light in late medieval and early modern London.

James Masschaele is Professor of History at Rutgers University (New Brunswick). His publications include *Peasants, Merchants, and Markets: Inland Trade in Medieval England, 1150–1350* (1998), *Jury, State, and Society in Medieval England* (2008) and a chapter in *A Companion to the Medieval World*, ed. Carol Lansing and Edward English (2009). He is currently working on a book dealing with English peasant revolts before 1381.

Ralph V. Turner is Professor of History Emeritus at the Florida State University. He has authored numerous articles and several books on twelfth- and thirteenth-century England. Among his books are *The English Judiciary in the Age of Glanvill and Bracton, 1176–1239* (1985, 2008), *King John* (1994), *Magna Carta* (2003) and *Eleanor of Aquitaine, Queen of France and Queen of England* (2009).

Abbreviations

Annales Monastici	Henry Richards Luard, ed., *Annales Monastici*, 5 vols, Rolls Series 36 (London, 1864–9)
BL	British Library
Bracton	George E. Woodbine, ed., *Bracton on the Laws and Customs of England*, tr. with revision and notes by Samuel E. Thorne, 4 vols (Cambridge, MA, 1968–77)
Chronique des rois	Martin Bouquet, ed., *Chronique des rois de France, Receuils des Historiens de Gaulle et de la France*, 2nd ed. Léopold Delisle, 24 vols (Paris, 1864–1904)
Coggeshall	Joseph Stevenson, ed., *Radulphi de Coggeshall Chronicon Anglicanum*, Rolls Series 66 (London, 1875)
CRR	*Curia Regis Rolls of the Reigns of Richard I and John*, 7 vols (London, 1922–35)
Fitz Nigel, *Dialogue*	Richard fitz Nigel, *Dialogus de Scaccario* and *Constitutio Domus Regis: The Dialogue of the Exchequer* and *The Establishment of the Royal Household*, ed. Emilie Amt and S. D. Church (Oxford, 2007)
Giraldus Cambrensis, *Opera*	J. S. Brewer, J. F. Dimock, and G. F. Warner, eds., *Giraldi Cambrensis Opera*, 8 vols, Rolls Series 21 (London, 1861–91)
Glanvill	G. D. G. Hall, ed., *The Treatise on the Laws and Customs of England commonly called Glanvill* (Edinburgh, 1965); repr. with guide to further reading by M. T. Clanchy (Oxford, 1993)
Histoire des ducs	Francisque Michel, ed., *Histoire des ducs de Normandie et des rois d'Angleterre* (Paris, 1840)
Howden	William Stubbs, ed., *Chronica Magistri Rogeri de Hovedene*, 4 vols, Rolls Series 51 (London, 1868–71)
HWM	Anthony J. Holden and David Crouch, eds, *History of William Marshal*, trans. Stewart Gregory, 3 vols, Anglo-Norman Text Society Occasional Publications Series 4–6 (London, 2002–7)
Liber Niger Scaccarii	Thomas Hearne, ed., *Liber Niger Scaccarii*, 2 vols (Oxford, 1728)
Matthew Paris, *Chronica Majora*	Henry Richards Luard, ed., *Matthaei Parisiensis Chronica Majora*, 7 vols, Rolls Series 57 (London, 1872–84)

MIC	Monumenta iuris canonici
ODNB	*Oxford Dictionary of National Biography* online (www.oxforddnb.com)
Pipe Roll	*The Great Roll of the Pipe for the* [named year] *Year of the Reign of King Richard I/John/Henry III*
PRS	Publications of the Pipe Roll Society
RCR	Sir Francis Palgrave, ed., *Rotuli Curiae Regis*, 2 vols (London, 1834–35)
Rolls Series	*Rerum Britannicarum medii aevi scriptores, or Chronicles and Memorials of Great Britain and Ireland during the Middle Ages*, 99 vols (1858–96)
Rot. Chart.	Thomas Duffus Hardy, ed., *Rotuli Chartarum* (Record Commission, 1837)
Rot. Litt. Claus.	Thomas Duffus Hardy, ed., *Rotuli Litterarum Clausarum*, 2 vols (Record Commission, 1833–4)
Rot. Litt. Pat.	Thomas Duffus Hardy, ed., *Rotuli Litterarum Patentium*, (Record Commission, 1835)
Rymer, *Fœdera*	Thomas Rymer, *Fœdera, Conventiones, Litterae et cujuscunque generis Acta Publica*, ed. Adam Clarke and Frederick Holbrooke, 4 vols in 7 (Record Commission, 1816–69)
SCP	William Paley Baildon, ed., *Select Civil Pleas*, Selden Society 3 (London, 1890)
Stubbs, *Select Charters*	William Stubbs, ed., *Select Charters and other Illustrations of English Constitutional History*, 9th edn rev. H. W. C. Davis (London, 1913)
TNA:PRO	The National Archives: Public Record Office
Walter of Coventry	William Stubbs, ed., *Memoriale Fratris Walteri de Coventria*, 2 vols, Rolls Series 58 (London, 1872)
Wendover	Henry G. Hewlett, ed., *Rogeri de Wendover Flores Historiarum*, 3 vols, Rolls Series 84 (London, 1886–9)
William of Newburgh	*Historia Rerum Anglicarum of William of Newburgh*, in Richard Howlett, ed., *Chronicles of the Reigns of Stephen, Henry II and Richard I*, 4 vols, Rolls Series 82 (London, 1884–9)

Introduction

JANET S. LOENGARD

IT IS CERTAINLY a testament to the vitality of Magna Carta that a conference invoking its name was held in Pennsylvania almost 800 years after Runnymede. This volume has its genesis in that conference, 'Magna Carta and the World of King John', at Pennsylvania State University in March 2008. As it happened, all the papers presented there dealt primarily with England, hence the change in the title of this book. Together, they explore the economic, social, political, and personal factors which ultimately affected the relationship of king and subjects. To borrow the title of a recent volume, their theme might be said to be 'Why Magna Carta?'[1]

In both the United States and the United Kingdom, books and articles with interpretations and analyses of the Charter have appeared regularly. Their focus has shifted over time. Nineteenth century work tended to concentrate on constitutional and political history, speculating on thirteenth-century political thought and often tracing the effect of various Charter provisions on one or more later periods in British history. There was also a tendency to inject an author's view of the morality of barons and/or king into the discussion; John Hudson touches on both points in his essay here when he speaks of historians' former tendency to write in terms of 'the nature of political thinking amongst the lay elite' and of 'the moral terms in which the question of ... lay ideals for reform in 1215 used to be posed – for example, how far were the barons of 1215 self-interested, how far altruistic.' Particularly in the second half of the twentieth century, that focus shifted. Historians concerned themselves with exploring the social and economic networks of early thirteenth century England, as well as tracing the background of specific grievances, which led the barons to embark on what David Crouch in his essay refers to as the Barons' Rebellion.[2] In part this

---

[1] Natalie Fryde, *Why Magna Carta?* (Münster, 2001).

[2] There have been various discussions of the Charter in which an author's particular interests or expertise have been emphasized; for example, recent work by two academics in the area of accounting focuses on Magna Carta as a tax rebellion: Jane Frecknall-Hughes and Lynne Oates, 'King John's Tax Innovations – extortion, resistance, and the establishment of the principle of taxation by consent', *Accounting Historians Journal* 34 no. 2 (2007), 75–107, and 'John Lackland: A Fiscal Re-evaluation', in John Tiley, ed., *Studies in the History of Tax Law III* (Oxford and Portland, OR, 2009), pp. 201–26. They are of course not alone in noting the significance of taxation as a factor; in this volume David Crouch quotes J. C. Holt's remark that the events of 1215 were 'a rebellion of the king's debtors'.

may reflect changing trends in the discipline of history, but in part it must be related to the vast increase in the number of primary sources readily available to historians, thanks to the publications of county record societies, The National Archives, the Selden Society, the Ames Foundation, and other groups both British and American. The plea rolls, charters, pipe rolls, and various administrative records have led to a more nuanced view of John's governance and its reception by his subjects, baronial or other. One might suggest that the shift in focus is encapsulated in the title of Helen Maud Cam's 1965 Selden Society lecture: *Magna Carta, Event or Document?*[3]

It is, of course, not only academics and scholars who continue to find Magna Carta of absorbing interest. Like the Declaration of Independence or the Constitution in the United States, the physical document itself – in one of its four existing 1215 copies and various later reissues and exemplars – exerts a popular fascination. Its iconic status could not be better illustrated than by the sight of crowds of people – at least one hobbling with the aid of two sticks – who streamed into Oxford's Bodleian Library in December 2007 to view the four copies it holds, briefly on view there.[4] In the same year, there was widespread dismay well reported in the American news-papers when a 1297 inspeximus of the Charter, which had been on loan to the United States National Archives in Washington, DC, was withdrawn and put up for sale; the same papers chronicled its 'rescue' when it was pur-chased by a buyer who immediately announced his intention to return it to the Archives.[5] Such interest alone would surely justify an attempt to explore the England which produced a parchment so freighted with mean-ing and interpretation.

The conference did not focus on the character and personality of King John, but his qualities are the background for the events of 1215 and for this book. In the opening essay, Ralph Turner sites John with relation to his father and brother. John was not simply the ill-favoured child of a well-beloved and benevolent royal family; Turner analyses the personality and character of two generations of the Angevin dynasty, finding them all lack-ing in most of the attributes necessary for successful kingship. They were, in his assessment, greedy, cruel, and violent. But he also points up circum-stances which a medieval chronicler did not take into account or perhaps generally did not recognize: the Angevins would have faced overwhelming

---

[3] 'Magna Carta, Event or Document?', Selden Society lecture delivered in the Old Hall of Lincoln's Inn, 7 July 1965 (London, 1965).

[4] *Telegraph*, 12 December 2007: http://www.telegraph.co.uk/news/ uknews/1572181/crowds-flock-to-see-Magna-Carta-Manuscripts.html; *Guardian*, 11 December 2007: http://www.guardian.co.uk/uk/2007/dec/11/maevkennedy.

[5] 'This Magna Carta to Remain in US', *New York Times*, 19 December 2007; 'Who Bought Magna Carta?', *Wall Street Journal*, 20 December2007.

difficulties even had they exhibited more desirable personal qualities. The size and diversity of their 'empire' – the quotation marks are Turner's – would have made it difficult if not impossible to administer, given the state of communications and transportation. Moreover, the wealth of the French king was increasing as that of the English monarchs was not, threatening the financial advantage which Henry II and even Richard had enjoyed. Finally, the French monarch himself was widely admired, benefiting to no small extent from comparison with the tumultuous personal lives of Henry II and John.

Nonetheless, Turner makes clear that even without a family background which had engendered distrust and dislike among segments of his subjects, John's behaviour and his alleged behaviour – murder of a nephew, torture to death of courtiers, harsh treatment of hostages and more – coupled with his military defeats would have been enough to bring barons and clergy to the brink of rebellion.

Two further essays, by John Gillingham and David Crouch, examine contemporary perceptions of the king. John has not lacked for analysis, from the vitriolic remarks of Matthew Paris in the thirteenth century and the startlingly intemperate ones of William Stubbs in the nineteenth,[6] to the more measured comments of the Tudor chronicler Raphael Holinshed, who could be said to write more in sorrow than in anger,[7] the somewhat more favourable but conflicted analyses of historians from V. H. Galbraith to W. L. Warren,[8] and the generally critical but balanced appraisals in essays collected in *King John: New Interpretations*.[9] J. C. Holt's carefully balanced assessment may sum up John's character most succinctly: he had a

---

[6]   *Walter of Coventry*, ii, Preface: '… there is nothing in him which for a single moment calls out our better sentiments; in his prosperity there is nothing that we can admire and in his adversity nothing that we can pity. … John has neither grace nor splendour, strength nor patriotism. His history stamps him as a worse man than many who have done much more harm …' (p. xi); '… he is savage, filthy, and blasphemous in his wrath …' (p. xv) and so on.

[7]   Hollinshed's summing up of John, despite its sixteenth-century diction, sounds familiar to modern historians: while John had a princely heart, he could not bridle his affections, 'a thing verie hard in a stout stomach, and thereby [he] missed now and then to compasse that which otherwise he might verie well haue brought to passe.' *Holinshed's Chronicles of England, Scotland and Ireland*, new intro. by Vernon F. Snow, 6 vols (New York, 1976), vol. 2: England, p. 339. The text is a reprint of the 1807–8 edition.

[8]   V. H. Galbraith, 'Good Kings and Bad Kings in Medieval English History', *History* 30 (1945), 119–32; repr. in his *Kings and Chroniclers* (London, 1982), pp. 119–32; W. L. Warren, *King John* (London, 1961; 2nd edn 1978) and W. L. Warren, 'King John and the Historians', *Journal of British Studies* 1:1 (1961), 1–15.

[9]   Stephen D. Church, ed., *King John: New Interpretations* (Woodbridge, 1999), especially essays by Jim Bradbury, John Gillingham, and Ralph V. Turner.

'genius for political negotiation, for intrigue, and the manipulation of men' and he was interested and able – if ruthless – in governance.'But he lacked what helps a man most in a crisis – a level head.'[10]

Holinshed's comment about John's inability to bridle his affections is a fitting complement – albeit perhaps more favourable to the king – to John Gillingham's detailed consideration of the early thirteenth century anonymous and somewhat neglected *Histoire des ducs de Normandie et des rois d'Angleterre*, attributed to an author in the retinue of Robert de Béthune. The *Histoire* lets the reader listen to the voice of King John, rather than hearing only an interpretation of his words; the king could be crude and cruel, but a measure of stubborn bravery also appears together with considerable administrative ability. He shows himself as in no way admirable – there is little in the *Histoire*'s narrative to invite admiration – but also in the end not simply 'a very bad man ... brim-full of evil qualities', as the anonymous author does characterize him at one point.[11] Reading Gillingham's detailed and even-handed analysis of the *Histoire* provides a measured picture of John, a man who emerges still not likeable but neither cowardly nor incompetent.

David Crouch also refers to the *Histoire des ducs de Normandie et des rois d'Angleterre* and its picture of John, this time using it as one of the sources which offer an insight into the circumstances which coloured the barons' view of the king. Their 'paranoia', which Crouch chronicles, seems to have been warranted by what might be thought of as the king's own paranoia: he was fearful of his subjects (sometimes not without justification); he trusted no one, as evidenced by his taking of hostages; he could justify even the most cruel of his actions. It is not surprising, then, that fear existed as well on the part of his subjects and Crouch comments that fear 'has always been the emotion that most compels human beings to fight'. He sees it as the key to the paranoia which in turn led to the events of 1215; it is unsurprising that there was a Barons' Rebellion. What is of interest to Crouch are the barons' failure to move against the king until late in the reign, and the events that eventually triggered their rebellion. His assessment of the first is complex, dealing with both the barons' individuality and inability to form a unified faction and the benefits which John's favour conferred. On the second point, he offers a commentary on the tradition of counsel and its ability to influence kingly behaviour, the lack of meaningful consultation as a basis for policy formation in John's reign, and the attempt on John's life in 1212 which caused the king to modify his behaviour and which Crouch implies empowered the baronial opposition.

[10] 'King John', in J. C. Holt, *Magna Carta and Medieval Government* (London and Ronceverte, 1985).

[11] *Histoire des ducs*, p. 105.

One of the significant modifications Crouch mentions was a relaxing of the forest law, whose harshness in both prescription and administration had been one of the barons' longtime grievances. Its injustice affected more than noblemen and was widely felt; Ralph Turner here quotes the complaint of a monk of Eynsham Abbey about the punishment inflicted on peasant poachers. The particulars of forest law administration are set out in detail by David Crook, whose essay leaves little doubt in the reader's mind of both its brutality and the financial hardship it imposed. The 1198 assize of the forests, with its reiteration and explication of the penalties of the brutal Assize of Woodstock, while instituted under Richard would have formed the basis for the repeated visitations of the chief forester and his assistants. Crook's carefully constructed outline of the forest eyres from 1198 to 1212 and of the sums they produced makes clear their success as a fund-raising venture, although apparently the severity of the visitations abated after 1212. As Crook explains, following the crisis when the plot against the king's life was discovered in mid-August of that year, John ordered that his senior foresters demand only what had been customary under Henry II. In any event, the 1217 Charter of the Forest, echoing themes raised in the Articles of the Barons, was the eventual remedy for the excesses of the former reign.[12]

The essays by James Brundage and John Hudson look at the impact of non-English developments on the British Isles. Both take up the question of the *ius commune* and its influence, on the English church in Brundage's case and on Magna Carta itself in Hudson's. Brundage traces the rise of teaching of both canon and Roman civil law in England, leading to what he calls 'the takeover of the church by lawyers' and the result of their presence on the entire system of church courts. As more men studied law at Oxford and Cambridge, more men learned in canon and civil law were appointed to significant positions in the church administration and hierarchy and some of them came to dominate the increasingly formal and complex system of church courts. Brundage finds the influence of the *ius commune* significant, although he is of two minds about the beneficial results of a church court system increasingly dominated by lawyers. Although he mentions it only in passing – it is not the point of his essay – another result of the 'managerial takeover' was the concomitant presence of churchmen with training in Roman law as justices in the king's courts in the earlier part of the

---

[12] In a recent wide-ranging, and speculative book, Peter Linebaugh argues for the original importance of the Charter of the Forest, which he sees as having left only 'local and customary practices' over the centuries. He traces the early relationship between Magna Carta and the Forest Charter, stressing the importance of the latter in a society which depended on wood as its source of fuel and building material: Peter Linebaugh, *The Magna Carta Manifesto: Liberty and Commons for All* (Berkeley, 2008), esp. the chapter 'Two Charters'.

thirteenth century. The Roman law elements in Bracton's treatise, set out by Maitland in his *Bracton and Azo*,[13] come to mind, and with them the long-debated question of *ius commune* influence on English law.

John Hudson enters that debate in analysing *ius commune*'s place in the drafting of Magna Carta. The poles of the debate, for him, are Richard Helmholz's 1999 article 'Magna Carta and the *ius commune*'[14] and the second edition of J. C. Holt's *Magna Carta*, published in 1992.[15] Helmholz argues from a detailed analysis of various chapters that not only did drafters of the Charter know the *ius commune*, they borrowed from it when formulating a significant number of provisions; the wider point is *ius commune* influence on English common law. Holt would allow the *ius commune* a narrower role, and Hudson takes a similar position: he suggests that much of Magna Carta was derived from earlier custom and practice and '[A]s with Magna Carta, any influence [on the common law] generally seems to have been on underlying thinking or on discussion of parallel problems, rather than through the adoption of procedures from the *ius commune*.' In an appendix whose sources range from the Bible to the *Leges Willelmi* he offers some of the evidence for his conclusions.

The other three essays in the volume deal with less theoretical topics. Barbara Hanawalt investigates the administration of justice before 1215, in a world where a majority of criminal matters were brought to the courts by private appeal rather than by jury of presentment although both modes of initiating action existed,[16] and where many or most of those initiated were not decided by judgment of either judge or jury. The number of plaintiffs who failed to appear following their initial appeal, the parties who put themselves on the king's mercy and paid a fine, and the frequent court-sanctioned settlements between the parties of essentially criminal charges, might suggest an impotent judicial system but might better be seen as a legacy of Anglo-Saxon legal thinking and attitudes toward dispute settlement.[17] Hanawalt speculates that the apparent malfunctioning of procedure – ordeals which never took place or failure of clear-cut findings of guilt, for example – may mean, rather, that people initiated appeals for

---

[13] F. W. Maitland, ed., *Select Passages from the Works of Bracton and Azo*, Selden Society 8 (London, 1895).

[14] R. H. Helmholz, 'Magna Carta and the *ius commune*', *University of Chicago Law Review* 66 (1999), 297–371.

[15] J. C. Holt, *Magna Carta* (Cambridge, 1965; 2nd edn 1992).

[16] The jury of presentment of course offered a path to greater involvement in criminal cases by royal justices since a jury was obliged to voice its suspicions to them, under threat of penalty for failure to do so.

[17] See Doris M. Stenton, 'The Anglo-Saxon Inheritance', in *English Justice between the Norman Conquest and the Great Charter, 1066–1215* (Philadelphia, 1964 repr. 1966) pp. 6–21.

reasons other than seeing a criminal brought to justice. That theory goes far to explain the behaviour of both parties and judges in many instances. Because Hanawalt is interested primarily in why people behaved as they did within the framework of the courts as they found them, rather than what that behaviour meant for the development of legal institutions, she moves behind the terse accounts in the plea rolls to speculate on the parties' motivation and relationships.

Janet Loengard examines the background to clauses 7 and 8 of Magna Carta 1215, the provisions protecting widows' dower and their right not to remarry. She finds that despite the well-known occurrences recorded in the pipe rolls and early plea rolls, royal interference was not the force behind most dower litigation. While widows of all men who had held freehold land could claim dower, there was a divide between the widowed heiresses and widows of tenants-in-chief on the one hand and widows of lesser men on the other, and the king rarely interfered with the latter. It was the barons who were most concerned about their wives' dower and remarriage – and it is they whose concern is reflected in clauses 7 and 8 of the 1215 Charter (c. 7 of 1225), which deal with dower, maritagium, inheritance, and remarriage. Clause 60 of that Charter (c. 7 of 1225), which decrees that customs and liberties granted by the king to his men are to be observed by them towards their own men, may well have affected many more women. But in fact most dower litigation did not involve a dead husband's lord, and in many cases the provisions of Magna Carta may not have been a deciding factor.

James Masschaele provides a survey both detailed and sweeping of the economic condition of England in the early years of the thirteenth century. He offers a critique of several scholars' views of both inflation and deflation during the reign, finding that the first decade of the thirteenth century was actually a period of significant commercial growth, a period which began in the mid-twelfth century. His conclusion is that Magna Carta thus falls in the middle of an exceptional period of overall expansion related to a rise in commercial activity: he discusses the founding of new towns and the acquisition of commercial privileges by established towns; the burgeoning of markets and fairs; and the development of transportation. Masschaele notes that in each of these areas, it is possible to find strong evidence for growth, and that various clauses of Magna Carta in fact deal with commercial matters – an indication that commerce had become of national concern rather than simply a local preoccupation. The question of inflation – the period over which it took place and its severity – is, of course, important because it would have resulted in an increased cost of government and it has been suggested that John's escalating financial demands resulted from those rising expenses. But Masschaele argues that knowledge of price trends 'cannot really serve as a proxy for general trends or developments'. He cautions that the links between the economy and the barons' revolt against King John are not simple and draws no certain conclusions.

Finally, after discussion of him ranging from the thirteenth century to the twenty-first, there is the voice of King John himself. The king's open letter concerning William de Braose or Briouze,[18] translated with notes by David Crouch, provides compelling evidence of John's character – an insistence on procedure, a petulant conviction of his own victimization, an apparent concern for criticism by his barons – as the king makes his case against a former favourite courtier, although, as Crouch points out, the letter was written before the death of William's wife and son in Windsor Castle at the king's hands.

Something should be said to acknowledge what is *not* covered in the volume. There is no effort to assess or explain the importance of the Charter through the centuries in either its impact on political thought or its effect on governance. Additionally, the book does not present an all-inclusive picture of England even in the early thirteenth century: most importantly, the peasantry is underrepresented, touched on only tangentially in several essays. The omission was dictated by the content of contributors' papers, and is not meant to imply that peasants were an unimportant group, although admittedly they played little or no role in the formulation of the Charter and had very little short-term benefit from it, being carefully left out of its most significant provisions.[19]

It would be wrong to end this introduction without reference to two significant historians who spent much time working on King John and whose influence hovers over this volume. Doris Mary Stenton appears in the footnotes of many essays; she edited not only most of the pipe rolls for John's reign but numerous volumes of plea rolls of the same period for county record societies and the Selden Society. Her familiarity with the sources led her to a relatively positive evaluation of John in relation to the courts and the emerging common law, even as she made no attempt to assess the king's character or justify his sometimes unjustifiable conduct.[20] Sir James

---

[18] William's name is spelled in various ways and contributors to this volume have elected one or another of them. I have not attempted to impose uniformity on the point.

[19] Perhaps most importantly, it is free men who are not to be detained, arrested, deprived of freehold, outlawed or banished except by judgment of peers and law of the land (c. 39 of 1215, c. 29 of 1225). One of the few specific protections for villeins is in c. 20 of 1215 (c. 14 of 1225): if amerced for a grave offence, a villein is to be spared his agricultural implements and he is not to be amerced except by oath of honest men of the neighbourhood.

[20] 'King John and the Courts of Justice', the Raleigh Lecture of the British Academy, 1958, repr. in Stenton, *English Justice between the Norman Conquest and the Great Charter, 1066–1215*, pp. 88–114.

Clark Holt has had a significant influence on several generations of scholars. His work is cited and quoted frequently here; his *Magna Carta, The Northerners*,[21] and the essays collected in both *Magna Carta and Medieval Government* and *Colonial England, 1066–1215*,[22] among other of his publications, form a starting point for discussion of issues as diverse as the Charter's debt to the *ius commune*, the meaning of fines paid by widows for leave not to remarry, a comparison of English and French royal finance, and the state of mind of John's rebellious barons.[23]

---

[21] J. C. Holt, *The Northerners* (Oxford, 1961, paper 1962; repr. 1965, 1991).

[22] J. C. Holt, *Colonial England, 1066–1215* (London and Rio Grande, 1997).

[23] I owe thanks to Ralph Turner for reading an earlier draft of this introduction and making suggestions; any remaining errors and infelicities are of course my own.

England in 1215: An Authoritarian Angevin Dynasty Facing Multiple Threats

RALPH V. TURNER

I N SPRING 1215 King John faced a confrontation with his barons that resulted from more than his personal failings, numerous as they were. As J. E. A. Jolliffe wrote a half-century ago, Magna Carta was 'a judgment, a grand inquest upon the whole past of Angevin kingship'.[1] John faced intractable problems in defending the Angevin 'empire' assembled by his father Henry II. Under John, as under his father and his brother Richard I, England with its precocious professionalization or bureaucratization would be the 'nerve centre' of their domains. England, together with Normandy to a lesser extent, was the three Angevin monarchs' primary source of funds, a vast treasure trove for funding military campaigns, fighting off rebellions, and repelling Capetian attacks on their French possessions. Each generation had to make more excessive demands on the English, and John's rule over England differed only in degree from his two predecessors' authoritarian governance.

Even with the rich English kingdom under firm control, the Angevins found governing an 'empire' incorporating both the British Isles and Continental domains covering half of western France an impossible goal, given its size and diversity.[2] By the end of the twelfth century, the French ruler's resources were beginning to match those of Richard Lionheart, threatening his financial advantage. Richard was brutal and unrelenting in his financial exactions on both the English and the Normans, and the combination of ruthless taxation and repeated French invasions was exhausting the Normans, alienating them from their duke. Their indifference would turn into outright hostility in John's early years, causing Norman nobles' defections to the Capetian king. Under Philip II of France basic changes in the structure of French royal government brought increases in royal revenues, giving him an income close to parity with the Angevin monarchs by the first years of the thirteenth century.

John's revenues were already lagging behind Richard's in the years before his loss of Normandy in 1204, and its loss reduced his resources further.

---

[1] J. E. A. Jolliffe, *Angevin Kingship*, 2nd edn (New York, 1963), p. 349.

[2] Ralph V. Turner, 'The Problem of Survival for the Angevin "Empire": Henry II's and his Sons' Vision versus Late Twelfth-Century Realities', *American Historical Review* 100 (1995), 78–96.

Despite raising enormous sums in the years before his great campaign to recover his lost French lands in 1214, he could not match the Capetian king's growing wealth, which now included Norman revenues.[3] As the nature of Richard's and John's rule increasingly took on a 'strong military colour',[4] both engaged in a gigantic shakedown of great landholders to extort money and military service, despite doctrines of royal responsibility for the realm's general welfare. Royal records abound with evidence of arbitrary seizures of land at the Angevin king's command, referring routinely to confiscations 'by the king's will' or measures taken 'unjustly and without judgment'. For victims of the king's ill will, their only recourse was to purchase restoration to his good will by offering gifts of horses, falcons, or cash.[5] Unlike on the Continent, the English nobility endured harsh royal exactions; not only the common people suffered from the Angevin kings' predatory rule.

Although Angevin predatory practices under Richard differed only in degree from those of his brother later, it was King John who would bear greatest blame. Adding to his infamy was his failure to hold the Angevins' French lands, as he was defeated by Philip II first in 1204, then again in 1214. Possibly only Richard's early death in 1199 prevented him from having to confront a rebellion by his English subjects sometime in the new century. A chronicler wrote shortly after Richard's death, 'No age can remember or history tell of any king, even one who ruled for a long time, who demanded and took so much money from his kingdom as this king extorted and amassed within five years after his return from captivity.'[6]

Impersonal issues of shifting balances of power and resources are not the whole story in the early dissolution of the Angevin 'empire', the

---

[3] Since earliest surviving French royal accounts date only from 1202–3, comparisons of earlier Plantagenet and Capetian revenues are surmises. Comparisons are found in John W. Baldwin, *The Government of Philip Augustus: Foundations of French Royal Power in the Middle Ages* (Berkeley, 1986), and J. C. Holt, 'The Loss of Normandy and Royal Finance', in J. C. Holt and John Gillingham, eds, *War and Government in the Middle Ages* (Woodbridge, 1984), pp. 92–105. Nick Barratt analyses their figures in 'The Revenues of John and Philip Augustus Revisited', in Stephen D. Church, ed., *King John: New Interpretations* (Woodbridge, 1999), pp. 75–99. See also Barratt, 'The English Revenue of Richard I', *English Historical Review* 116 (2001), 644–56; Vincent Moss, 'Normandy and the Angevin Empire: A Study of the Norman Exchequer Rolls 1180–1204' (PhD. diss., University of Wales, Cardiff, 1996); and an earlier work, J. E. A. Jolliffe, 'The Chamber and Castle Treasures under King John', in R. W. Hunt, W. A. Pantin, and R. W. Southern, eds, *Studies in Medieval History Presented to Frederick Maurice Powicke* (Oxford, 1948), pp. 100–42 at p. 118.

[4] J. O. Prestwich, 'War and Finance in the Anglo-Norman Realm', *Transactions of the Royal Historical Society*, 4th ser. 4 (1954), 20.

[5] Jolliffe, *Angevin Kingship*, chs 2 and 3.

[6] *Coggeshall*, pp. 92–3; trans. in John Gillingham, *Richard the Lionheart* (New York, 1978), notes, p. 303.

uprising of John's English barons, and their demands for a charter of liberties. Prominent among the three Angevin kings' problems was their inability to win their subjects' hearts, due in large part to their own personalities.
Willing to resort to intimidation and violence to collect funds and compel
services, they not surprisingly aroused their subjects' fear and anger. As a
result, mutual respect and trust between the ruler and his great men was
flimsy, and in John's reign fear of the king predominated among the barons.
The Angevins' subjects, whether English or French, did not share their kings'
dedication to Henry II's creation, an Angevin 'empire' straddling the English
Channel. As Bishop William Stubbs noted in the late nineteenth century, 'a
lack of sympathy with the people he ruled ... robbed the character of Henry
II of the title of greatness'.[7] Henry and his sons failed to find a means of
binding themselves to their diverse subject peoples or of fostering any sense
of unity among them. In contrast to the Capetian kings, they had no reservoir of good will that they could draw on when making new demands
on their subjects. Unlike the favourable reports circulated about Louis VII,
malicious rumours of the sexual immorality of Henry II and his family
were widespread.[8] Henry II appeared unfavourably in any comparison of
his character with the pious and good- natured Louis. Ralph Niger wrote
that the French king 'was most clement in his character, a father to clerics, a
lover of peace, a zealot for justice, an example of kindness, guardian of the
Church, consoler of the poor, supporter of the oppressed, drinker of wine'.[9]
Louis's son Philip II sought, like his father, to present himself as a protector
of ecclesiastical liberties and a model of good lordship.

The early Plantagenets themselves acknowledged their quarrelsome
nature; Richard often joked that 'They had all come of the devil, and to
the devil they would go.'[10] One of Henry's younger sons, Count Geoffrey
of Brittany, maintained that the sons' quarrels were 'a natural property,
engrafted and inserted in us by hereditary right'.[11] To disclose what the
English thought of Henry II and his sons' rule, we can turn to chronicles
surviving from the late twelfth and early thirteenth centuries, a period that

---

[7] H. G. Richardson and G. O. Sayles, *The Governance of Mediaeval England from
the Conquest to Magna Carta* (Edinburgh, 1963), p. 265, quoting William Stubbs,
Constitutional History of England, 3 vols, 5th edn (Oxford, 1896–7), ii, p. 104.

[8] Nicholas Vincent, 'Isabella of Angoulême, John's Jezebel', in Church, *King John:
New Interpretations*, pp. 165–219 at p. 204.

[9] Robert Anstruther. ed., *The Chronicle of Ralph Niger*, Caxton Society 13 (London,
1851), *Chronicle II*, pp. 166–7, my translation.

[10] Giraldus Cambrensis, *Opera*, viii: *De principis instructione*, p. 309; trans. Joseph
Stevenson, *Gerald of Wales Concerning the Instruction of Princes* (London, 1843;
reprint Felinfach, Dyfed, 1991), p. 98.

[11] Stevenson, *Instruction of Princes*, p. 99.

has been dubbed the 'golden age' of medieval English history writing.[12] Of course, chroniclers were clerics; and beginning their careers late in Henry II's reign, they felt the after-shocks of Archbishop Thomas Becket's 1170 martyrdom that had shattered the king's reputation throughout Europe. They followed criteria established by earlier churchmen for evaluating rulers and, drawing on conventional portraits of the 'good' king, they found the Angevin kings falling short. But despite the chroniclers' biases, they can reveal something of contemporaries' expectations of their monarchs.

The forging of strong ties between Henry II and his family with the nobilities of their disparate collection of lands should have been a key goal, essential for holding together the Angevin 'empire'. Quarrels between Henry II and his sons and between siblings complicated this goal, for the sons' dissatisfactions always aided the cause of rebellious nobles, who readily allied with the sons against their father. In any case, both Anjou and Aquitaine were under-administered, and the aristocracy regarded their own lands as independent of any higher authority, limiting the Angevins' ability to raise revenues from them. Furthermore, reliance on English and Norman administrators made Angevin rule in Anjou and Aquitaine appear almost 'colonial'.[13]

Nor did the Angevin monarchs win over their English barons, who were forced to bear the military and financial burden of defending Angevin territories farther south. Unlike Louis VII of France or other Continental monarchs too weak to control their nobility, Henry II loaded ever-heavier military and fiscal burdens on his English magnates as conditions for holding their estates. Gerald of Wales declared that Henry was 'from beginning to end the oppressor of the nobility'.[14] English barons were finding their own property rights diminished at the same time that Henry's legal innovations were placing lesser freemen's property under the common law's protection and, far from finding protection for their landholdings in the royal courts, they were experiencing insecurity as the king increasingly interfered in baronial successions and marriages to extort money.[15]

---

[12] Antonia Gransden, *Historical Writing in England c. 550–1307* (Ithaca, 1974), p. 219.

[13] Martin Aurell, *L'Empire des Plantagenêt, 1154–1224* (Paris, 2003), p. 209.

[14] Giraldus Cambrensis, *Opera*, viii: *De principis instructione*, p. 160; Stevenson, *Instruction of Princes*, p. 14.

[15] From offerings averaging about £117 under Henry to over £770 under Richard, and over £2,000 under John: Scott L. Waugh, *The Lordship of England: Royal Wardships and Marriages in English Society and Politics, 1217–1327* (Princeton, 1988), pp. 157–8. Thirty-nine widows' fines were offered to Richard Lionheart totaling £1,125 in 1198: Janet S. Loengard, 'Of the Gift of her Husband: English Dower and its Consequences in the Year 1200', in Julius Kirshner and Suzanne F. Wemple, eds, *Women of the Medieval World* (Oxford, 1985), pp. 215–55 at pp. 234–5.

For centuries Henry II was labelled as a despot who paved the way for his sons' tyranny, but he has won good marks since the late nineteenth century as a ruler with a genius for efficient management and sound government, an opinion reinforced by late twentieth-century admirers of 'administrative kingship'.[16] Yet Henry's contemporaries gave him little credit for being a law-giver or administrative innovator, seeing him instead as an irresistible force whose anger aroused terror. A bishop who experienced his ill will wrote that he 'has neither superior who can frighten him nor subject who can resist, nor is he attacked from outside by foreign assaults, which might cause him to tame his innate ferocity at home'.[17] English peasants had to endure an arbitrary forest law that subjected them to death or mutilation as punishment for poaching. An Eynsham Abbey monk complained of the injustice of Henry's forest law: 'In revenge for irrational wild animals, which ought by natural law to be available to all in common, he had either punished by death or cruelly mutilated in their limbs human beings, who employ reason, are saved by the same blood of Christ, and share the same nature in equality.'[18] Henry appeared to his subjects as their oppressor and as the English church's oppressor, complicit in Archbishop Thomas Becket's death. Only after Henry's death did the English look back on him fondly. One chronicler writing in Richard's time recalled the 'good old days' of his reign, 'Indeed the experience of present evils has revived the memory of his good deeds, and [Henry], who in his own time was hated by almost all men, is now declared to have been an excellent and profitable prince.'[19]

Medieval queens could soften a harsh king's reputation among his subjects with charitable activities, pious acts, or moderation of their husband's severity with pleas for mercy. The Anglo-Norman queens had acted as intercessors, and they had enjoyed general approval as models of piety and purity, devoted wives and conscientious mothers. The Angevin queens, however, did not leave the English with such favourable impressions. Eleanor of Aquitaine offered Henry II little help in winning over his English subjects,

---

[16] C. Warren Hollister and John W. Baldwin, 'The Rise of Administrative Kingship: Henry I and Philip Augustus', *American Historical Review* 83 (1978), 867–905. For Henry II's historical reputation, Nicholas Vincent, 'Introduction: Henry II and the Historians', in Christopher Harper-Bill and Nicholas Vincent, eds, *Henry II: New Interpretation* (Woodbridge, 2007), pp. 1–23 at pp. 9–11.

[17] Frank Barlow, ed., *Letters of Arnulf of Lisieux*, Royal Historical Society, Camden 3rd ser. 61 (1939), pp. 72–3; cited by Anne J. Duggan, *Thomas Becket* (London, 2004), p. 255.

[18] Robert Bartlett, *England under the Norman and Angevin Kings, 1075–1225* (Oxford, 2000; paper, 2002) p. 674, citing *Vision of the Monk of Eynsham*, ed. H. E. Salter, *Eynsham Cartulary*, 2 vols, Oxford Historical Society 51 (1907–8), ii, p. 348.

[19] *William of Newburgh*, i, pp. 280–3, my translation.

arriving in England at the end of 1154 with the baggage of scandalous rumours about her conduct on the Second Crusade.[20] Exaggerated tales of Eleanor's shocking behaviour spread from Paris to the English royal court, although most of Eleanor's new subjects knew little more than that she came from the south of France, a region that they associated with worldly attitudes and easy morals. Late twelfth-century English chroniclers, who likely reflect popular opinion, found Henry II's queen falling short of the standard for queenly conduct established by Anglo-Norman consorts, especially Henry I's pious queen.[21] Eleanor would never win contemporaries' praise for her charity, piety, or mercy. Nor would Richard's bride, who never set foot in England, while John's (second) wife, Isabelle of Angoulême, like her mother-in-law, was viewed as a foreigner and a wanton woman, 'more Jezebel than Isabel', in Matthew Paris's words.[22]

The issue in Henry II's reign most troubling to chroniclers was his lack of respect for the English Church's liberties, especially its right to select prelates without royal interference. Soon many of the higher clergy, including Archbishop Theobald of Canterbury, were terrified of his anger. Early on, Henry removed two heads of royal abbeys whom he found too closely associated with his predecessor, King Stephen: Stephen's illegitimate son from Westminster Abbey and the late king's keeper of his seal from Reading.[23] In 1156–7, a member of Theobald's household, the writer John of Salisbury, provoked the king's ill will, and he wrote that 'such a storm of indignation against myself [had arisen] that it is not safe for me to remain in England and impossible, or at least very difficult, for me to leave it.'[24] Henry's anger against John was a means of intimidating his master, Theobald of Canterbury, and the aged archbishop was deeply fearful.

The king's bitter quarrel with Thomas Becket leading to the archbishop's murder at the end of 1170 epitomizes his oppression of the Church.

---

[20] Edmond-René Labande, 'Pour une image véridique d'Aliénor d'Aquitaine', *Bulletin de la Société des antiquaires de l'ouest*, 4th ser. 2 (1952), pp. 175–235; reprinted in Labande, *Histoire de l'Europe Occidentale XIᵉ–XIVᵉ siècles* (London, 1973); Martin Aurell, 'Aux origines de la légende noire d'Aliénor d'Aquitaine', in *Les Royautés imaginaires: Colloque de l'Université de Paris X-Nanterre du 26 au 27 septembre 2003* (Tournhout, 2005), pp. 89–102.

[21] Lois Huneycutt, *Matilda of Scotland: A Study in Medieval Queenship* (Woodbridge, 2003) and Lois Huneycutt, 'Intercession and the High-Medieval Queen: The Esther Topos', in Jennifer Carpenter and Sally-Beth Maclean, eds, *Power of the Weak: Studies on Medieval Women* (Urbana, 1995), pp. 126–46.

[22] Vincent, 'Isabella of Angoulême', pp. 164, 204, citing Matthew Paris.

[23] Richardson and Sayles, *Governance*, pp. 414–21, for Gervase of Blois, abbot at Westminster, and pp. 256–7 for Abbot Reginald of Reading.

[24] W. J. Millor, H. E. Butler, and C. N. L. Brooke, eds, *The Letters of John of Salisbury*, 2 vols (Oxford, 1986), i, p. 30, no. 18, to Pope Adrian IV.

It clouds Henry's image as an apostle of the rule of law, exposing him as a tyrant whose harshness paved the way for his two sons' despotism.[25] His complicity in Becket's martyrdom deeply shocked all western Christendom, and it came to be the most important fact remembered from his reign among late twelfth- and thirteenth-century churchmen. The dramatic scene of knights in armour striking down a defenceless prelate in his own cathedral was an unforgettable image. Thomas Becket's martyrdom shattered Henry's reputation, darkening contemporaries' view of the entire royal family; for Becket was an international figure, known personally by the pope, the cardinals, prelates, and lesser clerics throughout Europe.[26]

Henry II's fierce reaction to what he saw as Becket's betrayal of their friendship is a prime example of his temper, and his rage against those he considered traitors was notorious. A letter written to Archbishop Thomas Becket in exile gives a description of one of Henry's fits of rage. The king, angered by a courtier's speech in favour of one of his enemies among Becket's friends, 'broke out in abusive language ... calling him a manifest traitor'. Then, 'flying into his usual temper, [he] ... threw off his cloak and clothes, grabbed the silken coverlet off the couch, and sitting as [if] on a dung heap started chewing pieces of straw.'[27] Later Peter of Blois writing an imagined dialogue depicts Henry explaining and justifying his anger to an abbot; he has the king asking, 'Have I no right to become angered when rage is a virtue of the spirit and a natural power? By nature I am a son of anger: how therefore could I not become enraged? God himself becomes enraged.'[28]

Even after Henry's 1170 truce with Thomas Becket, he refused to give him the kiss of peace, an essential part of the ritual for ending conflicts.[29] He extended his vengeance against Becket to the cleric's friends, servants and their kin. One of his writs commanded seizure of the wealth and property of the archbishop's hapless clerks, and also that 'the fathers and mothers, brothers and sisters, nephews and nieces of all the clerks who are with the archbishop shall be laid under safe pledges with their chattels'. Also banished from England were Becket's relatives, among them his sister and

[25] Vincent, 'Introduction', p. 9.

[26] Duggan, *Becket*, pp. 266, 268.

[27] James C. Robertson, ed., *Materials for the History of Thomas Becket*, 7 vols, Rolls Series 67 (1875–85), vi, p. 72, a letter of 1166, quoted in W. L. Warren, *Henry II* (Berkeley, 1977), p. 183; see also pp. 210, 211.

[28] Jolliffe, *Angevin Kingship*, p. 100, quoting Peter of Blois, *Dialogus inter Regem Henricum II et Abbatem Bonaevallensem*, in J. P. Migne, ed., *Patrologiae cursus completus ... series Latina* [*Patrologiae Latina*], 221 vols (Paris 1844–1903), ccvii, col. 978.

[29] Aurell, *L'Empire des Plantagenêt*, pp. 272–4.

her children, forced to find shelter in a Flemish abbey.[30] Later King John would take similar reprisals against the Canterbury monks who had defied him by accepting Pope Innocent III's choice for archbishop of Canterbury, and against the papal nominee Stephen Langton's friends and relatives.[31] A few years after Becket's death in 1174–5, Henry harried out of episcopal office Bishop Arnulf of Lisieux, one of his longtime counsellors. The aged Norman bishop wrote, 'Our lord the King has long been moved against me, and … he harasses me at every turn, allowing me to be most miserably oppressed by his ministers and taxers, so that nowhere in the province can I find safety.'[32]

Medieval rulers' anger cannot be dismissed as staged, ritualized performances that were part of dispute settlements with their great men.[33] The Angevin kings' subjects knew that a willingness to use force lay behind royal anger, and they accepted it as inevitable, comparable to God's wrath. Indeed, Henry II in one of his charters equated his anger with divine wrath and indignation.[34] All three Angevin kings extorted crippling fines from royal officials unlucky enough to have lost their good will. The Angevins' anger became almost institutionalized, reflected in pipe roll entries in which the king remitted his anger and indignation against individuals in exchange for money.[35] Courtiers seeking advancement paid a heavy price for loss of royal favour, since it 'was the passport to prosperity', postponing justice for them, standing in the way of their inheritances, denying them advantageous marriages and profitable privileges.[36]

---

[30] Warren, *Henry II*, p. 492, citing Robertson, ed., *Materials for Becket*, v, pp. 151–2; Frank Barlow, *Thomas Becket* (Berkeley, 1986), pp. 126–7.

[31] Kate Norgate, *John Lackland* (London, 1902), pp. 127, 136–7, citing *Wendover* ii, p. 223–4, iii, p. 214, and *Walter of Coventry*, ii, p. 199.

[32] Barlow, *Letters of Arnulf of Lisieux*, p. 194; cited by Jolliffe, *Angevin Kingship*, p. 107.

[33] E.g. Richard Barton, 'A "Zealous Anger" and the Renegotiation of Aristocratic Relationships in Eleventh- and Twelfth-century France', in Barbara H. Rosenwein, ed., *Anger's Past: The Social Uses of an Emotion in the Middle Ages* (Ithaca, 1998), pp. 153–70, at p. 162: 'The performance of lordly anger was frequently linked to compromise and negotiation.' Also Stephen D. White, 'The Politics of Anger', in ibid., pp. 127–52.

[34] Jolliffe, *Angevin Kingship*, p. 98, citing Léopold Delisle and Élie Berger, eds, *Recueil des actes de Henri II*, 3 vols (Paris, 1916–27), ii, p. 244, no. 633.

[35] White, 'Politics of Anger', p. 146, citing *Pipe Roll 28 Henry II*, PRS 31 (London, 1910), p. 94, and *Pipe Roll 20 Henry II*, PRS 21 (London, 1896), p. 135. When one of Richard's officers allowed a French prisoner to escape, he had to offer the king 1,200 marks to escape imprisonment and recover his lands, and the prisoner's guard was hanged: Doris M. Stenton, ed., *Pipe Roll 9 Richard I*, PRS 46 n.s. 8 (London, 1931), pp. xviii, 61.

[36] Warren, *Henry II*, p. 388.

The Angevin kings' anger erupted into acts of outright cruelty. Each of them ordered enemies imprisoned under such cruel conditions, starved and weighted down with irons, that they died. Henry II ordered a Poitevin rebel imprisoned, kept in heavy irons and given only bread and water until he perished. On Richard's return to England from his crusade, he commanded that one of the supporters of his brother John's rebellion be starved to death, although luckier partisans of John purchased the king's good will with massive offerings, some amounting to more than £1,300.[37] Best known, however, are John's punishments; allegedly he ordered one of his clerks, a former exchequer official, 'dressed in so much iron that he died', or according to another chronicler, clad in a cope of lead. John marred his most noteworthy military success, the rescue of his mother at Mirebeau in 1202, by shameful treatment of his prisoners, twenty-two of whom died from their harsh incarceration.[38] The most important of John's prisoners, his nephew Arthur of Brittany, soon disappeared, likely murdered at his command. Next to Arthur's disappearance, John's most monstrous deed was his pursuit of the Braose family. The king's former favourite, William de Braose, had incurred a royal debt of over £13,000, and John applied to him the full force of the law of the exchequer and beyond, imprisoning and starving to death his wife and son and forcing him to flee the kingdom and die in exile.[39]

King John was even less likeable than his two predecessors. The chronicler of Béthune, in England with John's Flemish allies in 1215 and a relatively detached observer, wrote, 'A very bad man was King John: he was cruel toward all men, he was too covetous of beautiful women; he brought much shame on great men of the land by whom he was much hated.' Like the rebel barons, he viewed John as untrustworthy, lecherous and vicious, with a fearsome personality.[40] The rebels viewed their king as less courteous or chivalrous than his father or his brother, with a thirst for revenge and a streak of pettiness or spitefulness that made him take relish in humiliating

---

[37] *Howden*, iii, pp. 239, 287; D. E. Desborough, 'Politics and Prelacy in the Late Twelfth Century: The Career of Hugh de Nonant, Bishop of Coventry, 1188–98', *Historical Research* 64 (1991), 6. For example, 2,000 marks each from Gerard de Camville and Hugh de Nonant: Doris M. Stenton, ed., *Pipe Roll 7 Richard I*, PRS 44 n.s. 6 (London, 1929), p. 191; *Pipe Roll 9 Richard I*, p. 100; 300 marks from Roger de Montbegon and 500 marks from Geoffrey Esturmi, ibid., pp. 114, 216.

[38] Sidney Painter, 'Norwich's Three Geoffreys', in Fred A. Cazel, ed., *Feudalism and Liberty: Articles and Addresses of Sidney Painter* (Baltimore, 1961), pp. 185–94; Ralph V. Turner, *King John* (Harlow, Essex, 1994), pp. 120–1.

[39] Turner, *King John*, pp. 220–1.

[40] *Histoire des ducs*, p. 105, my translation. See Olivier de Laborderie, 'Convergences et divergences de points de vue: La Conquête de la Normandie en 1204 dans les deux chroniques de l'Anonyme de Béthune', in Anne-Marie Flambard Héricher and Véronique Gazeau, eds, *1204, La Normandie entre Plantegenêts et Capétiens* (Paris, 2007), pp. 205–10.

weaker men, although he also revelled in humbling powerful and popular rivals. Since John could not win his barons' affection, he tried to coerce them into obedience, demanding charters of prospective fealty that required them to surrender their lands if they fell under suspicion or failed to perform services – in effect forcing them to renounce in advance rights to due process. John also demanded his barons' sons as sureties for their faithful service, but fear and distrust made fathers reluctant to hand them over as hostages, especially once rumours spread of Arthur of Brittany's fate. The killing of one's kin, even a dangerous political rival, outraged medieval aristocrats with their strong sense of family solidarity. The king's hanging of twenty-eight sons of Welsh chieftains in 1211 made handing over hostages even more risky. John's action recalls his father's earlier command that males among his Welsh hostages 'should be blinded and castrated, and that the females … should have their ears and noses cut off'.[41] Yet when John demanded additional hostages of his barons in 1212, they surrendered them, 'not daring to resist his commands'.[42]

Both Richard and John were engaged in a desperate struggle to defend their father's legacy from the aggressive French monarch, Philip II. In John's reign, the connection between his unquenchable thirst for money to defend his French territories and his English barons' disenchantment is clear, as his need for funds forced him to load his subjects with heavier and heavier financial burdens. After John's loss of Normandy by 1204, he suffered a disadvantage not borne by his predecessors. His enforced residence in England meant that John's subjects experienced his financial extortions first-hand, while his largely absentee predecessors had succeeded in blaming their ministers for their subjects' oppression. John's barons resented his over-zealous enforcement of their obligations, and their alienation was complete after his decisive defeat in France in the summer of 1214. After that, military humiliation coupled with insolvency weakened his hand, handing the initiative to militant barons. The result would be John's submission to rebel demands and his grant of Magna Carta in May 1215, followed by a civil war still raging on his death in October 1216.

The Angevin kings' chief rivals, the Capetian kings of France, are sometimes credited with an ideological advantage. Certainly they benefited from their dukes' and counts' acknowledgment of some sense of belonging to the larger French kingdom and their recognition of the monarch's superiority as the crowned and anointed successor to the Carolingian rulers.[43] Louis VII cultivated an image of himself as model Christian monarch, a pious

---

[41] Norgate, *John Lackland*, p. 169, citing *Walter of Coventry*, ii: 207. For Henry II, see Bartlett, *England under the Norman and Angevin Kings*, p. 49.

[42] Norgate, *John Lackland*, p. 171, citing *Wendover*, iii, pp. 238, 239.

[43] No other great French prince of ducal rank was anointed in such a religious

peacemaker whom churchmen could place on a pedestal. One of his contemporaries wrote, 'He was so pious, so just, so catholic and benign, that if
you were to see his simplicity of behaviour and dress, you would think that
he was not a king, but a man of religion. He was a lover of peace, a defender
of the weak.'[44] Henry II had no historically sanctioned rationale for his
rule over his assemblage of lands, depending rather on right by inheritance,
marriage, or conquest; a major obstacle to creating such a rationale was the
status of his Continental territories as part of the French kingdom.

Certainly Henry and his sons spent lavishly on royal splendour as a
means of impressing their subjects with their wealth and power, but evidence is thin for any sustained effort at formulating an ideology of kingship
to unify the diverse lands and peoples of the Angevin 'empire'. Henry had
an early ideological advantage, for the eleventh-century reform movement
of the Church had barely blunted the sacred character of his predecessors,
the Anglo-Norman kings. According to John of Salisbury, Henry II had
boasted in 1168 that 'he had at last regained the privileges of his grandfather,
Henry I, who was king, apostolic legate, emperor, and all that he wished in
his land.'[45] After Thomas Becket's martyrdom claims of kingship's sacred
character were hardly appropriate, however. Yet Henry and his sons made
desultory attempts to counter the blow to royal prestige, pointing up the
monarch's special character. Henry introduced a new vocabulary of power
into royal documents in 1172, adding to his titles the term *Dei gratia Rex*,
'king by grace of God', on his charters, and his son Richard later would
adopt the plural of majesty in his documents. Also Richard had some success employing the primitive 'media propaganda' of his day to promote himself and create his own legend, advertising himself as a chivalric crusader
king by circulating newsletters and forged letters.[46]

A few English royal clerks would continue to support royal supremacy
in the late twelfth century, promoting near-absolutist ideas of kingship
lingering from the late Roman Empire. The author of the *Dialogue of the
Exchequer*, a royal financial official late in Henry II's reign, stated that God
entrusts the king with 'the general care of his subjects'; he admitted that
rulers sometimes act arbitrarily, but denied that their subjects had a right 'to

---

ceremony. Geoffrey Koziol, 'France in the Central Middle Ages, 900–1200', in
Marcus Bull, ed., *Short Oxford History of France* (Oxford, 2002), p. 44.

[44] Elizabeth M. Hallam, *Capetian France, 987–1328* (London, 1980), p. 119, citing
Stephen of Paris.

[45] Millor, Butler, and Brooke, *Letters of John of Salisbury*, ii, p. 581.

[46] John Gillingham, 'Royal Newsletters, Forgeries and English Historians: Some
Links between Court and History in the Reign of Richard I', in Martin Aurell,
ed., *La Cour Plantagenêt, 1154–1204* (Poitiers, 2000), pp. 171–85. Also Jean Flori,
Richard Coeur de Lion (Paris, 1999), pp. 2–4, 465, 473–5.

question or condemn their actions'.[47] King John found a pseudo-theologian who preached that the king was 'the rod of the wrath of the Lord, ruling his people like a rod of iron and dashing them in pieces like a potter's vessel', words recalling John's own threat in 1191 to 'come and visit [William Longchamps] with a rod of iron'.[48] John would apply the Roman doctrine of the emperor's power to himself in a 1202 letter to the English clergy in which he claimed that 'the English kingdom is equal to an empire'.[49]

All of this was too little too late in light of the papacy's growing power and its ever more extravagant claims to supremacy. Secular princes in reacting to papal claims could only appeal to ancient custom, and John, who had read some early English history, turned to the Anglo-Saxon past in his dispute with Innocent III over the Canterbury election (1205–13). He pointed out that 'all my predecessors conferred archbishoprics, bishoprics and abbeys in their chamber', and he cited Edward the Confessor's appointment of St Wulfstan as bishop of Worcester.[50] John even attempted to disguise his authoritarian innovations by maintaining that they lay within the law and had the sanction of ancient custom. He claimed that the law of the exchequer enforcing his financial demands was part of the law of the land, although the barons saw it as little more than enforcement of the royal will. In 1215 John was confident that he had ancient custom on his side, defending what he saw as ages-old monarchical prerogatives. In his view, the rebel barons were the real revolutionaries, attempting to place unprecedented limitations on royal power.

A particular propaganda problem confronting Henry and his sons was the need for a unifying myth or ideology to justify their heterogeneous collection of subjects who shared in common only their rule by a Plantagenet dynasty. Their diverse subjects lacked a myth of a common origin or descent from an ancient hero, such as the Capetians' connections to the Franks and to Charlemagne. The counts of Anjou had never claimed a mighty forefather from mythical times. If Henry and his sons grasped the need for some principle of unity, they made no more than half-hearted attempts to devise one. Henry did seek to accent his Norman ancestry, however, sponsoring

---

[47] Fitz Nigel, *Dialogue*, pp. 2–3, 152–3.

[48] *Wendover*, ii, p. 53; also Matthew Paris, *Chronica Majora*, ii, p. 527. See F. M. Powicke, 'Alexander of St. Albans: A Literary Muddle', in H. W. C. Davis, ed., *Essays in History Presented to Reginald Lane Poole* (Oxford, 1927), pp. 246–60; and Norgate, *John Lackland*, p. 31.

[49] Rymer, *Fœdera*, i, pt 1, p. 87. For other references to England as empire, see Walter Ullmann, *Principles of Government and Politics in the Middle Ages* (London, 1961), p. 160.

[50] *Annales Monastici* i, p. 211; trans. F. M. Powicke, *Stephen Langton* (Oxford, 1928), pp. 86–7.

histories of the early dukes written in the Anglo-Norman vernacular.[51] Yet by John's time, the prospect of peaceful rule under Philip of France appealed to the Normans, especially the clergy.

Some scholars looking for links between Henry II's literary patronage and the Arthurian romances propose that the Angevins turned to King Arthur as such a legendary hero, trying to raise up the Briton prince as a rival to Charlemagne, the Capetians' celebrated ancestor. They attempt to show that Henry and Eleanor gave patronage to romance writers reworking Arthurian materials.[52] Yet romance authors' interest in Arthurian legends hardly amounts to a Plantagenet campaign to create a myth countering Capetian propaganda, and the contention that Henry viewed Arthur as a predecessor offering him an imperial mythology, cannot be substantiated.[53] King Arthur and Arthurian legends served better the purposes of rebellious English nobles. For the nobility, Arthur with his faithful men seated at his round-table presented an idealized view of early medieval royal government centred on great councils that contrasted with the reality of low-born professionals advising the Angevin kings.[54] Arthurian tales had an especially subversive effect on inhabitants of the Celtic fringes. To quote one authority, 'In the reign of Henry II, political "Arthurianism" remained far more Welsh or Breton than Angevin or English'.[55] A clear indication of this is the Bretons' hunger for freedom from Angevin rule. Brittany's infant duke, Henry's grandson, was named Arthur as a sign of hostility toward the Angevin monarch at the Breton nobles' insistence.

The aristocracy of the duchy of Aquitaine always chafed under Angevin rule, and the duchy's place within the Angevin empire was problematic. The 1172 consecration ceremony for Richard as duke at Limoges was by no means aimed at cementing Plantagenet power over Aquitaine. Rather it was a public recognition that young Richard's authority had nothing to do with Henry II, and that his ducal title descended from God and from the Carolingian rulers of Aquitaine through his mother Eleanor's lineage. It was devised by monks at Saint-Martial Abbey with no love for Henry, who had twice punished them by levelling their city's walls; and it was approved by

---

[51] John Gillingham, 'The Cultivation of History, Legend, and Courtesy at the Court of Henry II', in Ruth Kennedy and Simon Meecham-Jones, eds, *Writers of the Reign of Henry II: Twelve Essays* (New York, 2006), p. 28.

[52] E.g. Georges Duby, *The Three Orders: Feudal Society Imagined*, trans. Arthur Goldhammer (Chicago, 1980), p. 287.

[53] Gillingham, 'Cultivation of History, Legend, and Courtesy', pp. 28, 36.

[54] John W. Baldwin, 'The Capetian Court at Work under Philip II', in Edward Haymes, ed., *The Medieval Court in Europe* (Munich, 1986), pp. 80–1.

[55] Aurell, 'Henry II and Arthurian Legend', in Harper-Bill and Vincent, *Henry II: New Interpretations*, p. 388.

the queen-duchess Eleanor, who shared the monk's interest in a ceremonial expression of Aquitaine's autonomy.[56]

Undermining any Angevin attempt to make themselves the focus of unity for their empire was the fact they had a royal title only in England; Normandy, Anjou and Aquitaine lay within the French kingdom, and the Capetian kings' claims to lordship were irrefutable. By the late twelfth century, feudal doctrine was placing the Capetians at the apex of a feudal pyramid above all French principalities, presenting an insoluble problem. Henry II had long avoided doing homage to Louis VII, but in 1183 in a weakened position, he found himself doing homage to Philip II for Normandy.[57] Afterward, Henry seems to have tried to reassert his royal majesty. He understood well the usefulness of ostentatious court ceremonial as a means of displaying royal power, and at his 1186 Christmas court, his earls performed duties at table recalling coronation banquets and other solemn feasts of earlier English kings.[58] Yet the fact of Capetian lordship over them was undeniable, and Henry and his sons were never able to overcome that disadvantage.[59] The Angevin kings could devise no adequate response, no propaganda to reconcile their diverse subjects in their French lands to their rule over them or to inspire them to reject Capetian claims to lordship. Worse, the French king made himself available as an alternative authority to whom their French subjects could appeal against them.

The crisis of 1215 that resulted in Magna Carta followed the collapse of the Angevin 'empire' in France. The ignominy of John's 1214 loss of all the Angevins' French lands north of the Loire river as well as parts of Poitou, squandering a reservoir of funds extorted from the English in a futile effort, freed his English subjects from their fear. Two groups in England that were alienated from Angevin rule joined together. One group consisted of English clerics who had been estranged since Thomas Becket's murder in

---

[56] Geoffroi de Vigeois, in Martin Bouquet and Leopold Delisle, eds, *Recueil des historiens des Gaules et de la France*, 24 vols (Paris, 1869–1904), xii, pp. 442–3; also pp. 451–3, order blessing the duke of Aquitaine. Also Daniel F. Callahan, 'Eleanor of Aquitaine, the Coronation Rite of the Duke of Aquitaine and the Cult of St. Martial of Limoges', in Marcus Bull and Catherine Léglu, eds, *The World of Eleanor of Aquitaine: Literature and Society in Southern France between the Eleventh and Twelfth Centuries* (Woodbridge, 2005), pp. 29–37.

[57] John Gillingham, 'Doing Homage to the King of France', in Harper-Bill and Vincent, *Henry II: New Interpretations*, pp. 63–84.

[58] William Stubbs, ed., *Gesta regis Henrici secundi Benedicti abbatis*, 2 vols, Rolls Series 49 (London, 1867), ii, p. 3. At Pentecost two years later, he had the *laudes regis* sung at court: R. W. Eyton, *Court, Household, and Itinerary of King Henry II* (London, 1878) pp. 286–7; *Pipe Roll 34 Henry II*, PRS 38 (1925), p. 19, cited by Matthew Strickland, 'The Upbringing of Henry, the Young King', in Harper-Bill and Vincent, *Henry II: New Interpretations*, p. 198.

[59] Aurell, *L'Empire des Plantagenêt*, p. 290.

1170. Becket's former circle and their successors were revolutionaries, advocating princes' submission to the priestly power and resistance against rulers defying the Church. Frustrated that the archbishop's martyrdom had made little difference in the king's power to place his preferred candidates in English bishoprics, Becket's circle continued to influence later generations' hostility toward the Angevin line.[60] Clerical opposition was muted during the crusader king Richard's reign, but rose up again almost four decades after Becket's death in John's reign. Disaffected English clergy saw John's struggle with the papacy over the Canterbury succession as part of a long ideological struggle over secular princes' proper sphere in Christian society that had begun with St Anselm's prelacy at the beginning of the twelfth century and culminated in Archbishop Thomas Becket's assassination.[61]

The barons who feared and loathed King John found common cause with discontented clerics and were emboldened to defy him in 1215. Both groups would find the principle of due process or no punishment without judgment a means of curbing John's excesses. The Scholastics' *sine sententia* was their equivalent of the Anglo-Norman *absque judicio*.[62] Stephen Langton, during his long struggle with John, had urged the English knights to support his position with their swords. As early as 1207, he pointed out to the English in a pastoral letter that their fealty to the king was secondary to their 'loyalty to the superior Lord, the eternal king who is king of kings and lord of lords', and that 'whatever service is rendered to the temporal king to the prejudice of the eternal king is undoubted an act of treachery'. Later, at Winchester in 1213 as part of Langton's absolution of King John, he had obliged the king to swear to abolish all evil laws and restore good ones, and also to judge all men by the just sentences of his court.[63] At the core of both English churchmen's and barons' concerns was subjecting King John to the law, defining and limiting his authority. The chronicler Ralph of Coggeshall makes clear a linkage of ecclesiastical and baronial interests, writing that the Great Charter's purpose was to end 'the evil customs which the father and brother of the King had created to the detriment of the Church and kingdom, along with those abuses which [King John] had added.'[64]

English barons considered themselves defenders of the custom of the realm, by which they meant 'the good old law' of Edward the Confessor

---

[60] Aurell, *L'Empire des Plantagenêt*, pp. 285–6.

[61] Natalie Fryde, *Why Magna Carta? Angevin England Revisited* (Münster, 2001), pp. 102, 109.

[62] John W. Baldwin, 'Master Stephen Langton, Future Archbishop of Canterbury: The Paris Schools and Magna Carta', *English Historical Review* 123 (2008), 836.

[63] Powicke, *Stephen Langton*, pp. 94–7; Baldwin, 'Master Stephen Langton', pp. 827–9.

[64] Quoted by J. A. P. Jones, *King John and Magna Carta* (London, 1971), p. 101.

and Henry I, not Angevin innovations. They looked longingly to the years
before 1154, when they imagined England to have been a 'truly feudal' society, disrupted under Angevin rule. They had access to documents circulating widely in the first decades of the thirteenth century, Anglo-Norman
French translations of the *Leges Edwardi Confessoris* and coronation charters of Henry I, Stephen and Henry II.[65] Any number of English clerics
could have shared these documents with noble and knightly acquaintances,
and together they fashioned the principles of the rule of law underlying the
Great Charter. Part of a forged letter interpolated into the *Leges*, allegedly
from an early pope to a pre-Saxon king of the Britons, rejected authoritarian rule by the king's will: 'Right and justice ought to reign in the kingdom
rather than perverse will; law is always what does right; for will and force
and violence are not right.' It goes on to place the king under God's law: ' the
king ought to fear and love God above all things and keep his command-
ments throughout all his kingdom.'[66]

The passage adds that the king must maintain justice 'through the advice
of the nobles of his kingdom', voicing an ideal of good government that
English barons and their knights learned from traditional lord-vassal relationships.[67] Good governance for them was an idealized version of an eleventh-century great lord's court, with the king surrounded by his leading vassals, making decisions and settling disputes with their counsel, the principle
of *commune consilium*. Members of the baronage extrapolated from their
experiences in baronial courts a conviction that the king ought to govern
'by judgment' and 'by counsel'. Instead, at the Angevin royal court they saw
the king taking counsel with low-born and foreign courtiers and familiars.
It was not a large step for the barons to move on to taking up arms against
King John. There is a genre of Old French literature, so-called 'rebellious
baron epics', in which a hero becomes so disillusioned with his king, so dis-
gusted by his abuses, that he abandons his loyalty to him and goes to war.[68]

It appears that Jolliffe's term 'unrealized absolutism' still describes best
Angevin political thought. Over fifty years ago, he described the Angevins
as authoritarian in practice, applying their centralizing power without
theoretical justification and making only desultory attempts at indoctri-
nating their subjects through propaganda. The price of their failure to win
their subjects' affection and loyalty was John's loss of an empire in France,

[65] Bruce R. O'Brien, *God's Peace and King's Peace: The Laws of Edward the Confessor*
      (Philadelphia, 1999), pp. 106–8.

[66] Felix Liebermann, ed., *Die Gesetze der Angelsachsen*, 3 vols (Halle, 1898–1916), i,
      653; *Leges Edwardi Confessoris*, my translation.

[67] Liebermann, *Gesetze*, i, 653.

[68] Baldwin, 'Capetian Court at Work', pp. 80–1, citing William C. Calin, *The Old
      French Epic of Revolt* (Geneva, 1962).

rebellion by his English barons, and Magna Carta. On John's death in the midst of a stalemated civil war, loyal barons and churchmen protecting his minor son Henry III reissued the Charter as a conciliatory gesture, and it was renewed in a definitive version in 1225. During the thirteenth century Magna Carta would become 'a kind of fundamental law which governed the thinking of the Crown's opponents whenever kingship provoked opposition'.[69] Three crises would cement it in the English people's consciousness: first, in 1232 to 1234 at the beginning of Henry III's personal rule; second, the baronial reform movement,1258 to 1265; and third under Edward I, the 1297 Confirmation of the Charters and the Articles on the Charters in 1300.

[69] J. R. Maddicott, '"1258" and "1297": Some Comparisons and Contrasts', in *Thirteenth Century England IX* (Woodbridge, 2003), p. 3.

The Anonymous of Béthune, King John and Magna Carta

JOHN GILLINGHAM

O NE OF THE most frequently met generalizations about King John is that he was unfortunate to have lived at a time when those authors who chronicled the events of their own day were churchmen, and that in consequence, above all because of his quarrel with Pope Innocent III, he was doomed to be condemned. 'Contemporary chroniclers who first sketched King John's character were subject to prejudices or preconceptions that distorted their perceptions. They were churchmen following criteria established by earlier clerical writers for evaluating medieval kings.'[1] Ralph Turner is in good Protestant company in expressing this view of 'Papist' chroniclers. Henry VIII's quarrel with the papacy led to a new and more positive perception of John as an illustrious predecessor of the Tudors. In John Bale's play *Kynge Johan* (*c.* 1540) Verity complains of the untruths told by historians. But with the emergence of the cult of Magna Carta in the seventeenth century, John's reputation sank again. For David Hume, John was 'mean and odious, ruinous to himself and destructive to his people'.[2] In the twentieth century the increasing preference of historians for judicial and financial records led to a tendency to rehabilitate John and a corresponding return to the Protestant view of medieval chroniclers. W. L. Warren, for example, began his lively and deservedly influential book with a chapter entitled 'The genesis of a sinister reputation' in which he analysed the differing ways in which chroniclers had treated John and his predecessors. He concluded that the two authors most responsible for 'the terrible verdict' on John were two monks of St Albans: Roger of Wendover and, a generation later, Matthew Paris.[3] Admittedly not all chroniclers were monks, and some indeed were critical of the papacy, but since nearly all were ecclesiastics of one sort or another and wrote in Latin, it was easy enough to characterize them as authors who had little or no sympathy for secular values.

Some, however, wrote in French, the language of aristocratic society.

I am much indebted to Ian Short for improvements to my translations from the Anonymous's French; all surviving blunders are entirely my own work.

[1] Ralph V. Turner, *Magna Carta* (Harlow, 2003), p. 31.

[2] David Hume, *History of England*, 3 vols (London, 1786; repr. 1871), i, p. 313.

[3] W. L. Warren, *King John* (Harmondsworth, 1961), pp. 25–31. His statement (p. 23) that 'all the chroniclers were members of religious orders' is erroneous.

Warren mentioned *L'Histoire de Guillaume le Maréchal*, claiming that it 'assumes a unique importance because it sometimes, but all too rarely, takes us into John's presence'.[4] Yet there is another work, probably written slightly earlier than the biography of the Marshal, also composed in French, and it too sometimes takes us into John's presence: the *Histoire des ducs de Normandie et des rois d'Angleterre*.[5] This *Histoire* was given a very low profile in Warren's *King John*, appearing neither in the introductory chapter on sources nor in his index.[6] J. C. Holt, on the other hand, in his masterly Historical Association pamphlet (1963), *King John*, drew an explicit contrast between the *History of William Marshal* and the *Histoire des ducs*. Whereas the former's portrait of John as a resentful, suspicious monarch had to be treated with caution because its author was anxious to explain William Marshal's differences with the king, no such doubts could be raised against the author of the latter. He 'came to England with John's Flemish allies in 1215, had no such axe to grind, and he was even more critical. In his view John was cruel, vicious and lecherous, a king who committed many shameful acts against the nobles of the land; he was not only wicked but petty, a man who could be upbraided by his wife and openly contradicted and challenged by his barons.'[7] As long ago as the 1890s two great French scholars, Léopold Delisle and Charles Petit-Dutaillis, insisted on the accuracy and precision of his narrative of events after 1212; in 1902 Kate Norgate described him as 'strictly contemporary … one of the best, and certainly the most impartial, of our informants on the closing years of John's reign'.[8]

In the circumstances we might expect to find a considerable secondary literature on this author's perception of King John and Magna Carta. This, however, is far from being the case. Already described as a neglected work in the 1890s, it was still being referred to in these terms as recently as 2007.[9] True, a book by Gabrielle Spiegel published in 1993 contained a

---

[4] Warren, *King John*, p. 21.

[5] *Histoire des ducs*. It begins with the arrival of the Northmen in France and ends in 1220. A new edition is badly needed.

[6] It has an equally low profile in Ralph V. Turner, *King John* (Harlow, 1994).

[7] Reprinted in J. C. Holt, *Magna Carta and Medieval Government* (London, 1985), pp. 85–109, at p. 99. He went too far, however, in describing the author as 'a member of the king's camp': J. C. Holt, *The Northerners* (Oxford, 1961), pp. 217–18.

[8] C. Petit-Dutaillis, 'Une nouvelle chronique du règne de Philippe Auguste, l'Anonyme de Béthune', *Revue historique* 50 (1892), 63–71; L. Delisle, in *Histoire littéraire de la France*, 32 (1898), pp. 189–90; Kate Norgate, *John Lackland* (London, 1902), pp. 291–2.

[9] Petit-Dutaillis, 'Nouvelle chronique', 65; C. Petit-Dutaillis, *Studies and Notes Supplementary to Stubbs' Constitutional History* (Manchester, 1923; trans. of 1908 edn), p. 131; Olivier de Laborderie, 'Convergences et divergences de points de vue: la conquête de la Normandie en 1204 dans les deux chroniques de l'Anonyme de

substantial analysis of the anonymous author, but relatively little notice of this was taken by historians of English government – perhaps because her book's title and subtitle appeared to indicate that it was not for them. She reinforced the received view that he was 'at the center of the major political events of his era' and concluded that he understood the workings of the English court (as well as that of France).[10] More could have been said on the subject but, given her main theme, an intensive study of the author's understanding of English politics would have been out of place. The later articles on the *Histoire des ducs* by Seán Duffy and Olivier de Laborderie focused on earlier events, the expedition to Ireland in 1210 and the loss of Normandy in 1203–4, rather than on the Magna Carta years towards the end of John's reign.[11] Here I shall argue that although the *Histoire* was written after John's death and with the benefit of hindsight, it looks as though his informant or informants changed their views of the king over time and, in particular, that Magna Carta played a significant part in bringing about that change of mind.

We do not know the author's name, but the language and content of his work suggest that he came from Artois and was attached to the household of Robert of Béthune, a younger son of William II, advocate of Arras and lord of Béthune in Artois, and lord of Dendermonde in Flanders by virtue of his marriage.[12] It seems clear that it was composed to be read by or to Robert. We are given information about Robert which only someone very close to him would have thought of interest – for instance his whereabouts when he heard of his father's death or the fact that a recently dubbed knight, Hugh de la Bretaigne, was his cousin.[13] In consequence the author has long been known as the Anonymous of Béthune. His first editor reckoned that he must have been an eyewitness of some of the events described.

Béthune', in Anne-Marie Flambard Héricher and Véronique Gazeau, eds, 1204: *la Normandie entre Plantagenêts et Capétiens* (Caen, 2007), pp. 189–213, 190–4, 212. In Laborderie's view it was principally the historians who engaged in the rehabilitation of John characteristic of the later twentieth century who tended to omit some of this author's most damaging comments.

[10] A 'completely original account of events during the reign of King John' within a work which 'achieves real value, both as a narrator of history and as an index of the attitudes and concerns of the aristocratic audience for whom his histories were destined': Gabrielle M. Spiegel, *Romancing the Past: The Rise of Vernacular Prose Historiography in Thirteenth-Century France* (Berkeley, 1993), pp. 224–68, 232, 243.

[11] Seán Duffy, 'King John's Expedition to Ireland, 1210: The Evidence Reconsidered', *Irish Historical Studies* 30 (1996), 1–24; Laborderie, 'Convergences et divergences'.

[12] On his mother's death in 1224, Robert became lord of Dendermonde; in 1227 he succeeded his brother Daniel as head of the family: Robert VII, advocate of Arras and lord of Béthune.

[13] *Histoire des ducs*, pp. 133, 139.

In 1882 Oswald Holder-Egger even suggested that it may have been the Anonymous himself who read out letters sent to Robert by King John in August 1215.[14] What is clear is that the Anonymous presented Robert as someone who knew John well. No less than five dialogues between Robert de Béthune and King John are reported, all containing direct speech, more than between John and any other individual. This is 'a chronicle with close access to sources at court'.[15]

Whether the Anonymous was a clerk or layman cannot be known for certain.[16] But whatever his status, the values he espoused appear to have been more secular than ecclesiastic. There is no subject on which he dwelt more lovingly than warfare, particularly in Flanders, the scene of many a beautiful – as he saw it – chevauchée.[17] It was doubtless this aspect of his work which made Kate Norgate dub him 'the Flemish soldier-chronicler'.[18] This did not prevent him from writing about great religious and social occasions such as the translation of Becket's body in 1220, or from taking an interest in the politics of religion as when he remarked on how few London churches respected the ban on religious services in the summer of 1216.[19] But in his account of the disputed Canterbury election, the author criticized those monks who went against the king's wishes and his praise for Hubert Walter, whom he twice called 'the good archbishop', is strikingly secular in tone: 'very generous and very valiant and very courteous'.[20] According to Spiegel: 'He employs a vigorous language aimed at pleasing a lay audience in a graceful and lively manner, creating a narrative through which he scatters

---

[14] *Histoire des ducs*, pp. i, 153; O. Holder-Egger, ed., *Ex historiis ducum Normaniae et regum Angliae*, Monumenta Germaniae Historica Scriptores 26 (Hanover, 1882), p. 700. If so he may also have read the letter sent to Louis of France by William Marshal late on Saturday 9 September 1217: *Histoire des ducs*, p. 203.

[15] Nicholas Vincent, 'Isabella of Angoulême: John's Jezebel', in Stephen D. Church, ed., *King John: New Interpretations* (Woodbridge, 1999), pp. 165–219, at p. 200.

[16] Most scholars have thought him a layman, but Delisle, before changing his mind, had thought him a clerk, and Duby preferred to sit on the fence: Georges Duby, *The Legend of Bouvines* (Berkeley, 1990), p. 58. In his essay in this volume, David Crouch presents evidence which tends to hint at clerical status.

[17] For the fighting in Flanders in May–June 1213 and the 'beautiful chevauchées', see *Histoire des ducs*, pp. 130–9, 141–2, 173, 200. These and similar passages reinforce the likelihood that the Anonymous was male.

[18] Norgate, *John Lackland*, p. 276; 'on croirait lire les mémoires d'un soldat', Petit-Dutaillis, 'Nouvelle chronique', 69. But there is no mention of the Anonymous or his opinion of John as a soldier in Ralph Turner, 'King John's Military Reputation Reconsidered', *Journal of Medieval History* 19 (1993), 171–200.

[19] *Histoire des ducs*, pp. 171–2, 208–9.

[20] Although aware of Stephen Langton's learning, he was noticeably less enthusiastic about him, possibly because of his role in the making of Magna Carta: *Histoire des ducs*, pp. 101, 105, 110, 149.

amusing anecdotes, proverbial sayings and memorable dialogues'.[21] *Prima facie* then the *Histoire des ducs* appears to provide direct evidence for contemporary secular opinion – hence what should be its fundamental importance in any assessment of King John, a king who, after all, was brought down in 1215–16 not by the church and papacy, but by laymen acting in defiance of the pope.

One possible explanation for the relative neglect of the *Histoire des ducs* is that it may have been assumed that because the author came from Artois he can have understood little of English politics. Formally Artois was part of the kingdom of France, and King Philip's son, Louis, was count of Artois; the Anonymous clearly recognized this, calling Louis's wife Blanche 'ma dame'.[22] But from the 1180s onwards Artois had been at the heart of tension and war between the king of France and the counts of Flanders and the Anonymous consistently referred to Robert of Béthune and his friends as men of Flanders.[23] Their loyalty to Flanders brought them into close contact with the man who was generally their count's most important ally, the king of England. Robert's father, William, received grants of estates in England from Henry II, Richard and John, estates to which Robert himself succeeded in 1214.[24] One of his uncles was Baldwin of Béthune, a man whose prowess and friendship with Richard I led to him being raised to the heights of the Anglo-Norman aristocracy as count of Aumale and lord of Holderness.[25] Another uncle was Jean de Béthune, provost of Douai, whom Richard I had wanted to make dean of York.[26] As Capetian pressure on Artois and Flanders mounted, the aristocracy of that region increasingly found themselves forced to make potentially dangerous political choices. They needed to keep a close eye on the English court.

But they needed to watch what was happening at the French court as

---

[21] Spiegel, *Romancing the Past*, p. 230. On his knightly values, see Laborderie, 'Convergences et divergences', pp. 195, 199–200.

[22] *Histoire des ducs*, pp. 198, 200.

[23] *Histoire des ducs*, pp. 127–8 and thereafter *passim*. On the beginnings of Capetian pressure on Artois, see Daniel Power, *The Norman Frontier in the Twelfth and Early Thirteenth Centuries* (Cambridge, 2004), pp. 406–12.

[24] *Rot. Litt. Claus.*, i, p. 208b, for King John's order to the sheriffs of Nottingham, Northampton, Kent, Gloucester and Hertford to admit Robert as heir. Robert became the best rewarded of the Flemings in John's service, G. G. Dept, *Les Influences anglaises et françaises dans le comté de Flandre au début du XIIIᵉ siècle* (Ghent, 1928), pp. 128–9.

[25] On Baldwin, see Barbara English, *The Lords of Holderness, 1086–1260* (Oxford, 1979), pp. 32–6. He went to Ireland in 1210, so it may have been through him, or one of his knights, that the Anonymous derived his information on that expedition, Duffy, 'King John's Expedition', 8–9.

[26] *Howden*, iii, p. 221. Another of Robert's uncles was Conon of Béthune, the wellknown trouvère and a leading figure on the Fourth Crusade.

well. It may have been this that led the Anonymous to write a second chronicle, a *Chronique des rois de France*, beginning – as was traditional with histories of France – with the fall of Troy and continuing up to his own day.[27] The fact that the Anonymous wrote two overlapping but distinct versions of the same story, one focusing on the ruler of Normandy and England, the other on the king of France, enabled him, as Spiegel put it, 'to set forth the political forces and choices that weighed on the house of Béthune' during a 'turbulent era'.[28] Whereas the *Histoire's* account of the battle of Bouvines is cursory in the extreme, the *Chronique* contains a long narrative of King Philip's greatest victory.[29] Common to both, however, is the care and detail with which the Anonymous wrote about the relationships between his people and the kings of France and England. After Bouvines, he commented, the land of France enjoyed great peace, but Nevelon, the bailli of Arras, reduced all of Flanders to such servitude that all who heard about it were amazed at such suffering.[30] Robert of Béthune is less prominent in the *Chronique* than in the *Histoire*, doubtless because he came into much closer contact with the king of England than with the king of France. But he does appear. It was he, apparently, who knighted his cousin, Hugh de la Bretaigne. Most strikingly it is reported that he was captured in the battle of Bouvines (1214), but persuaded a knight called Flamenc de Crespelaines to release him and put him in safety.[31]

It is to the advantage of historians that the Anonymous's overriding attachment to Flanders and Artois meant that he was able to take a fairly detached view of the kings of both England and France, but that historians of England should have turned to the *Histoire* rather than to the *Chronique* is entirely understandable, especially since it is the more entertaining of the two. It is as though the author had already used up most of his best stories by the time he began to compose his second narrative. Not all of them fortunately. His account of John's visit to Fontainebleau in 1201 when Philip put both his palace and wine cellar at the king of England's disposal ends with the king of France and his people having a good laugh when they saw that John's followers had drunk all the bad wines and left the good.[32] But

---

[27] *Chronique des rois*, xxiv pt 2, pp. 750–75. The case for one author being responsible for both works was made by Delisle and Petit-Dutaillis in the 1890s and has been accepted ever since. For his insights into the French court, see John Baldwin, *The Government of Philip Augustus* (Berkeley, 1986) pp. 123, 336.

[28] Spiegel, *Romancing the Past*, pp. 229, 235.

[29] Translated into English in Duby, *Legend of Bouvines*, pp. 194–7.

[30] *Chronique des rois*, p. 770. Compare Baldwin, *Government*, p. 135.

[31] *Chronique des rois*, pp. 765, 769. The silence of the *Histoire des ducs* on the subject had led Holder-Egger, writing before the *Chronique* was known, to conclude that Robert cannot have been at Bouvines, *Ex historiis*, p. 700.

[32] *Chronique des rois*, p. 760.

one consequence of English historians ignoring the Anonymous's 'other work' is that several of his most critical comments concerning John have gone largely unobserved. In his narrative of the events of 1206 he called John a coward; in his account of John's retreat from La Roche-au-Moine in 1214 he said that he acted 'molt vilainement'. According to the *Histoire*, John imprisoned his nephew Arthur in the tower at Rouen where he died; according to the *Chronique*, he put him in the tower and then murdered him.[33]

It is generally believed that the *Histoire* was composed very soon after the date (1220) of the last events recorded in it; there is at any rate no indication that it was written much later.[34] The Anonymous was clearly writing after John's death. Referring to the king's quarrel with Robert FitzWalter, he observed that 'he committed wrongs for as long as he lived.'[35] But although his whole narrative was composed after the event, it is very far from being all of a piece. On the contrary, its coverage of the years between 1199 (John's accession) and 1217 (Louis of France's departure from England) falls into two distinct parts: the first part up to May 1213, the second from May 1213 to September 1217. In the printed edition the fourteen years of the first part take up about forty pages; the four and a half years of the second about seventy-five. The author evidently wanted to follow chronological order throughout, but for his first part he had no written sources available and was unable to supply precise dates. Events are dated only approximately with such phrases as 'before one Christmas', 'at this time', 'during the interdict'.[36] But in the second part there are passages sprinkled with dates such as 'Monday after Pentecost' or 'Thursday, the fourth day after the feast of St Matthew' which allow us to date sequences of events very precisely – in 1213 from 28 May until 6 June; in 1215 from 24 to 27 September; in 1216 from 18 May to 14 June; in 1217 from 21 April to 30 May and from 24 August to 13 September.[37] This degree of precision suggests that irrespective of whether or not the Anonymous was himself an eyewitness of events from 1213 to 1217, when he came to compose his chronicle he must have been able to use diary-style written notes.[38] This means that the *Histoire* from May 1213

---

[33] *Histoire des ducs*, p. 95; *Chronique des rois*, pp. 762, 767.

[34] Although it breaks off in 1217, the *Chronique des rois* is generally thought to have been written a little later than the *Histoire des ducs*. It refers, by implication, to the death of Bishop Stephen of Noyon (September 1221): Petit-Dutaillis, 'Nouvelle chronique', 70. Unfortunately virtually nothing is known – at least to me – about Robert of Béthune's career in the early 1220s.

[35] *Histoire des ducs*, p. 119.

[36] *Histoire des ducs*, pp. 105, 107–9, 111, 115–16, 121.

[37] *Histoire des ducs*, pp. 130–8, 154–6, 168–73, 188–96, 200–5.

[38] Moreover a list such as that enumerating the number of knights brought by each

onwards contains the bones of some strictly contemporary narratives, some of them composed before John's death.

In these circumstances it is not surprising that the two parts treat John in very different ways. Part Two consists very largely of a narrative of what he did and said up until May 1216, when it ceases to follow him (for reasons which are explored below), but it offers no character sketch or generalizations about him – not even in the form of an obituary notice when recording his death. Part One, by contrast, where the *Histoire* is both less contemporary and less well informed, contains a character sketch and a number of anecdotes illustrating his relations with queen, barons and ministers. The beginning of Part Two in May 1213 coincides – evidently not coincidentally – with the first mention of Robert of Béthune. At this date he was already in John's service, one of the six Flemish 'high men' who, together their followers, were still in bed when Baldwin of Nieuwpoort arrived at their quarters near Dover. Baldwin had been sent to England by Count Ferrand of Flanders to ask for help against an invasion by King Philip. On hearing their count's message, the Flemings chose Robert as their spokesman. There then follows an account of the conversation, with the king's words given in direct speech, between King John and Robert, the first of the dialogues between them. Here John appears as a well-informed and sensible man, anticipating the request for licence to return to Flanders, and taking counsel as a good lord should before delivering his own, helpful message. He was both properly appreciative of the Flemings and businesslike. The help he promptly sent under the command of his half-brother, Earl William of Salisbury, succeeded in destroying the French fleet at Damme.[39]

After narrating the Franco-Flemish war of May–June 1213 in great detail, the chronicle then fast-forwards to January 1214 and to Windsor, where the next conversation between Robert and John took place. When the king told Robert that his lord the count of Flanders had landed at Sandwich, Robert asked why he wasn't already on his way to see him. 'Listen to the Fleming!' said the king, 'he thinks his lord the count really counts for something.' 'By St Jacques!' replied Robert, 'I'm right, that he does!' John laughed and rode so fast to Canterbury that most of his staff, their horses exhausted, were left behind. He went straight to Ferrand's lodgings, greeted him courteously and invited him to dine with him the next day; the alliance between them was confirmed and strengthened.[40] Robert then returned to Flanders

---

lord who accompanied Louis's invasion in May 1216 suggests another type of written source: *Histoire des ducs*, pp. 165–7.

[39] *Histoire des ducs*, pp. 127–30. Record evidence confirms that Robert was in John's service by May 1213: *Rot. Litt. Claus.*, p. 133.

[40] *Histoire des ducs*, pp. 139–40. Spiegel's account of this incident, covering only John's initial jibe and commenting that his disdain for the protocols of honor

with Ferrand. After a narrative of the war they waged in the spring of 1214, the Anonymous switched to a brief account of John's campaign in western France and his reception of the news of the battle of Bouvines.

From Bouvines he turned directly to the subject of the rebellion against John.[41] This brought Robert, accompanied by his brother William and many knights, back to England in John's service again. They arrived in May 1215, just as London fell to the rebels, the 'Northerners'. John immediately sent them, together with the earl of Salisbury, to relieve the siege of Exeter, but at Sherborne they received reports which indicated that their way led through a wood where the road was blocked by a makeshift but strongly defended palisade. The earl took counsel and retreated, much to John's irritation. 'So you fell, did you, at the first hurdle', he jeered. These words, the Flemings felt, were deeply shaming. Soon afterwards the earl and the Flemings were ordered to go to Exeter again, and this time Robert's reminder of John's jibe persuaded them, though outnumbered, to go forward to win or die rather than retreat 'vilainement'. In the face of their bold advance, the Northerners retreated.[42] In this episode (the third 'conversation' between John and the Flemings) the king's sharp tongue is represented as having the desired effect. On the whole the author's treatment of John during the period from May 1213 to May 1215 was a positive one. He observed, for example, that Robert of Dreux, taken prisoner at Nantes during John's expedition to France in 1214, was held 'molt honnerablement', being allowed to enjoy the pleasures of hunting and hawking.[43]

But while Salisbury and the Flemings were at Exeter, John met the rebels at Staines and agreed peace terms. From then on a more critical note is heard. When the king next met the Flemings,

> he no longer showed them as friendly a countenance as formerly. None the less they went with him to Marlborough. There he did a villainous thing (*grant vilonnie*). He had a great quantity of his treasure taken from the tower and brought into his chambers, in the sight of all the knights of Flanders, but didn't give any of it to them. After this villainy which the king did, the Flemings took their leave from him and returned to Flanders.[44]

---

governing relations between allies courted disaster', is misleadingly abbreviated: *Romancing the Past*, p. 249.

[41] *Histoire des ducs*, pp. 141–6.

[42] *Histoire des ducs*, pp. 147–9.

[43] *Histoire des ducs*, pp. 143–4. Although no doubt intended as a contrast to his comments on deaths of Arthur of Brittany and the Briouzes, it may also have reflected how Robert of Béthune felt in 1214.

[44] *Histoire des ducs*, pp. 149–51.

Despite this, a few months later Robert of Béthune was prepared to enter John's service again, though not before, according to the Anonymous, he had received a letter containing the king's abject apology.[45] After Robert joined John, the king advanced to besiege Rochester. *En route* the two of them had their fourth conversation, in which John expressed contempt for his enemies: 'Even if we had fewer men than we do have, we might safely go to fight against them.'[46] Whether or not Robert was impressed by John's bold words, he was doubtless pleased to be promised possession of a great estate belonging to one of the rebels, the earldom of Clare. At Rochester John and Robert talked again, this time about bringing over more aid from Flanders. While John laid siege to Rochester, Robert captured the Clare family castle of Tonbridge, enabling the king, in the sixth of their conversations, to greet him as 'My lord of Clare' and remind him that he still had to take possession of the castle of Clare itself.[47] According to the Anonymous, when Rochester surrendered John planned to hang the knights of the garrison, but the 'high men' who were with him dissuaded him, saying that would be a bad mistake, for if he hanged some of their enemies, they would reply in kind.[48] Since the Anonymous does not name any of these 'high men', it seems unlikely that Robert was among them, but he would doubtless have approved the argument.[49]

In his narrative of 1216 the Anonymous described King John backing away from confronting his enemies on no fewer than four occasions – in ironic contrast to his bold words on the way to Rochester.[50] Much the most critical of those retreats was his flight as Louis's fleet approached the shore at Sandwich on 22 May 1216. According to the Anonymous, John had his trumpets sounded, but then lost heart and made off at such speed to Dover that he had gone a league before his men knew anything of it, giving them no

---

[45] *Histoire des ducs*, p. 153.

[46] In this exchange John expressed his shame that foreigners should witness the wickedness of English people: *Histoire des ducs*, pp. 158–9.

[47] *Histoire des ducs*, pp. 159, 162–3. According to Roger of Wendover, Tonbridge was captured on 28 November by, presumably, those besieging Rochester: Matthew Paris, *Chronica Majora*, ii, p. 638. Neither Roger nor any English chronicler ever mentions Robert de Béthune by name. But record evidence confirms the grant of Richard de Clare's earldom: *Rot. Litt. Claus.*, pp. 251, 268.

[48] *Histoire des ducs*, p. 163.

[49] According to Wendover, it was Savari de Mauléon who made this argument: Matthew Paris, *Chronica Majora*, ii, p. 626. It may be that conversations between him and Robert (or between their staffs) in 1215–16 lie behind the stories of Savari's earlier exploits in western France: *Histoire des ducs*, pp. 96, 100–103.

[50] *Histoire des ducs*, p. 165 (from London), p. 169 (at Sandwich), p. 173 (at Winchester, with extra details in his other work, *Chronique des rois*, pp. 771–2), p. 179 (near Reading).

choice but to follow after.[51] The decision not to oppose Louis's landing was one that could be, and was, defended.[52] The way it was implemented was, however, disastrously inept. The mood of Robert and his fellow Flemings, those whom twelve months earlier John had urged to be bold, was, as the Anonymous emphasizes, one of despair, irritation and displeasure. They were ordered to act as his rearguard as he made for Winchester, and in so doing they suffered a mauling at the hands of the men of the Weald. At this point Robert disappears from the story. We hear no more of his actions or of his conversations. Moreover at precisely this point there is an abrupt change in the narrative thread. From now on, instead of following King John and Robert of Béthune as hitherto, it focuses on Louis and follows his movements until he returned to France in September 1217.[53] Did Robert also switch sides and follow Louis?[54] If he did, this must have made some things easier. Among those who came with Louis in May 1216 was Robert's older brother, Daniel, the head of the family.[55] To change sides was to reunite the house of Béthune. But to some it may have smacked of disloyalty. The Anonymous had made much of Robert's loyalty when discussing his relations with the count of Flanders.[56] In a work written for Robert, even after 1220, when allegiance to Louis was presumably much more palatable, so sudden a reversal of allegiance was perhaps better passed over in silence.

In the light of the close-up view which Robert of Béthune had of John's retreat in May 1216, it is not in the least surprising that the Anonymous should have been one of the king's sharpest critics.

> He was a very bad man, more cruel than all others; he lusted after beautiful women and because of this he shamed the high men of the

---

[51] *Histoire des ducs*, pp. 169–70.

[52] To English chroniclers such as Roger of Wendover and the 'Barnwell' and Dunstable annalists, it seemed that too many of John's troops were foreigners owing allegiance to the king of France to be trusted to fight against Louis: Matthew Paris, *Chronica Majora*, ii, 654; *Walter of Coventry*, ii, pp. 229–30; *Annales Monastici*, iii, p. 46. But aristocratic Flemings such as Robert of Béthune and his fellow commanders had spent the last few years doing precisely that.

[53] *Histoire des ducs*, pp. 170–205. John, of course, could hardly disappear altogether until October 1216: *Histoire des ducs*, pp. 163, 179–81.

[54] As Petit-Dutaillis thought, 'Nouvelle chronique', 66; C. Petit-Dutaillis, Étude sur la vie et le *règne de Louis VIII* (Paris, 1894), pp. xx, 106. On the other hand Holder-Egger believed that Robert's disappearance meant that he had returned to the continent: *Ex historiis*, p. 700.

[55] In the campaigning which followed the Anonymous found several occasions on which to record the contribution made by Daniel's men: *Histoire des ducs*, pp. 166, 172, 175, 178, 188, 190–1.

[56] *Histoire des ducs*, pp. 128–9. A point well made in Spiegel, *Romancing the Past*, pp. 251–2, 259.

land, for which reason he was greatly hated. Whenever he could, he told lies rather than the truth.[57] He set his barons against one another whenever he could; he was very happy when he saw hate between them. He hated and was jealous of all honourable men (*preudomes*); it greatly displeased him when he saw anyone acting well. He was brim-full of evil qualities.[58]

Some of the Anonymous's most vivid stories, those relating to Matilda de Briouze and Robert FitzWalter, illustrate John's cruelty and lust. His Matilda was an impressive woman, a rancher who ran huge herds of cattle and boasted of her cheese production, a successful war leader against the Welsh and a good servant to the king; 'moult sage et moult preus et moult vighereuse' – phrases usually used to praise outstanding men; but she was also a 'biele dame'. John, after quarrelling with her husband, imprisoned her and her eldest son in Windsor Castle, where they starved to death. In phrases presumably intended to move his audience to pity, he painted a vivid picture of the discovery of their bodies, the son sitting against a wall, she sitting between his legs and leaning on his chest, so desperately hungry that she had eaten his cheeks. The fact that, according to the Anonymous, Matilda had boasted of her thousands of cows to her nephew, Baldwin de Béthune Count of Aumale, both indicates a likely source for the gruesome details and suggests that her death was a matter of special concern to his patron's family.[59]

The Anonymous's anecdotes about the quarrel between John and Robert FitzWalter contain the most circumstantial evidence for the king's lusts.[60] According to this account, FitzWalter fled to the Continent claiming that John had driven him abroad because he had opposed John's attempt to force his elder daughter to have sex with him. Since he left his wife and children at Arras while he went on to repeat the tale to Philip Augustus, this was a story which the Anonymous could have heard from the FitzWalters themselves.[61] Although modern historians have sometimes written as though John was accused of sexual profligacy, he was not. The charge made at the time and as it developed in subsequent decades was that he dishonoured

---

[57] John's preference for untruths is illustrated by his malicious attempt to unsettle William Marshal in 1207, a story well told in David Crouch, *William Marshal*, 2nd edn (London, 2002), pp. 104–11, based on *HWM*, i, lines 13801–51.

[58] *Histoire des ducs*, p. 105.

[59] *Histoire des ducs*, pp. 111–15.

[60] In making a similar charge, Roger of Wendover named no names. 'There were many nobles whose wives and daughters John had violated, despite the objections of their husbands and fathers': Matthew Paris, *Chronica Majora*, ii, p. 535.

[61] *Histoire des ducs*, pp. 117–21. For discussion, see Norgate, *John Lackland*, pp. 289–93.

some of the most powerful men in his kingdom by subjecting their wives and daughters to forceful sexual harassment.[62]

But the Anonymous's picture of John was not all bad. After his most scathing criticism, his next word was 'but'.

> But he spent lavishly; he gave plenty to eat, and did so generously and willingly. People never found the gate or the doors of John's hall barred against them, so that all who wanted to eat at his court could do so. At the three great feasts he gave robes aplenty to his knights. This was a good quality of his.[63]

Although there are no extant records of the royal court's routine daily expenditure on food and drink before the 1220s, the ample scale of provision at John's great feasts can be inferred from Exchequer records. This mattered. In David Carpenter's words: 'The food and drink which the household provided were integral to the political process, allowing the king to display his magnificence and demonstrate his generosity.'[64] In this respect John did well. Matthew Paris notoriously had few good words for him, but when Henry III made cutbacks in order to save up for a crusade, it seemed to Matthew that he had 'unwisely deviated from his father's footsteps'.[65]

Twice the Anonymous observed that John was devoted to pleasure. If, as other evidence suggests, he ate and drank too much, this did not figure in the *Histoire*. Possibly Robert of Béthune had been too well entertained at court to want to make this criticism.[66] In both instances the Anonymous remarked on John's delight in hunting and hawking; in one instance he added the king's pleasure in a queen whom he much loved.[67] His portrait of John's relations with the queen, Isabella of Angouleme, is a remarkable one. If his John is a sharp-tongued king, he more than met his match in her.

> On receiving news of some loss or other he said to her, 'You hear, my

---

[62] Painter, who made more use of the *Histoire des ducs* than John's later biographers, commented that since the Anonymous also gave another account of the outbreak of John's quarrel, he 'obviously doubted' FitzWalter's story: Sidney Painter, *The Reign of King John* (Baltimore, 1949), p. 234. I don't follow the logic of this.

[63] *Histoire des ducs*, p. 105. The robes he gave to his knights at Christmas 1201, 1207 and 1213 were thought worthy of special note even by Roger of Wendover: Matthew Paris, *Chronica Majora*, ii, pp. 475, 520, 571.

[64] David Carpenter, 'The Household Rolls of King Henry III of England (1216–72)', *Historical Research* 80:207 (2007), 22–46, at 41–2.

[65] Matthew Paris, *Chronica Majora*, v, p. 114.

[66] An audit of King John's wine taken in 1201 revealed that he had over 700 tuns (180,000 gallons: a tun = cask containing 252 gallons) stored in fifteen castles and houses: Doris M. Stenton, ed., *Pipe Roll 4 John*, PRS 53 n.s. 15 (London, 1937), pp. 82–4.

[67] *Histoire des ducs*, pp. 104, 109.

lady, all that I have lost for you.' To which she immediately replied, 'And I, my lord, have lost the best knight in the world for you.'[68] After some more news, he said, 'My lady, don't worry, for by the faith I owe you, I know a corner where you won't have to watch out for the king of France for 10 years, not for all his power.' 'Indeed, my lord', she said, 'I really think you are keen to be a king who is mated in a corner'.[69]

Although she bore John at least five children between 1207 and 1215, it is a remarkable fact that after leaving England in 1217 she made not a single reference to him, or to prayers for his soul, in all the charters issued in her name over the next thirty years; thus it appears that she felt no affection for him at all.[70]

According to the Anonymous, in 1210 both John and his followers were very amused by the king of Connacht's habit of riding bareback.[71] This episode from Part One fits in with Part Two's depiction of a king quick to mock and jeer. Other contemporary narratives note the same tendency. According to a Canterbury chronicle, for example, in 1207 in a dispute over the king's right to tax the church, the archbishop of York went to see John. He fell at his feet, begging for exemption. By way of reply, 'John fell at the archbishop's feet, laughing and saying, "You see, my lord archbishop, I have done for you just as much as you have for me." And thus he dismissed him, not with consolation but with ridicule.'[72] It appears, not surprisingly, that he surrounded himself with like-minded courtiers. According to Ralph of Coggeshall, Cistercian abbots were worried about approaching the king's household 'in case they should be ... received with ridicule by the triflers

---

[68] An allusion to the fact that she had been betrothed to Hugh of Lusignan when John carried her off in August 1200. On this, see Vincent, 'Isabella', 165–75, and *Histoire des ducs*, p. 91.

[69] *Histoire des ducs*, pp. 104–5. Compare Roger of Wendover's report (under the year 1203) that John spent all morning in bed with his wife: Matthew Paris, *Chronica Majora*, ii, pp. 482, 489.

[70] Vincent, 'Isabella', p. 198. The Anonymous believed she was pregnant when John died: *Histoire des ducs*, pp. 180–1.

[71] *Histoire des ducs*, p. 112. Given the widespread view that Irish practices were outlandish, even barbarous, this reaction was probably commonplace. Even so, Gerald de Barri had believed that John's followers went too far during his expedition to Ireland in 1185: 'there came to meet him the Irish of those parts, men of some note hitherto loyal to the English ... But they were treated with contempt and derision, pulling them about by their beards, large and flowing according to the native custom', Giraldus, *The Conquest of Ireland*, ed. and trans. A. B. Scott and F. X. Martin (Dublin, 1978), p. 237.

[72] Pope Innocent III was shocked by reports of this incident: William Stubbs, ed., *The Historical Works of Gervase of Canterbury*, 2 vols, Rolls Series 73 (London, 1879–80), ii, pp. lix–lx.

of the royal hall'.[73] The most basic rule throughout courtesy literature in all languages is: do not do or say anything to humiliate others. Don't mock. Don't ridicule.[74] That John and his entourage seem to have flouted this rule is ironic in view of the evidence linking the most comprehensive of courtesy poems, 'The Book of the Civilized Man' by Daniel of Beccles, with the court of Henry II.[75] This book takes the form characteristic of much courtesy literature, that of a father's advice to his son. But although John's father was praised for his courtliness, he evidently failed to teach his son this fundamental rule.[76] In the Anonymous's account of John's reign the one man whose courtliness is explicitly admired is Archbishop Hubert Walter, displaying that quality most clearly in his ability to rise above John's jealous attempts to impoverish and humble him.[77]

The king's feebleness in May 1216 plainly proved to be the last straw for Robert of Béthune, but equally plainly Magna Carta had provoked an earlier crisis in their relationship – despite the fact that as a peace treaty it allowed the Flemings to secure the release of their servants who had earlier been trapped in London.[78] So far as the Anonymous was concerned, the treaty which John made with the rebels 'without waiting for the advice of his brother and the Flemings was 'la vilaine pais' – a phrase he used three times in the space of five sentences.[79] It may well be that in this wholehearted condemnation there was in part the self-interest of Robert and his knights made redundant by the peace. If so, this is an aspect of the treaty about which the Anonymous preferred to keep quiet.[80] But about other aspects of the charter he was much more forthcoming – in marked contrast to our

---

[73] *Coggeshall*, pp. 104–5.

[74] See John Gillingham, 'From *civilitas* to Civility: Codes of Manners in Medieval and Early Modern England', *Transactions of the Royal Historical Society*, 6th ser. 12 (2002), 267–89, at 277–8.

[75] J. G. Smyly, ed., *Urbanus Magnus Danielis Becclesiensis* (Dublin, 1939). For a seminal analysis of 'the earliest English courtesy book' and its link with the Angevin court, see Robert Bartlett, *England under the Norman and Angevin Kings, 1075–1225* (Oxford, 2000), pp. 582–8.

[76] John Gillingham, 'The Cultivation of History, Legend and Courtesy at the Court of Henry II', in Ruth Kennedy and Simon Meecham-Jones, eds, *Writers of the Reign of Henry II: Twelve Essays* (New York, 2006), pp. 25–52, 39–40. According to Raimon Vital de Besalú, Henry II and three of his sons, Henry, Richard and Geoffrey, were all paragons of courtliness: J.-C. Huchet, ed., *Nouvelles occitanes du moyen âge* (Paris, 1992), pp. 50–5, 86. Just what should be read into Raimon's omission of John depends upon the (uncertain) date of the poem.

[77] *Histoire des ducs*, pp. 101, 105–7. See C. R. Young, *Hubert Walter, Lord of Canterbury and Lord of England* (Durham, NC, 1968), pp. 151–2.

[78] *Histoire des ducs*, pp. 147, 150.

[79] *Histoire des ducs*, pp. 149–51.

[80] Whether they felt that c. 51, in which John promised to expel all foreign soldiers,

only other evidence for secular opinion, the *History of William Marshal*, which says little more than that the trouble began when 'The barons came to the king and asked him to grant them their privileges, which he refused.'[81] The Anonymous evidently regarded the rebels with some distaste, observing that 'They required him [the king] to observe faithfully what he had agreed with them; but what they had previously agreed with their men they were unwilling to observe.'[82] Nonetheless, in picking out four concessions to which John was forced to agree, he chose issues on which he tended to sympathize with the barons. First, a woman should never be disparaged by being married to a man beneath her station. 'This', he wrote, 'was the best agreement which he made with them, had it been well kept.' Second, John 'had to agree that he would never cause a man to lose life or limb for any wild beast that he took, but that he should be able to pay a fine.'[83] To this too the Anonymous raised no objection. 'These two things could readily be tolerated.' The wording of his third item – that the king had to fix reliefs which heirs paid for estates, which were too high, at the rates which the barons demanded – suggests that he shared the belief that many reliefs were indeed too high. His fourth item was that the barons insisted that they should enjoy the highest powers of jurisdiction in their lands. His comments on the first three concessions and the absence of any comment on the fourth, suggests that he thought none of these was intolerable. Indeed, he noted that they demanded many other things 'with much reason'.[84]

But there is not the slightest doubt that he thought that overall Magna Carta was a wretched document. And it is very clear why.

> Over and above all this they wanted 25 barons to be chosen, so that the king should treat them in all matters and by the judgement of these 25. He would redress through these 25 all the wrongs that he did them, and they likewise would through the 25 redress all the wrongs that they might do to him. And they also wished that

was directed against them is a moot point, since Robert of Béthune was one of the king's tenants.

[81] The author was very uncomfortable about Magna Carta, stating that he would not say more, since 'to do so might result in harm to myself': *HWM*, i, line 15035.

[82] *Histoire des ducs*, p. 151.

[83] In fact this concession first appeared in the Forest Charter of 1217 (ch. 10), not in the charter of June 1215. That the Anonymous was impressed by the severity of John's forest law is shown by his image of England as a land in which wild animals were able to graze as safely as sheep; if chased, they merely trotted away; whenever the hunter stopped, they stopped too: *Histoire des ducs*, p. 109. In his essay in this volume, David Crook suggests on evidence of Pipe Roll entries that fines may have been the normal penalty even before 1217.

[84] *Histoire des ducs*, p. 150.

the king would never appoint a bailiff in his land except through the 25.[85]

The Anonymous's version of Magna Carta concentrated on the powers of the Twenty-Five, even to the extent of attributing to them the power – not explicitly given them in the charter itself – to appoint bailiffs.[86] He saw as clearly as any subsequent commentator that the sanctions clause (clause 61) was the most startling and revolutionary change proposed in Magna Carta. 'What', asked Fritz Kern,

> is the essence of Magna Carta, in virtue of which it has become a landmark in history? Not the fact that a king once again, as so often, admitted certain legal duties, and promised to fulfil them ... The only fundamentally new thing in the treaty... is the establishment of an authority to see that the king carries out his obligations, and if he fails, to coerce him. ... The sixty-first article deserves its fame ... It incorporated the right of resistance in the written public law of a nation, and the creation of a committee of resistance gave it the vitality necessary for institutional development.[87]

This, in Holt's words, was the 'sledge-hammer' which, if used, 'would amount to civil war'.[88]

The Anonymous described or imagined a scene in which this was expressed in Symbolic (Timothy Reuter's name for the pan-European language of political theatre).[89]

> One day the 25 came to the king's court to give a judgement. The king's feet were giving him so much trouble that he could not walk and so he stayed in bed. He ordered the 25 to come to his chamber to give their judgement since he could not go to them. They replied that they would not for that would be against their right (*droiture*). If he could not walk, he must have himself carried. So since he could do nothing about it, he was carried into their presence, and they did not rise to meet him, for it was said that had they done so, it would have been contrary to their right.[90]

---

[85]　My translation is based on those in Petit-Dutaillis, *Studies and Notes*, 132–3, and in J. C. Holt, *Magna Carta*, 2nd edn (Cambridge, 1992), p. 271.

[86]　Holt, *The Northerners*, p. 118.

[87]　Fritz Kern, *Kingship and Law in the Middle Ages*, trans. S. B. Chrimes (Oxford, 1956), pp. 127–9. Compare Warren, *King John*, pp. 259–60.

[88]　Holt, *Magna Carta*, p. 346.

[89]　Timothy Reuter, *Medieval Polities & Modern Mentalities*, ed. Janet L. Nelson (Cambridge, 2006), pp. 169–70.

[90]　'On the strength of this wretched peace they treated him with such pride as must move all the world to pity': *Histoire des ducs*, p. 151.

As Holt noted, 'Within this highly coloured and dramatic picture there was a real kernel of truth'.[91] Several decades later Matthew Paris, in one of his additions to Roger of Wendover, went to the heart of the matter, imagining John in the weeks after Magna Carta being mocked as now just one of twenty-five kings in England, in effect king no longer.[92] But none of the other contemporary commentators, not Roger of Wendover, nor the 'Barnwell' chronicler, nor Ralph of Coggeshall, saw this kernel of truth as clearly and vividly as the Anonymous of Béthune.

---

[91] Holt, *Magna Carta*, p. 361.

[92] Matthew Paris, *Chronica Majora*, ii, pp. 610–11. Matthew attributed this derisive laughter to John's paid troops. Moreover in his later and more condensed history, the only part of the charter which Matthew quoted in full was c. 61: Frederic Madden, ed., *Matthaei Parisiensis Historia Anglorum*, 3 vols, Rolls Series 44 (London, 1866–9), ii, pp. 158–9.

Baronial Paranoia in King John's Reign

DAVID CROUCH

THERE COMES A POINT in some political crises when talking stops and the parties mobilize for conflict. Civil war is rarely inevitable, and right up to the last moment it may well seem avoidable and resolvable. The descent into civil war in England in 1215 is well documented and, in the light of that documentation, looks abrupt at first sight. Unreasoning fear and persection mania – paranoia – played a powerful part in the preliminaries to the conflict, as in several other outbreaks of civil war. The king's own disposition showed such features in 1215. It has to be said that there has not been a shortage of commentators on King John's state of mind in the last years of his reign over recent decades, and I do not intend to focus particularly on *that* aspect of the crisis. What I do want to do is look at the collective state of mind of his opponents amongst the barons in and before 1215, so far as it is possible to do so. Fear has always been the emotion that most compels human beings to fight, and my suggestion here will be that it was unresolved and unchecked suspicion on both sides that led to the paranoia which triggered the Barons' Rebellion of 1215.

The key work in appreciating the baronial agenda and state of mind was published as long ago as 1955 by James Holt, then a young lecturer at the University of Nottingham. His *English Historical Review* article, 'The Barons and the Great Charter', was a singularly lucid and informed analysis of the run-up to Runnymede, and the basis of his landmark monograph, *The Northerners*, published in 1961. Holt located a number of issues which have since been visited and revisited by other historians, and which indeed I am going to revisit once again here.

Holt's remarkable article summed up a mass of arguments and developments in a mere twenty-four pages and presented them with enviable clarity. It is not surprising therefore that it has been the basis of much of the discussion that has succeeded. His points were as follows. Despite the older tradition that the barons were puppets in the hands of the Church – and especially Archbishop Stephen Langton – when it came to putting forward their agenda for reform in 1215, Holt presented good evidence that the agenda was generated within the aristocracy. He believed that the various causes of the barons' discontent were the product as much of the reigns of Henry II and Richard I as of John's, though John much worsened the problems.[1] John did not himself believe he was asking of his realm more than established custom allowed. Barons and knights had a history of combining to negotiate with the king at a county level for a decade before Magna Carta, and were agitating on Magna Carta's agenda as early as the 1190s. Holt even offered some evidence that the terms of the coronation charter of Henry I – the rallying call of the barons in 1215 – were being appealed to in northern England nearly a decade before the Barons' Rebellion.[2]

It follows from Holt's work that the baronial agenda in the crisis of 1215 was not by any means the work of anger or the moment, but the end result of a long process of friction, discontent, and negotiation. This paper is not going to differ very radically on this issue from Holt's position in what it says. Its purpose is to look at how the barons were suddenly impelled to act on that agenda, and at that level, as we will see, reason and the deep sediment of generations of discontent and discussion had little to do with things. Fear impelled them to arms, not a considered desire for reform.

There are two particular sources which bring us quite close to the state of mind of the baronial party in the latter years of John's reign. The first was written by a Picard Frenchman, who was most probably a clerk associated with the household of the Flemish magnate, Robert de Béthune, a magnate who came to England in the winter of 1215–16 when he was hired to fight for John.[3] The allusions in the work of this anonymous writer tell us that he had been himself in England in 1216 and 1217. He had certainly

---

[1] In this volume, Ralph Turner comments on the earlier Angevin reigns as sources for later rebellion. I wish to record my thanks here for the help and advice offered in the revision of this paper by Hugh Doherty, John Gillingham, John Hudson, and Richard Sharpe.

[2] J. C. Holt, 'The Barons and the Great Charter', *English Historical Review* 70 (1955), 1–24.

[3] There is extended discussion about the author and his work in John Gillingham's essay in this volume. Some basic points were made about this author in Francisque Michel's introduction to his edition of *Histoire des ducs de Normandie et des rois d'Angleterre*, pp. i–iv. Michel established that the author was an eyewitness to the campaign of 1216–17 and derived from Artois. It cannot be established for certain whether he was a layman or clerk. He was certainly well read in the vernacular histories of Normandy composed by Wace and Benoit, whose work forms the basis of a quarter of his own. He repeats the castle list of Robert de Torigny's chronicle (p. 70) and quotes the prophecies of Merlin (p. 68), so he plainly also used Latin sources. He was very familiar with the diplomatic forms of the day (p. 153) so had been educated for business. His opening disquisition on the *mappa mundi* indicates a man who had received a liberal education. His work features nothing in the way of learned scriptural allusion, though one would not expect that in a vernacular history (compare Wace). He is however very keen to note and describe liturgical events – he ends his work with a description of the translation of Becket in July 1220, all of which tends to hint at a clerical status, if not a high one.

been in Kent, where he did a bit of tourism, visiting for instance the tombs of King Stephen and his queen, Mathilda of Boulogne, in Faversham Abbey, perhaps because of an interest in local Boulonnais history.[4] He subsequently wrote two prose historical works. One was a history of the dukes of Normandy and kings of England, a mostly derivative work up until it considers Richard's reign. The other was a complementary history of the kings of France, not quite so useful for our purposes. He clearly hoped for literary fame on both sides of the Channel. A pity he has not left us his name.

This observant commentator was a meticulous worker, researching Latin and French accounts of the past history of England and Normandy to get the background of his story. He was close enough to the baronial party in the south-east of England in 1216 to have been able to take notes of its version of the events that led up to Louis of France's invasion. His account of the years from 1212 to 1217 is particularly full. His take on John is generally hostile, although it has to be said that a sudden shift of sympathy towards the king becomes evident once the war had broken out; we even see John briefly as a noble figure at bay, joking with Robert de Béthune that he was less bothered by the damage the war was doing to him than by his feeling of embarrassment that his foreign friends would see at first hand how low his subjects had sunk.[5] The clerk certainly believed that the king was unreasonably treated by the Twenty-five barons who were the guarantors of the Magna Carta settlement.

Our second source close to the barons wrote for a lord on the other side, the royalists. This was the young man called John who, between 1224 and 1226, wrote a biography of the late loyalist baron, William Marshal, earl of Pembroke, the baron who in fact defeated the baronial party and ousted Louis of France from England after King John's death. Though the biographer knew little at first hand of what had happened in John's reign – he was most likely a Frenchman from the Loire valley – nonetheless he was provided with the memoirs of several barons who were associated with the Marshal, and was employed and paid by the Marshal's eldest son, who had in fact fought on the other side from his father, joining Louis's court in 1216, before King John's death.[6] John the biographer too is uniformly hostile to the king, even though Marshal was a loyalist throughout the reign. But again, as King John was brought to bay in his last year, the criticism ebbs and the king is portrayed at the last as a redoubtable and resourceful

---

[4] *Histoire des ducs*, pp. 80–1.

[5] *Histoire des ducs*, pp. 158–9.

[6] For the biography and its author, see *HWM*, iii, pp. 23–41; David Crouch, 'Writing a Biography in the Thirteenth Century: The Construction and Composition of the "History of William Marshal"', in David Bates, Julia Crick, and Sarah Hamilton, eds, *Writing Medieval Biography: Essays in Honour of Frank Barlow* (Woodbridge, 2006), pp. 221–35.

warrior. The biographer goes so far as to condemn many of the barons who turned against the king in 1215 as opportunists with no reasonable grudge against John.

Both these writers have a lot to say about paranoia. The Marshal biographer gives us the famous portrait of John skulking through the back lanes of Normandy in 1203 because he feared ambush by dissidents on the main roads, and commented that 'A man who does not know whom he has to fear and who always thinks he is in an inferior position is bound to fear everybody.'[7] His assessment of John's character was that the king lacked common sense (*saveir*), was possessed by arrogance (*orgels*), and was snide (*despleisante*).[8] He had several quite striking things to say about the way the king conducted relations with the Marshal, to which we shall return. The Béthune clerk also remarks on John's craven behaviour in Normandy in 1203. He talks of John's fears of Geoffrey fitz Peter, the justiciar, because he both distrusted the extent of Geoffrey's power and envied him his wealth. He talks also of the way John feared his own people as much as his Capetian enemies.[9] For the Béthune clerk, John was dishonest, lecherous, envious, and a spendthrift, even if people benefited from his liberality:

> He set his barons against each other whenever he could. He was delighted when he saw them at each other's throats. He hated all *preudommes* through envy; he was most unhappy when he saw a good deed done for anyone. He was brimming with bad qualities, but he spent freely, he gave plenty to eat and did so generously and willingly. Neither gate nor the entrance to his hall was ever closed to diners; all those who wanted to could eat in his court.[10]

These two writers get us as close as we can to the baronial view of the king against whom they rebelled. And neither says anything positive about him till he showed himself curiously redoubtable in the last months of his reign. As is well known, there is no contemporary source which has anything approving to say about John's character. The most sympathetic comment comes from a writer traditionally associated with Barnwell Priory in Cambridgeshire, and it is hardly unqualified: 'a great prince certainly, but not a happy one'.[11] The efforts of W. L. Warren to rehabilitate John's reputation as king were very necessary in their day. As he pointed out, previous

---

[7] *HWM*, ii, lines 12579–84.

[8] *HWM*, ii, lines 11966–98, 12105–10, 13579–88.

[9] *Histoire des ducs*, 97, 116

[10] *Histoire des ducs*, 105; my thanks to John Gillingham for the translation. Note the verdict of the Barnwell chronicler, that John was 'munificus et liberalis in exteros sed suorum depraedator': *Walter of Coventry*, ii, p. 232.

[11] 'princeps quidem magnus sed minus felix': *Walter of Coventry*, ii, p. 232.

writing on John's character depended rather too much on the ill-opinion of Roger of Wendover and Matthew Paris, whose verdicts were neither balanced nor – in Paris's case – contemporary.[12] But the verdict on John's character by strictly contemporary writers were – as we have just seen – anything but balanced either.[13]

What do we make of this? My feeling is that at the root of John's unhappiness was his defective ability to interact with his principal subjects. For all Holt's belief that John's problems were essentially a legacy of the reigns of his brother and father, John undeniably made things far worse by his inability to manage men and his mania for amassing money. Time again we see his wilfulness, suspicion, and lack of restraint. John was not a courtly ruler and was out of sympathy with the social habitus of his age. Martin Aurell has pointed out the telling and calculated exclusion of John by the noble poet Raimon Vidal de Besalú, a Catalan who wrote a verse reflection on courtliness – an *ensenhamen* – during John's reign. When Raimon was evoking avatars of courtliness he said that a noble man should display three virtues: bravery, generosity, and courtesy. 'These three virtues', he said in his dialogue,

> increased the acclaim of that Henry king of England your father must have mentioned, as you yourself said he had, as much as his three sons – men I myself do not forget – my lords Henry, Richard, and Geoffrey. They had twice as many virtues as I could list in a year. I myself saw them entering court at their father's side, men fit for lordship and war.[14]

Notice that John does not make it onto the Occitan poet's list of Henry II's four sons who are worthy of recall and imitation. The implication is

---

[12] W. L. Warren, *King John* (London, 1961), pp. 11–16. Warren was responding perhaps ultimately to the positive view projected in Lady Stenton, summarised in her 'King John and the Courts of Justice', *Proceedings of the British Academy* 44 (1959 for 1958), 103–28, itself doubtless influenced by the call for reassessment in V. H. Galbraith, 'Good and Bad Kings in Medieval English History', *History* 30 (1945), 119–132 at 128–30; see for comment, John Gillingham, 'Historians without Hindsight: Coggeshall, Diceto and Howden on the Early Years of John's Reign', in Stephen D. Church, ed., *King John: New Interpretations* (Woodbridge, 1999), pp. 1–26. The rehabilitation of John on the grounds of his administrative competence is briskly and intelligently reviewed in the brief historiographical assessment by James C. Holt, *King John*, Historical Association 53 (London, 1963), pp. 12–16.

[13] Holt, *King John*, pp. 21–2, makes this point. Gillingham, 'Historians without Hindsight', pp. 1–26, points out that John was receiving more criticism early in his reign than has been appreciated.

[14] J.-C. Huchet, ed. and trans., *Nouvelles occitanes du moyen âge* (Paris, 1992), pp. 52–4. For comment, M. Aurell, *L'Empire des Plantagenêt, 1154–1224* (Paris, 2003), p. 100.

perfectly clear: John was *not* a courtly man and no one was to imitate *his* conduct.

We are fortunate to have a revealing statement from John himself as to how he conducted his relationship with one very significant Anglo-Norman baron, William de Briouze, a man who was for the first years of his reign one of his closest intimates. At the end of the year 1210, having driven William from England and imprisoned his family, the king dictated in Latin a statement as to why his relations with William had come to that point. It was copied into the Black Book of the Exchequer in the thirteenth century, possibly under the erroneous belief that it was written by Henry II and was therefore worth keeping.[15] To John, the whole wretched business had been about money. In 1203 William had taken the lordship of Munster in Ireland from the king, for which he continued to owe 5,000 marks and a further unspecified sum for the rents of the city of Limerick. William had paid very little of the debt by 1208 when the king decided to collect it from his goods and estates. The king's account makes much of his forbearance and willingness to negotiate, at first with William, then as the crisis deepened, with his relatives and his wife, Mathilda of Hay. By the end of the king's account, in 1210, after endless delays, rebellion, and confrontation, John had been stalled for two years and a settlement of 40,000 marks was on the table. John's last plaintive word on its collapse, when Mathilda would no longer play the game was: 'She told me curtly that she would pay me nothing and she had no more money to pay towards the fine than twenty-four marks of silver, twenty-four gold coins, and fifteen ounces of gold. So neither then nor subsequently did she, her husband, or anyone else on their behalf, pay me anything of the debt.'[16] Poor John.

On one level, there seems little doubt that John's weary account of his troubles with Briouze is reliable: after all, he got six earls and many barons to add their seals to authenticate the document's account. Not only that, but one of the earls was Briouze's nephew and one of the barons was his brother-in-law, while the leader of the later rebellion, Robert fitz Walter, was the first of the barons to put his seal to it. The king is emphatic not just about his tolerance of Briouze's stonewalling but that due process of law had been followed. As Ralph Turner notes, when John moved against Briouze in 1208, the king insisted that 'It was decided that, *according to the custom of England and the law of the Exchequer*, he should have his possessions in

---

[15] *Liber Niger Scaccarii*, i, pp. 377–85; another edition is to be found in Rymer, *Fœdera*, i pt 1, pp. 52–3. There is no modern treatment of this fascinating document previous to my edition of it in this volume, though see for context, Brock W. Holden, 'King John, the Braoses and the Celtic Fringe, 1207–1216', *Albion* 33 (2001), 1–23.

[16] *Liber Niger Scaccarii*, i, p. 384.

England seized for non-payment and I should recover my money.'[17] Yet even in asserting that position John betrays the true state of affairs – the state of affairs that led him to issue the justification in the first place. '*Consideratum fuit,*' he says: 'It was decided.' He distances himself from the decision by use of the passive voice; as far as he was concerned it was all done by due process. Why? Because the truth was that the king had been happy to condone this debt and many others over several years while Briouze was in favour, but in 1207 the king had abruptly turned against three of his former closest advisors: Briouze, William Marshal, and Walter de Lacy. The scale of his debts meant that all he had to do to break Briouze was to call them in.[18] To expect Briouze to pay the astonishing sum of 40,000 marks for a settlement was beyond unrealistic: it is still an impressive sum when translated into the sterling equivalent. It was not an amount that could ever have been raised and everyone knew it. The king's moves against Briouze were personal and intended to finish him for good to the king's profit, though the king doubtless kidded himself otherwise, thinking that he was just recovering what was rightly his.

Why had he done it? There are several theories, and none of them can be conclusively proved, but since we are dealing with paranoia in this paper let us simply return to the verdict of the vernacular chroniclers. Not for nothing did the Marshal biographer depict John in 1208 calling Briouze his 'mortal enemy': he hated him till death.[19] That was what the barons believed to be the root of the difference between the king and his baron. It was that irrational capacity for abrupt, extravagant, and uncontrolled resentment that put John outside the courtly world. He was unpredictable and unreliable. The Marshal biographer says that it was John's way to keep even his loyal friends at arm's length until the situation became desperate.[20] He could not trust them, and in return he was not trusted.

Yet for all this, it is I think a very significant fact that it took the political community well over a decade to unite against the 'felon', as the dying Marshal seemingly called John to the face of the young Henry III.[21] The Marshal biographer himself seems to find this delay odd. In his account of the first great argument between the king and William Marshal in 1205 he

---

[17] *Liber Niger Scaccarii,* i, p. 378, and see Ralph V. Turner, *King John* (Harlow, 1994), pp. 197–8.

[18] For a treatment of this fiscal exigency and its relation to the Briouze case, see J. C. Holt, *The Northerners* (Oxford, 1961), pp. 181–5, and see his comment (ibid., p. 34) that the events of 1215 were a 'rebellion of the king's debtors', as noted in Turner, *King John,* pp. 218–20.

[19] *HWM,* ii, line 14293.

[20] *HWM,* ii, lines 14480–3.

[21] *HWM,* ii, line 18083, 'alcun felon ancestre'.

has the Marshal turning to his fellow barons at court and haranguing them: 'My lords, look at me, for, by the faith I owe you, I am for you all this day an exemplar and model. Be on your alert against the king: what he thinks to do with me he will do to each and every one of you, or even more, if he gets the upper hand over you!'[22] Now this is an odd speech to put in the mouth of a man who was one of the most prominent loyalists in the crisis of 1214–16, and in truth it may well be a fiction intended to align the Marshal with the prevailing baronial sentiment about John. He had to be given credentials which identified him with the predominant feeling amongst his social class. But whether or not it was spoken in 1205, the speech certainly encapsulates what must have been a widespread baronial belief that the king was out to get them, and that the king's favour was a transitory and uncertain thing. Yet it was not until 1212 that we find the first stirrings of a corporate attempt to move against this felon king, and it was not a reality till 1214.

For the rest of this paper I want to focus on two questions. The first is the protracted inability or reluctance of the barons to combine against so undeniably unpleasant and untrustworthy a king. The second is the trigger that finally set them off in 1214 on the road that would lead to Runnymede, and beyond that to a very different relationship between the English king and the political community of his realm.

It is indeed an odd thing that nothing much happened in England to oppose King John between 1204 and 1213. It is odd on several levels. We have already looked at the first thing which makes it odd: the king's irrationality, unpredictability, and personal animus. Yet despite living on a knife edge of his displeasure, the magnates of the court still worked with him for years at a time. There were several reasons why they did. The potential gains from John's generosity were enormous. He was renowned for being a spendthrift as well as greedy. The Béthune clerk talks of his gluttony and partying, but says that at least he was generous with what he had: 'There was no watch kept on the gates and doors of his hall when there was feasting: anyone could eat at his court who wanted to.'[23] A spendthrift king was not necessarily a bad thing. He might direct a highly profitable stream of money to those he liked. We have already seen the extent to which William de Briouze gained from John's patronage between 1199 and 1205. He was showered with lands, wardships, and offices to the extent that he was wealthier than most earls. William Marshal in the same period acquired Pembrokeshire and the title of earl which went with it, as well as offices, privileges, and new lordships in Wales.[24]

---

[22] *HWM*, ii, lines 13167–74.

[23] *Histoire des ducs*, p. 105.

[24] David Crouch, *William Marshal: Knighthood, War and Chivalry, 1147–1219*, 2nd edn (Harlow, 2002), pp. 86–7.

At a lower level the example of Hugh de Neville is even more instructive. Hugh came from a Norman family long in Angevin service, and since 1198 he had occupied the office of chief forester. As chief forester he administered that part of John's governance that his subjects found the most arbitrary and extortionate: the forest eyres, and he did so without conscience or compunction, turning the forest into a money-making machine for the king. He did well out of his service to King Richard and continued to profit from his service to John. He held shrievalties, kept royal castles and manors, and had custody of the vacant diocese of Salisbury; all of them were licences to coin money. He was ruthlessly efficient in the king's interest as both sheriff and forester, but he too suffered from the king's unpredictability and animus. There is some evidence that in 1204 the king brazenly seduced Neville's wife, Joan, and made a humiliating joke of it around the court. In 1202 and 1210 Hugh had amercements of 200 and 1,000 marks slapped on him at the king's will. Although the later of these was pardoned, and may never have been intended to be collected, there is no doubt that the major amercement of 6,000 marks with which he was confronted in 1211 as a consequence of allowing two state prisoners to escape his custody was a serious imposition calculated to break him. The king had turned against him, and what followed the amercement were loss of office, enquiries into his maladministration, and further punitive measures. As it happened, little of the huge sum of 6,000 marks *was* ever collected, but its existence was a sword over Neville's head, just as the debt for Munster had hung over Briouze's. The 6,000 marks formed the basis of the king's further relations with Neville; he used pardons for part of it in 1214 to signal a partial return to favour and other pardons as a means to get Neville to raise troops for him. Nicholas Vincent has demonstrated how this insecurity influenced Neville's behaviour. In 1215 he had five state prisoners in his care. Once bitten, twice shy. He made them seal bonds that they would indemnify him for any financial losses he incurred should they escape his custody and he be amerced as a result.[25]

Huge potential profit was one reason certain barons continued to live on the edge of the volcano that was King John's temperament. But there were other reasons. The barons – by whom I mean the magnates attached to the court – were not a united group. The Béthune clerk said as much. John was renowned for playing one baron off against another. An example is the way John employed the Anglo-Welsh baron, Meilyr fitz Henry, as his auxiliary in Leinster against the disgraced William Marshal in 1207 and 1208. Meilyr seems to have despised Marshal as an intruder into the established community of Irish barons and an obstacle to his control over the region of Uí

[25] Nicholas C. Vincent, 'Hugh de Neville and his Prisoners', *Archives* 20 (1992), 190–7.

Fáeláin, which he was labouring to turn into his own fiefdom, but which was within Leinster. So John condoned and covertly supported Meilyr's military campaign against Marshal in the winter of 1207–8, summoning Marshal back to England to get him out of the way, and attempting to intimidate the principal Marshal supporters. So successful was the king in this that he managed temporarily to detach the Marshal's own nephew, John Marshal of Hockering, from his uncle's affinity at court in Tewkesbury in the autumn of 1207. The king had the bully's instinct for the weaknesses of others.[26] The Marshal case is not the only instance of this internal problem in the loyalty of aristocratic followings. When William de Briouze finally decided that he had more to gain than to lose from rebellion in 1208, and raised his banner against the king, he was embarrassed to find that most of his tenants in Wales refused to support him, and it was that – according to the Marshal biographer – which forced Briouze to flee with his family to Ireland.

Not only were barons individualistic, they had to depend on affinities of knights who might temporize with the king rather than support them at need. The lower level group which we call the county knights – local aristo-crats with no direct connection with the court – did not necessarily embrace baronial concerns wholeheartedly. Historical thinking is as yet unresolved on the way local knights behaved in the crisis of John's reign. Holt's studies point to a high degree of loyalty to their lords in certain of the great honors, but more recent writers – notably Kathryn Faulkner and John Maddicott – see them to a greater or lesser extent as a body with concerns which were independent of those of the barons, and even opposed to them.[27] What seems clear is that uncertainties about the behaviour of their dependents was another factor inhibiting the barons from moving against the king. The fact that Briouze's tenants did not rally to him is particularly significant. He was not a pushy upstart and new man, but a man of Norman lineage and high nobility. Yet he was clearly unable to gain the allegiance of the knights of the Marcher lordships he had inherited from the Hereford family, and had to seek refuge and support from men of his own class: relatives and barons with similar court connections.

Another of the king's expedients can only have added to the insecurity

---

[26] Crouch, *William Marshal*, pp. 108–13. For further observations about the situation of Meilyr fitz Henry, see for a modified view Marie Therese Flanagan, 'Defining Lordships in Angevin Ireland: William Marshal and the King's Justicier', in Martin Aurell and Frédéric Boutoulle, eds., *Les Seigneuries dans d'espace Plantagenêt (c. 1150–c. 1250)* (Bordeaux, 2009), pp. 44–59.

[27] Holt, *The Northerners*, pp. 35–60. For ideas of knightly solidarity, John R. Maddicott, 'Magna Carta and the Local Community, 1215–1259', *Past & Present* no. 101 (1984), 25–65; Kathryn Faulkner, 'The Knights in the Magna Carta Civil War', in Michael Prestwich, Richard Britnell and Robin Frame, eds, *Thirteenth Century England* 8 (Woodbridge, 2001), pp. 1–12.

among the barons. The taking of hostages for good behaviour was an ancient stratagem to use against people thought to be untrustworthy. Although the word for hostage – 'obses' – became chiefly used in the twelfth century to mean a guarantor of a transaction, who would suffer a financial penalty in case of a default, John revived the old sense of the expedient. He took wives, children and relatives of his barons as hostages for their good behaviour, keeping them at the royal court if they were lucky, or in prison if they were not. He might also demand control of baronial castles as a way of neutering them. The chroniclers tell us that it was John's demand for Briouze's sons as hostage that was the immediate trigger for the family's defiance of the king.[28] The king asked for Marshal's two elder sons as hostages and the trepidation the demands caused was intentional on the king's part. We are fortunate in that echoes of the household debates the demands caused are to be found in the Marshal biography; they are the reactions given to the biographer by men who were in the earl's council.

John took first the Marshal's eldest son, William, a boy of fifteen in 1205, and kept him at court till 1211. The biography says that the Marshal 'surrendered him readily to the king, since he was a man who would have nothing to do with evildoing or ever thought of it as such'.[29] However, when in 1208 John demanded the second son, Richard, then around thirteen, the Marshal's council was perturbed. It called the request a *felonie*, a disgrace. Some relics of the debate are to be found scattered through the biography. The boy's mother apparently was set against compliance, and some representations were made about Richard's delicate health. Indeed, he was seriously ill during his enforced stay at the royal court, when as a squire of nineteen he accompanied King John in the 1214 campaign in Poitou. Nevertheless, Marshal handed Richard over, and when he was challenged by the king in Dublin in 1210 to hand over his vassals and castles he summed up his compliance by saying 'You have my sons as hostages and you hold all my castles in England. If here in this land of Ireland you wish to have my towns and castles I shall hand over plenty to you, and I shall also surrender to you many of the sons of my worthy followers. A man can afford to proceed boldly in this manner who has no intention of doing harm.'[30] The king nonetheless took the hostages, and – as was always likely to happen – one of them, Geoffrey fitz Robert, held in Hereford Castle, died just before the Marshal was received back into favour in 1212 and all the others were released.

All these reasons and doubtless more besides kept the barons for years from combining as a group against the felon king with whom Fate had

---

[28] *Wendover*, ii, pp. 48–9.

[29] *HWM*, ii, lines 13274–6.

[30] *HWM*, ii, lines 13385–406, 14565–78, 14334–42.

saddled them. I want to move on now to consider how it was that the majority of then did finally combine against John, and what was the rationale and process behind their action. The first thing to say is that the *potential* for them to unite against the king was always there. Baronial dialogue with the king had deep roots in England. Kings had long sought out baronial opinion in their council, as John Hudson has recently illustrated for the reign of Henry I, and a king always welcomed expressions of corporate support. It was not therefore unusual for twelfth-century writers to talk of the 'magnates of England' or the 'barons of Normandy' thinking or doing something. From the eleventh century onwards, by talking to them, the king actually projected an identity on the upper nobility associated with his court: as John Hudson says, counsel 'reinforced the solidarity of the small but extremely powerful group around the king, and helped define its members against outsiders.'[31] Barons did it too, taking counsel with their own men, as we have already seen William Marshal doing. Of course, we are not usually party to the actual debates between king and barons, though it does seem from chroniclers that the intention and hope was that the barons should unite behind the eventual decision. Whether they did or not is always open to question. An important example of this is when Henry I issued his coronation charter in 1100. The document proudly states that Henry had been crowned by God's mercy and 'the common counsel of the barons of the entire realm of England'.[32] In fact we know very well – as did the audience of this document when it was read out in the county courts of England – that Henry had grabbed the crown with the support of a tiny cadre of the court nobility at hand when his brother was killed, and that he was consecrated in a hurry by the bishop of London, as the archbishop of Canterbury was nowhere nearby.[33] But the form of words was necessary, even if it was a pious fiction. Wace of Bayeux puts into a king's mouth the words: 'What can be undertaken and accomplished if his followers – who should assist a king – let him down? A fine following makes a king strong and feared.'[34] Appearance was everything.

Of course, the value of the advice given by the barons might be disputed or diluted by the king. The opinion of one romance writer of the 1150s was that barons had the responsibility to give advice when asked and say as

---

[31] John G. Hudson, 'Henry I and Counsel', in John R. Maddicott and David M. Palliser, eds, *The Medieval State: Essays Presented to James Campbell* (London, 2000), pp. 109–26 at 124–5. For the conciliar rule of Angevin England, see David Crouch, *The English Aristocracy, 1070–1272: A Social Transformation* (New Haven, 2010), ch. 4.

[32] Stubbs, *Select Charters*, p. 117.

[33] For an account, C. Warren Hollister, *Henry I* (New Haven, 2001), pp. 102–10.

[34] Wace, *Le Roman de Rou*, ed. Anthony J. Holden, 3 vols, Société des anciens textes français (1970–3) i, pt 2, lines 1090–2. The king was Charles the Simple.

much if they thought the king's proposed actions were foolish.[35] All well and good, but putting yourself at odds with the king had its dangers, especially if the king was as uncourtly and suspicious as John was. So a wise courtier might temporize. Thus Alexander Neckam, who knew John and his court very well, reflected on the matter of counsel that 'great men are used to taking advice, but they only agree to that which serves their own interests.'[36] But John, as much as his predecessors, took counsel of his barons. Medieval monarchy remained consultative, even if the king was a man regarded as a capricious tyrant by his contemporaries.

Did counsel ever go that further step of producing a baronial agenda independent of the king's wishes? Again, it is difficult to say. But the historiography of twelfth-century England does admit that such things might happen. Ralph Davis suggested in 1967 that there was a point in Stephen's reign when the barons developed their own corporate idea of how the kingdom's problems should be solved, and by the 1150s the bishops and the barons associated with either side in the succession struggle proposed a settlement that both the king and his rival, Henry Plantagenet, eventually accepted, or were obliged to accept.[37] Davis's theory remains current, and my feeling is that it could be developed further, into the next reign. The language of King Henry II's principal acts up until 1170 are remarkably conciliar in tone. His assizes in particular read as the joint statement of three parties interested in the state of the realm: king, bishops, and barons. The clergy and barons are prominent in agreeing the two statements issued at Clarendon, and they are individually listed in the Constitutions of 1164.[38] Though the originals of none of these assizes survive, it may be that, like John's tract against Briouze in 1210 and Magna Carta in 1215, the seals of the prelates and barons present were applied to them.

I would suggest that the barons who settled – or believed they had settled – the problem of succession in 1154 would have been inclined to think that their voice remained important in the running of the realm. The leading characters in the rule of England after 1154, in the frequent absences of the king, were, as it happened, earls: notably the chief justiciar, Robert

---

[35] Francine Mora-Lebrun, ed., *Le Roman de Thèbes* (Paris, 1995), lines 9685–96.

[36] Alexander Neckham, *De naturis rerum libri duo*, ed. Thomas Wright, Rolls Series 34 (London, 1863), p. 314.

[37] R. H. C. Davis, *King Stephen*, 3rd edn (London, 1990), pp. 108–24. The dating of this is refined in David Crouch, *The Reign of King Stephen, 1135–1154* (Harlow, 2000), pp. 234–9.

[38] For texts, see Stubbs, *Select Charters*, pp. 163–7, 170–3. Garnier de Pont-Sainte-Maxence, one of Becket's clerks, comments often how the king demanded his master's appearance and submission 'in the sight of my barons' as if they were the required audience for his measures; see Emmanuel Walberg, ed., *La Vie de Saint Thomas le Martyr* (Paris, 1936), lines 914–15.

of Leicester, and the king's uncle, Reginald of Cornwall. Paul Brand has recently highlighted the process of discussion and consent before the magnates and bishops which can be distinguished behind the texts of these assizes, and in particular in the legal text called *Glanvill*.[39] Here we find a world view that sees law as declared *in consilio*, 'by the advice of the magnates and the supporting authority of the prince'. Henry II benefited from this appearance of conciliar rule. The accounts of the confrontation between the king and Becket in 1164 emphasize how baronial support for Henry II was vocal and near unanimous in that crisis.[40] This state of affairs did not continue, and may have been in decline before 1170. Certainly after 1174 the king had reason not to trust his barons implicitly. After 1174 the English aristocracy was in any case mostly sidelined by the Angevin kings, whose presence in England from then until John's reign was something of a rarity.[41]

By this reconstruction of relations between king and barons, the generation of barons which was faced with the rule of John would have had little experience of framing joint policy and objectives. This was much the same baronial generation which had floundered so badly in the problems which England had faced in the absence of King Richard between 1190 and 1194. Not surprising really that the magnates were spineless and hesitant under John's misrule for so many years.[42] But they did not remain spineless, and under severe pressure, just as the barons of Stephen's reign had united under the intolerable pressure of civil war, so John's barons finally found a voice and an agenda. The first question is as to when they found a voice. The year 1212 seems important, in that King John himself sensed a major threat to himself from the political community. The sources are united in their belief that rumours reached the king in August as he was preparing a campaign against Llywelyn ab Iorwerth of Gwynedd that there was a plot amongst the barons to do away with him when he was in the Marches of Wales. The source of the information was allegedly King John's daughter, the princess of Gwynedd. The Margam chronicler insinuated that the king was so terrified he shut himself away in Nottingham Castle for a

[39] Paul A. Brand, 'Henry II and the Creation of the English Common Law', in Christopher Harper-Bill and Nicholas Vincent, eds, *Henry II: New Interpretations* (Woodbridge, 2007), pp. 215–41 at pp. 229–30.

[40] Frank Barlow, *Thomas Becket* (London, 1986), pp. 109–14.

[41] For the effect of Angevin itineration on the taking of counsel, see Aurell, *L'Empire des Plantagenêt*, pp. 58–65.

[42] There is the apparent exception of 1201 when 'the English earls met for a conference at Leicester, and jointly informed the king that they would not cross to Normandy with him unless he restored their rights to them': *Howden*, iv, p. 161. The king is said to have been most displeased and ill-advised in his reaction. The dispute seems to have been on the point of the earls' rights to a proportion of the county farm.

fortnight.[43] This may either suggest that Llywelyn was a very artful man, or that Princess Joan had overheard things she should not have. John would be apt to believe such a rumour. Plots to assassinate English kings were by no means unprecedented. King Henry I had broken one which involved his chamberlain in 1118. Stephen survived an attempt on his life in 1149 by assassin knights disguised as members of the royal household. Three years earlier his advisors had detected an alleged plot to do away with him in a campaign against the Welsh of Gwynedd. Henry II survived a number of assassination bids. In fact Richard was the only twelfth-century king of England whose subjects did not try secretly to kill him (though one eventually managed it from the walls of Chaluz). North Wales was not the sort of place in which to travel lightly in the twelfth century.[44]

The reason 1212 may represent a change of mood in England is that it marks a sudden awareness by the king of how hostile the political community had become, and what is more, he demonstrated a perception of what was energizing them. We are told by the Barnwell chronicler that all of a sudden the king 'began to conduct himself more civilly to his people and the country subsided'.[45] We are also told he made a particular point of restraining his foresters and he pardoned the debts and fines incurred under forest law. Hugh de Neville was certainly made a scapegoat over his management of the northern forests. With the complaints over the forest we may be seeing the emergence of one of the principal items of the baronial agenda, and like all the items it had a long history. The barons had been suffering under forest law for generations, and when they began to move into opposition with the king, the forest would be one of the major items to address. Significantly, the king also began to make rapprochements with

---

[43] See *Wendover* ii, p. 61, for the most dramatic account. See for the Nottingham comment, *Annales de Margan* in *Annales Monastici*, i, p. 32.

[44] For the assassination plot by one H., a chamberlain, see Suger, *Vie de Louis VI le Gros*, ed. and trans. Henri Waquet (Paris, 1929), p. 190. For the consequences and identification, see now Richard Sharpe, 'The Last Years of Herbert the Chamberlain: Weaverthorpe Church and Hall', *Historical Research* (forthcoming). For the assassination attempt on Stephen at Bedford, Raoul C. van Caenegem, ed. and trans., *English Lawsuits from William I to Richard I*, 2 vols, Selden Society 106–7 (London, 1990–1) i, p. 289. Henry II was plotted against by Adam du Port in 1172: William Stubbs, ed., *Gesta regis Henrici secundi Benedicti abbatis*, 2 vols, Rolls Series 49 (1867) i, 35. The same king was lured into an ambush at Limoges in 1183 and shot at: Maurice Bouquet *et al.*, eds, *Chronicon Lemovicense*, in *Recueil des historiens des Gaules et de la France*, 24 vols (Paris, 1869–1904), xviii, pp. 216–17. For the alleged plot to assassinate Stephen on campaign in Wales, see Kenneth R. Potter and R. H. C. Davis, ed. and trans., *Gesta Stephani* (Oxford, 1976), p. 196. My thanks for his help to Hugh Doherty, who is currently preparing a study of the du Port plot and other attempts on Henry II's life.

[45] *Walter of Coventry*, ii, p. 207.

those formerly in disgrace. William Marshal was offered the chance to have his hostage sons transferred to keepers mutually acceptable to both him and the king. The manner of his reception back into favour is perhaps the most significant thing of all for our argument. The king had initially suspected Marshal of being involved in the 1212 plot. But when Marshal got the barons of Ireland to compose jointly and seal a letter protesting their loyalty to the king, John became remarkably effusive in his relief at this development. Indeed, he himself wrote a thank-you letter to Marshal which positively drips with *faux amitié*. Marshal went on to organize a petition in favour of John addressed to Pope Innocent. In 1213 he was summoned back to England and his former dominant position in the Welsh March was re-established.[46]

Now for me an important symptom in all this is the corporate baronial letters suddenly flying everywhere. If anything, statements of joint baronial positions and beliefs are the most evocative symbols of crisis. Things have to be really bad to get the barons to work that closely together. Such documents are very rare and usually survive only through notices of their existence. In fact the earliest reference to one from John's reign I have so far found is a joint petition of the barons of Normandy in 1203 protesting against John's mercenary captain, Loupescar. Ireland produces the next one in 1207, a letter from the barons of Leinster and Meath addressed to the king against his justiciar and Marshal's enemy, Meilyr fitz Henry. The king's reply to it – which is how we know it was sent – is incoherent with rage.[47] By 1213 these pieces of parchment were the ravens of civil conflict, and they would gather quickly.[48]

The collapse of John's position in France after the battle of Bouvines is

---

[46] Crouch, *William Marshal*, pp. 116–19.

[47] *Rot. Litt. Pat.*, pp. 35, 72.

[48] In 1213 the pope regarded the barons and magnates of England as a group to engage in dialogue in support of the king. Letters of the pope recognised the 'earls, barons and other magnates to be found in England' as a corporate body to be admonished and disciplined: Christopher R. Cheney and William H. Semple, ed. and trans., *Selected Letters of Pope Innocent III concerning England* (London, 1953), p. 154. In 1214 the same body of magnates dispatched three envoys to represent their corporate interests at Rome carrying letters of authority issued in their name. For the 'litterae magnatum Angliae' commissioning their agents in Rome early in 1214, see Rymer, *Fœdera*, i pt 1, p. 120. From 1215, baronial meetings issued corporate letters to kings and pope, and even to shires, saluting them in the – rather presumptuous – name of the 'barons of England'. See the inventory of the muniments of the kings of Scotland taken by Edward I's army in Edinburgh in 1291, which contained two letters of the *barones Anglie* to Alexander II of Scotland probably late in 1215 'against King John', a writ in their name directed to the citizens of Carlisle, and another letter to the tenants of Westmorland, Cumberland and Northumberland 'against King John': *Instrumenta et Acta de munimentis regni Scotie*, in Thomas Thomson and Cosmo Innes, eds, *Acts of the Parliaments of*

the obvious turning point in his position in England too, as Holt maintains. The precise way the barons mobilized against John is never going to be entirely clear, but some parts of the process can be established. The barons of the north of England began to be identified as a focus of resistance in 1213, specifically in the context of their hostility to serving in John's projected campaign in Poitou. John marched into the north in an attempt to intimidate the northerners in August 1213 after their refusal to serve, so he himself seems to have identified them as a core group of troublemakers. He went on to meet them at Wallingford in November of that year to negotiate about their grievances.[49] It may be significant that it is at that point that Ralph of Coggeshall says that 'nearly all the barons of England formed an association to fight for the liberty of the Church and the realm.'[50] For one contemporary observer at least, parties had begun to form well before John's reverses of 1214.

Even before the return of the King to England in October 1214, the core group of northerners had been augmented by other baronial sympathizers. According to Coggeshall, it was the 'barons of Northumbria' who met the king almost off the boat from France late in 1214 with demands that he embrace the agenda of the liberties of Henry I for reform of the realm.[51] It is true that their centrality to the process of coalescing opposition can be seen by the application of the Latin word *Norrenses* and the French *Norreis* to all the opposition barons in 1215, but by the end of 1214 they were only a minority, and the leaders were in fact southern earls and barons.

The agenda was now appearing. Wendover's account of the pressing of Henry I's Charter of Liberties on the barons by Archbishop Stephen Langton as the basis of an agenda late in 1213 may be in part discounted, but Coggeshall confirms that the barons were indeed researching earlier charters of liberties in 1214. And there exists, for instance, an early thirteenth-century bifolium of the liberties of Henry I, Stephen and Henry II, given first in Latin, and then in French translation, for the benefit of a secular audience.[52] Such a survival tallies nicely with Wendover's account of the explanation of Henry I's charter to the barons, and also the Béthune writer's comment that Stephen's confirmation of the liberties of Henry I was part of the baronial rationale for their programme.[53] In January 1215 agents of the barons were sent to Rome, presumably to widen the debate and

Scotland, 12 vols (Edinburgh, 1814–75) i, p. III. My thanks to Hugh Doherty for this last reference, and see also Holt, *The Northerners*, pp. 131–3.

49 See the reconstruction of this period in Holt, *The Northerners*, pp. 89–99.

50 *Coggeshall*, p. 167.

51 *Coggeshall*, p. 170.

52 BL MS Harley 458, a source brought to my attention by Richard Sharpe.

53 *Histoire des ducs*, p. 80.

represent their views to the pope. This in itself indicates that lines had now been drawn and conflict was in full flow. A programme and baronial leadership had emerged by January 1215, and by February the king was putting his castles in defence, spurred on to this by his own fears.

And that is as far as this paper goes. The fate of the aristocratic party that had formed by January 1215 is well enough known, as is the long-term significance of its agenda. My point here is that an examination of the pre-history of the rebellion can tell us a lot about the way an aristocracy behaved. Even under John's ham-fisted rule it was by no means predisposed to rebel, and it took a lot to bring it to the point of resistance. Its eventual agenda also was not revolutionary: tension over the forests, wilful royal amercements, uncontrolled taxation, and the king's attitude to the disparagement of male and female heirs. Most of them were baronial bugbears since the eleventh century. But the crux is that once the barons *were* energized, as they had been before in the 1140s, the aftermath could be protracted. In 1215 the majority of the barons were once again stirred to work as a group to an anti-royal agenda. And since it involved written manifestos, a process of politicization was initiated that perpetuated the agenda of 1215 into future generations of the baronage, in a way that the crisis of the 1140s had not done. The same can be said of the conflict that began in 1215, and in Britain the new and self-conscious reactionary dynamic it introduced between aggressive government and suspicious populace is being enacted just as vigorously in this, the present day.

The Forest Eyre in the Reign of King John

DAVID CROOK

AFTER SOME at least tentative beginnings in the reign of Henry I, intermittent judicial visitations of counties where there were royal forests, to hold their forest pleas, became a regular feature of forest justice in England from the time of the appointment of Alan de Neville as the Henry II's chief forester in 1166.[1] These 'forest eyres' began at about the same time as eyres for common pleas, for which the name 'general eyre' was later coined.[2] The latter dealt with both civil and crown pleas; and the crown pleas, the investigation of which was based on the terms of the Assize of Clarendon of that year, closely paralleled the forest eyre. In effect the forest eyre dealt with an extraordinary category of crown pleas, protecting the king's deer and their habitat rather than the lives and property of men and women. Instead of presentments of alleged offences made by a jury of prominent local men to the common pleas eyre, forest offences were brought to the justices in eyre of the forest by the local forest officials who were responsible for recording them, to be determined by the justices. The equivalent of the Assize of Clarendon in forest jurisprudence was the so-called 'Prima Assisa', undated but quite probably also promulgated at about the same time as a preliminary to the judicial activities of Alan de Neville in the royal forests. Just as the Assize of Clarendon was superseded by the Assize of Northampton in 1176, so the Prima Assisa was replaced by the Assize of Woodstock in 1184. The Assize of Woodstock and the appointment of Geoffrey fitz Peter as forest justice in 1184 brought in a new forest regime, and three series of forest eyres in many counties in 1185, 1187 and 1189. Although fitz Peter continued in office until 1198, there were no forest eyres for nearly a decade because of King Richard's long absence from England on crusade and then in captivity, and his subsequent concentration on Continental affairs, leaving government and justice in England largely in the hands of his ministers. This inactivity came to an end in 1198, with the beginning of a new period of judicial activity in the royal forests which ran on into John's reign.

---

[1] For a brief account of the earliest references to itinerant forest justices in the reign of Henry I, from the 1130 pipe roll, see Judith A. Green, *The Government of England under Henry I* (Cambridge, 1986), p. 128.

[2] Introduction to C. A. F. Meekings and David Crook, eds, *The 1235 Surrey Eyre*, 2 vols, Surrey Record Society 31, 32 (Guildford, 1979–83), i, pp. 4–10. For the earlier development of forest eyres before 1135, see W. T. Reedy, jr., 'The Origins of the General Eyre in the Reign of Henry I', *Speculum* 41 (1966), 688–724.

❮ Evidence for forest eyres, 1166–89

The evidence for the study of the forest eyres of 1166 to 1189 almost entirely consists of the records of their financial issues, preserved in the pipe rolls of the Exchequer, which were themselves based on the estreat rolls for each eyre – lists of financial penalties extracted from the records of the eyre, handed in to the Exchequer by the justices or their clerks. A single original estreat survives from Thomas fitz Bernard's Shropshire eyre of 1179–80,[3] and there are references to others in the pipe rolls. No other original estreat survives until that for the Northamptonshire forest eyre of 1221, but in three other respects the sources for the forest eyres of John's reign are better than those for the earlier ones. The pipe roll entries for individual debts are sometimes more informative in the details they give of the offences being punished, at least in the eyres of 1198–1200 and 1207–10, even though the entries are still often so heavily abbreviated as to pose problems of interpretation.[4] Much background evidence about many aspects of forest administration, although surprisingly little about the eyres themselves, is given in the charter, patent, and close rolls, begun in the royal Chancery at various dates from 1199 onwards to record charters and out-letters issued by the crown;[5] as well as the fine rolls, which record monetary or other offerings for favours from the monarch. These had been kept since at least 1195 and possibly much earlier.[6] Most significantly of all, official records of forest pleas survive for the first time, with a few original plea rolls and some transcripts from now lost rolls made at later dates in the thirteenth century.[7]

The records relating to forest eyres under John nevertheless provide much less information about the planning of the circuits and the dates of particular eyres than what is readily available for many of those held in the reign of Henry III after 1216, because the judicial commissions and related

[3] TNA:PRO E 32/143, printed in David Crook, 'The Earliest Exchequer Estreat and the Forest Eyres of Henry II and Thomas fitz Bernard, 1175–1180', in Nicholas Vincent, ed., *Records, Administration and Aristocracy in the Anglo-Norman Realm* (Woodbridge, 2009), pp. 29–44. Unpublished documents cited are in TNA: PRO.

[4] This point can be illustrated by comparing, for example, the entry for the offence by Geoffrey Gibewin, steward of the abbot of Peterborough, in the roll of the Northamptonshire eyre of 1209, with the entry in the related pipe roll account: G. J. Turner, ed., *Select Pleas of the Forest*, Selden Society 13 (London, 1900) p. 2; Doris M. Stenton, ed., *Pipe Roll 11 John*, PRS 62 n.s. 24 (London, 1949) p. 186. There is less difference between plea roll and pipe roll in the case of Benedict of Haversham or Faversham and Roger Moin in the Rutland eyre of that year: *Select Pleas of the Forest*, p. 7; *Pipe Roll 11 John*, p. 107.

[5] *Rot. Chart.*; *Rot. Litt. Pat.*; *Rot. Litt. Claus.*, i.

[6] Thomas Duffus Hardy, ed., *Rotuli de Oblatis et Finibus … Tempore Regis Johannis* (Record Commission, 1835); H. G. Richardson, ed., *Memoranda Roll 1 John*, PRS 59 n.s. 3 (1943), pp. xxi–xxxiii, 85–8.

[7] Many are printed in *Select Pleas of the Forest*.

instruments were not recorded on the Chancery rolls until the 1220s. For the eyres other than the few for which plea rolls survive, the only evidence of their date is, as before, the first appearance of the accounts of their financial issues in the pipe roll of a particular year, which were audited from the beginning of October onwards during that year. It is usual to refer to 'the [county name] eyre of [Exchequer/calendar year]', but it must be borne in mind that it might have been held during the previous calendar year or, in a few cases, earlier than that, if for some unknown reason the holding of an account for eyre penalties was delayed. This can be shown to have happened in the case of a Shropshire forest eyre, held on 14 March 1209 but not accounted for in the pipe roll of that year and, because there were no Shropshire accounts in the pipe rolls of the following two years, not accounted for until October 1213 or later.[8] There is a contrast here with common pleas eyres, which can be dated fairly precisely from the dates on the feet of fines made in civil cases, which sometimes survive in very large numbers.[9] Nevertheless, more can be known about the forest eyres of the reign of King John than those for any other period before the issue of the Charter of the Forest in 1217.[10]

We know the exact dates of only four of John's forest eyres, those at Northampton, Oakham, Huntingdon and Shrewsbury in 1209, because of the survival of the original plea rolls, or copies of them, with dated headings.[11] Additionally, we know the date of a taxing session held at Barnack in Northamptonshire for the 'forest of the marsh' in Lincolnshire, and there is a list of Leicestershire amercements also made at Oakham.[12] These documents give a unique and useful chronological picture of the forest eyres of Hugh de Neville and Peter de Lyons in February–March 1209.[13] Beginning with an eyre at Northampton on Friday 20 February, they drew up the amercements list on Monday 23 February. They then moved on to Oakham, where on 3 March they held an eyre for the forest of Rutland and the small contiguous area of eastern Leicestershire which formed part of it; a separate

---

[8] *Select Pleas of the Forest*, p. 8; Patricia M. Barnes, ed., *Pipe Roll 14 John*, PRS 68 n.s. 30 (London, 1955), p. 90.

[9] For the details, see D. Crook, *Records of the General Eyre*, Public Record Office Handbooks 21 (London, 1982), pp. 59–71.

[10] There is much useful information in J. Winters, 'The Forest Eyre, 1154–1368' (PhD diss., King's College London, 1999).

[11] *Select Pleas of the Forest*, pp. 1, 6, 8; E 32/62, 249, rots 11, 37 (not printed), 144.

[12] E 32/249, rot. 1, a copy made later in the thirteenth century; E 32/249, rot. 30. E 32/249, rot. 12 records 'Amercements of the pleas of the forest at Northampton Monday after St Peter in Cathedra 10 John', 23 February 1209.

[13] For the relevant accounts of these forest eyres, see *Pipe Roll 11 John*, pp. 23, 76, 107, 159, 186. Two of the headings of these accounts mention only Neville as the justice, three (Northamptonshire, Leicestershire and Lincolnshire) mention Lyons also.

list of Leicestershire amercements was prepared on the same day, needed because it was in a separate shrievalty and so would be collected by a different sheriff, the one for Warwickshire and Leicestershire. They then headed towards Huntingdon, but *en route* on 7 March they held the Lincolnshire session at Barnack. This indicates that they did not actually visit the Lincolnshire forest of the marsh of Kesteven and Holland to hold an eyre there, but simply met the forest officials at that convenient place and dealt with what was brought before them. Perhaps they could not face the chill of the March winds blowing across the fens, or perhaps it was normal to deal with such a relatively insignificant forest, off the beaten track, in that way. They then moved on to Huntingdon to begin an eyre there two days later, on 9 March. It cannot have lasted very long, because the justices moved rapidly over to Shrewsbury to begin another forest eyre there on 14 March.

The first clear evidence for the planning of a series of forest eyres is found in the close roll in October 1224. The same group of justices was to be at Reading in Berkshire on 14 November, at Wilton in Wiltshire on 25 November, at Ilchester in Somerset on 3 December, and at Sherborne in Dorset on 4 December that year.[14] The implication of the last two, in a joint shrievalty, being held on successive days only ten miles apart, is that only one day was normally allowed for a forest eyre in the 1220s. It is unlikely to have been longer twenty-five years earlier, although some eyres in major forest counties could have lasted several days. In the Northamptonshire eyre of 1209 the session began on a Friday and the amercements were listed on the Monday following, while five pleas were adjourned from Friday to Saturday, so the whole session lasted three or four days, depending on whether or not the justices sat on Sunday.[15] A whole series of county eyres could therefore be held very quickly, with the intervals between the individual sessions caused only by the travelling times of the justices between the various venues.

⟪ The Assize of 1198

On 11 July 1198 Geoffrey fitz Peter, chief forester since 1184, was made justiciar by King Richard. His successor as chief forester was Hugh de Neville, probably the grandson of Alan de Neville, and described by the Yorkshire chronicler Roger of Howden as 'summum justiciarium omnium forestarium regis'. According to Howden, he was ordered by the king to visit each county assisted by Hugh Wake and Ernis de Neville, and bring together archbishops, bishops, earls and barons, all free tenants, and the reeve and four men from each village for pleas of the forest, and to hear the king's

---

[14] *Rot. Litt. Claus.*, i, pp. 633, 655.

[15] *Select Pleas of the Forest*, pp. 1–5. For other records or probable records of this eyre, see E 32/249, rots. 16–17.

instructions. These are listed by the chronicler under the heading 'This is the assize of the lord king, and these are the instructions concerning his forests in England, made by the assent and counsel of the archbishops, bishops and abbots, earls, barons, and knights of all our realm'.[16] This resembles the heading of the Assize of Woodstock, the only significant difference being the addition of the knights to the list of those said to have assented to it.[17] This may be significant in its recognition of the growing political importance of the knights, who two decades later were the constituency who secured the large reduction in the extent of the forest in many counties.

The text of the new assize consisted of seventeen clauses, building on the earlier one. The first clause had a significant addition, in that where Woodstock merely stated that the punishment for taking venison should be as it had been under Henry I, the new assize defined this as the loss of the eyes and testicles. The third clause added verderers to foresters as those officials responsible for viewing the use of the resources of private woods for the legitimate needs of the owners to ensure that they did not cause waste by doing so. This was simply recognition of an office which had only come into existence since 1184 to record forest offences to bring before the justices, as the forest equivalent of the office of coroner, itself created in 1194.[18] The fourth clause, about private foresters, preventing the appointment of foresters in private woods outside the regard in which the king's venison lived in peace, was removed.[19] Clause 11, about the viewing of assarts, which were formerly wooded areas cleared for cultivation, added the provision that both old and new ones, as well as purprestures – illegal encroachments on the forest, including buildings – and waste, should be inspected every third year within the regard, so regulating and tightening up the administrative arrangements for controlling potential threats to the forest habitat. The last five clauses, 13–17, were additions to the provisions of the Assize of Woodstock. They included a prohibition on levying cheminage, a tax on

---

[16] *Howden*, iv, p. 63.

[17] The text of the Assize of Woodstock is conveniently available in Stubbs, *Select Charters*, pp. 186–8; a translation is in David C. Douglas and George W. Greenaway, eds, *English Historical Documents*, 2nd edn (London, 1981), ii, pp. 417–20.

[18] The earliest reference to a verderer so far found is in the assize of 1198. The office may have been created at the same time as that of coroner, but if not it must have come into existence within the next four years. The closeness of the two offices is further indicated by the fact that by the fourteenth century returns from elections for both coroners and verderers in the county court were filed in the same series of Chancery files, c 242. In the Forest of Dean in 1248 the verderers were referred to as 'coroners of the forest': R. F. Hunnisett, *The Medieval Coroner* (Cambridge, 1961), p. 146.

[19] A regard was both an official examination of a forest by forest officials and the area under the jurisdiction of such officials.

the passage of carts bearing goods through the forest; a prohibition on the presence of pigs there during fence month, two weeks either side of midsummer; a reiteration of the liability of convicted deer poachers to blinding and emasculation; a more detailed definition, listed below, of punishable offences against the vert (the open habitat in which the forest beasts lived); and a reiteration that the regard was to be held every third year, defining what the regarders were looking for and what action they should take, again detailed below. Finally, the seventeenth clause stated that under Henry II it had been permissible to create banks and ditches within the forest in the place of hedges.

The new assize, linked as it was by Howden with the holding of the first forest eyres since 1189, appears in some respects to have been the forest equivalent of the articles given to justices of the common pleas eyre to prompt the juries of presentment to report crown pleas that had arisen since the last eyre in the same county. The first surviving text of common pleas eyre articles comes from 1194, and the articles for the new series of common pleas eyres that commenced in September 1198 is given by Howden immediately before the new forest assize; the chronicler seems to have regarded them as two related although distinct enterprises.[20] They may have commenced at the same time, but for the forest eyres there are no dating sources equivalent to the final concords recorded in common pleas eyres. In the case of forest eyres there were no presentment juries, since forest offences were recorded by forest officials in order to bring them before the forest justices in their next eyre.

The most striking clauses of the new assize in relation to the forest eyre that was about to take place were those concerning offences against the venison, and those giving the fullest definition yet of types of offences against the vert, and the penalties that could be imposed. The specification in 1198 of blinding and emasculation for venison offences, when contrasted with the general reference in the Assize of Woodstock to the punishments used in the reign of Henry I, suggests that the penalties actually meted out during the reign of the younger Henry were less severe than those imposed by his grandfather. Some support for this view can be found in an unofficial source. When William of Newburgh, the Yorkshire chronicler of the Augustinian priory of that name, summed up the reign of Henry II at the point of the king's death in 1189, he concluded that, although his administration of the forest laws was severe, it was far less so than that of Henry I.[21] Newburgh lived from about 1135 to 1198, his adult life coinciding closely

---

[20] *Records of the General Eyre*, p. 59; *Howden*, iv, pp. 61–2.

[21] *William of Newburgh*, i, p. 280: Venationis delicias, aeque ut avus, plus justo diligens, in puniendis tamen positarum pro feris legume transgressionibus avo mitior fuit. Ille enim, ut suo loco dictum est, homicidarum et fericidarum in publicis animadverionibus nullam vel parvam esse distantiam voluit. Hic autem huiusmodi transgressores carcerali custodia sive exsilio ad tempus coercuit.

with Henry's reign, and as one of best and most critical historians of the twelfth century his view on this issue commands respect.[22] For Henry's reign we have a full set of pipe rolls, and they contain no evidence of the use of mutilation as a punishment, although as purely financial documents they cannot necessarily be expected to have done so. Similarly, no evidence of the carrying out of such penalties can be found in the pipe rolls or other surviving records of the period between 1198 and John's suspension of forest eyres after the crisis in the summer of 1212, and it was left to chapter 9 of the Charter of the Forest in 1217 to prescribe that 'henceforth no-one shall lose his life or members on account of the king's venison'.

That chapter adopted in full the demand for these penalties to be abolished, but without the specific reference to the forest which had appeared at the end of the 'Unknown Charter' (clause 9), a product of the negotiations preceding Magna Carta, but not included in Magna Carta itself. Instead, the forest charter provided that anyone convicted of taking deer could redeem himself (by paying a fine). If he could not afford to do so, he was to remain in prison for a year and a day, after which he would be released if he could find pledges for his future conduct; if he could not he would have to abjure the realm, that is, go abroad and never return. Financial issues seem to have been the main source of contention about forest eyres in the reign of King John, not severe punishments for offences against the venison, so the clause in the forest charter seems to represent legislative tidying up after the mutilation provision of the assize of 1198. The detailed clauses about offences against the vert and the procedure of the regard in the 1198 assize (clauses 14 and 16) give more information about those areas than any previous document. The list of possible trespasses includes the cutting of wood; the stripping off of branches; the digging of peat; the stripping of moors; the cutting of underwood; assarting; the creation of new purprestures by hedging or ditching; the removal of mills; the diversion of watercourses; the building of sheepfolds or other houses; and the mowing of hay outside the hedges or ditches. Offenders committing them were liable to monetary penalties, unless they were vouched for by the verderers or the king's foresters. These were in addition to the offences of carrying bows and arrows or leading dogs without a collar in the forest, which on conviction resulted in an amercement. The regard was to identify new assarts, and old ones sown with crops since the previous regard, and see what crops or legumes had been sown. New assarts were to be taken into the king's hands. If the old ones had been planted with wheat or rye, the king was to receive 12d. per acre of that crop; if they were sown with oats or barley, or beans or peas, or any other legume, 6d. was payable for each acre of that crop.

---

[22] On his life, see *William of Newburgh*, i, pp. xvii–xxii, and Antonia Gransden, *Historical Writing in England* (London, 1974), pp. 263–8, including a general appraisal of the content of his work and its quality.

ℂ The forest eyres of 1198 to 1201

Roger of Howden had himself served as a forest eyre justice in Yorkshire, Northumberland and Cumberland from 1185 to 1189, but despite this he severely criticized the great countrywide programme of forest eyres that began in 1198 to implement the terms of the new assize. He remarked that it reduced the whole of England from sea to sea to destitution (*inopiam*).[23] He himself lived to see the completion of the forest eyres of 1198–9, and of the further programme carried out in 1199–1201. He died in 1202, and it was only the last eyre, that in Cumberland, accounted for in the pipe roll for that year, that was not certainly completed before his death; all the others except Wiltshire (in the roll for 1201) had appeared in the accounts by 1200. The common pleas eyres which began in September 1198 were completed in October 1199, having covered thirty counties in twenty-five sessions; several were for closely related shires, some sharing a sheriff, in five distinct circuits proceeding simultaneously, and using a total of twenty-eight different justices. The former chief forest justice, Geoffrey fitz Peter, now justiciar, headed the justices in the south-east, who completed their work in January 1199, before the change of monarch in May. In September 1199, after John had taken the throne, fitz Peter – newly created earl of Essex by the king – became the chief justice of another circuit and sat at Northampton and Leicester.[24] Another programme of common pleas eyres began in May 1201 in counties missed in 1198–9, but then began in full in June 1202, at the beginning of a period of five years without forest eyres.[25]

In view of his activities in the common pleas eyre circuits, it is all the more remarkable that twelve of the thirteen forest eyre accounts entered into the 1198 pipe roll name Geoffrey fitz Peter as chief justice with Hugh de Neville as the other justice (in two cases with unnamed associates); one, for Rutland, names fitz Peter alone with unnamed associates.[26] He became justiciar on 11 July, so it seems likely that the forest eyres accounted for at the Exchequer of Michaelmas 1198 were held in the first part of the year before his promotion, leaving him free to lead common pleas eyres; he began his circuit on 17 September at Bedford. If so, the revival of forest eyres began under his chief forestership, and suggests that the new forest assize was drawn up under his supervision. He could then have been, after his promotion to the justiciarship, the directing force behind the planning

---

[23] Howden, iv, p. 62.

[24] *Records of the General Eyre*, pp. 59–63.

[25] *Records of the General Eyre*, pp. 63–8.

[26] Doris M. Stenton, ed., *Pipe Roll 10 Richard I*, PRS 47 n.s. 9 (London, 1932), pp. 16, 63, 72, 104, 124, 136, 149, 159, 164, 174, 186, 222, 227.

of the common pleas eyres that began in the autumn and the main beget-
ter of the eyre articles used by himself and the other justices to deal with
the crown pleas in those eyres. The fact that Howden mentioned the two
kinds of eyres in the reverse chronological order of that suggested by this
chronology does not make it any the less likely to be valid. The common
pleas eyre affected every county and locality, the forest eyre only particular
areas, so the former was of wider national importance. Two further forest
eyres, in Devon, where the justices are named as fitz Peter, Neville, Thomas
de Sandford (the forester of Chippenham), Hugh Wake and William
de Wrotham, clerk, and in Gloucestershire by Neville, Wake, Sandford
and Robert de Vieuxpont, both accounted for in 1199, upset the pattern.
This can be explained either by assuming that the account was somehow delayed for a year, or, more likely in view of the inclusion of the last
three justices (who do not appear explicitly in any of the eyres accounted
for in 1198), fitz Peter for some unknown reason decided to take part in
them.[27]

The forest eyre of circuits that began in 1198 ended in 1199, followed very
rapidly by the beginning of another series later in the year, which probably went on into 1201. The division between the two eyre programmes in
1199 cannot be dated, but its existence is revealed by new eyres, beginning
in 1199, in counties which had already been visited. In 1198 and early 1199,
twenty-one counties or joint counties received eyres. The joint shrievalties
of Bedfordshire/Buckinghamshire and Warwickshire/Leicestershire were
visited for a second time in 1199, and their penalties accounted for in the
pipe roll of that year. In 1200 six more second forest eyres were held, in
Berkshire, Cornwall, Devon, Essex/Hertfordshire, Surrey and Sussex; in
1201 there were two, Dorset/Somerset and Wiltshire; and in 1201 or 1202
Cumberland: nine in total. Other counties were visited only once during
the four-year period, four in 1198, six in 1199 and four in 1200. After the
Cumberland account of 1202, there were no more forest eyre accounts in
the pipe rolls until 1207. The only chronicle reference to royal activity in
the forests in the early years of the reign comes right at the end of these
eyres. Under February 1201, when the king was visiting Yorkshire and
Northumberland, Roger of Howden remarked that John made the men of
the realm ransom themselves because they had wasted his forest.[28] He was,
as at other points of the reign, carrying out forest activities in his own right,
independent of the continuing work of his forest administration, and nothing can be found in the 1201 pipe roll to document this more fully. At least

---

[27] Doris M. Stenton, ed., *Pipe Roll 1 John*, PRS 48 n.s. 10 (London, 1933), pp. 33, 192.

[28] *Howden*, iv, p. 157; J. C. Holt, *The Northerners* (Oxford, 1961), p. 197.

once early in the reign he accepted and imposed forest fines outside the forest eyres themselves, in Nottinghamshire and Derbyshire in 1200.[29]

Where a county was visited twice, the amount of money levied in penalties was, in some counties, broadly similar, in others markedly different.[30] For example, Dorset and Somerset yielded £154 in 1198 and £173 in 1201, while in the same years Wiltshire brought in £135 and £45 respectively. Overall the total for the first eyres in these counties was £918, in the second £868. Much the highest individual yield from any of the eyres of 1198 to 1201 was from Yorkshire, £425, with £367 from Hampshire. The overall total yield was £3,838, almost £1,000 a year for each of the four years. Every forest county in England had a forest eyre between 1198 and 1201–2. Westmorland and Lancaster do not appear in their own right, but the former's forest pleas usually appeared in the Cumberland account, and a Lancaster forest debt first appears in the account for the Yorkshire eyre of 1199 with a cross-reference to the Lancaster account, where it is also entered.[31] Bedfordshire was no longer a forest county, having been the first to free itself from forest law through a fine of £200 to King Richard in 1189 by the barons of the county 'for disafforesting that part of the county of Bedford which Henry I afforested'.[32] It did not escape entirely, however, for in the 1199 Buckinghamshire forest eyre the knights of Bedfordshire were charged with thirty marks for hunting in Bedfordshire 'on this side of the water' (*citra aquam*) before showing their charter of liberties.[33]

❰ The forest eyres of 1207 to 1210

There is no direct evidence to show why a new series of forest eyres began in 1207 after a gap of six or seven years, and went on continuously until 1210, but its coincidence with the levying of a general tax of a thirteenth

---

[29] Doris M. Stenton, ed., *Pipe Roll 2 John*, PRS 50 n.s. 12 (London, 1934), pp. 18–19.

[30] The following figures and other figures about eyre yields are taken from Winters, 'The Forest Eyre, 1154–1368', and relate only to the sum assessed and mentioned in the first account for each eyre.

[31] Holt, *The Northerners*, pp. 195, 199 n. 2; *Pipe Roll 1 John*, pp. 51–2, 71. For the Lancashire entries in the pipe rolls of Henry II, see William Farrer and J. Brownbill, *Victoria History of the County of Lancashire*, ii (London, 1908), p. 439.

[32] Doris M. Stenton, ed., *Pipe Roll 2 Richard I*, PRS 39 n.s. 1 (London, 1925), p. 145; Doris M. Stenton, ed., *Pipe Rolls 3 and 4 Richard I*, PRS 40 n.s. 2 (London, 1926), pp. 109, 201–2, 264. From the time payment was completed in 1192, there are no subsequent references to forest in the county.

[33] *Pipe Roll 1 John*, p. 116. It is almost certain that the Buckinghamshire forest eyre was held in Bedfordshire, because the Buckinghamshire common pleas eyre of 1202 was held at Dunstable, there being no obvious Buckinghamshire venue: *Records of the General Eyre*, p. 65. Later, but only from 1227 onwards, Newport Pagnell, High Wycombe, and once Aylesbury, were used.

suggests that financial considerations played a significant part.[34] A new programme of common pleas eyres, running concurrently with the forest eyres during the period it lasted, did not begin until October 1208 and ended in June 1209 after visiting only fourteen counties in three circuits. No more were held in John's reign.[35] There is no record of a new set of forest articles for these eyres, and in the absence of any it seems best to assume that the assize of 1198 still served. The eyres beginning in 1198 which provoked Howden's striking comment were surpassed in quantity.[36] The annals of Dunstable Priory described the situation in Essex, where John ordered the destruction of all ditches, hedges, and assarted houses, even ones already established, and eighty foresters were imprisoned before being allowed to ransom themselves.[37] The account of the imprisonment of foresters has some documentary support, because 128 foresters were taken as prisoners to the king at Winchester in 1209.[38] John was in that city in May that year, and it may have been then that he dealt with the miscreants, although there is no evidence of what punishments he imposed. The St Albans chronicler Roger of Wendover wrote that at Christmas 1208 John forbade the taking of birds, and that at Norham Castle on 28 June 1209 he ordered the burning of hedges and the levelling of ditches in all the forests of England, thus providing plentiful food for the beasts on every side to devour.[39] By the time these pronouncements were made the eyres were well under way, and no specific indications that these orders were carried out can be found among such details of the amercements imposed during the eyres as can be found in the pipe rolls for 1209 and 1210.

For the forest eyres of 1207–10 a systematic programme can be detected in the first two years, when all but five of the normal forest counties were visited. The exceptions were Lincolnshire, Nottinghamshire/Derbyshire, Shropshire, Staffordshire and Sussex; Sussex was the only county never visited at all in these years, while the remaining four were finally dealt with in 1209. The apparent logic of the programme was disrupted only slightly, in that three counties of those visited in 1207 – Hampshire, Northumberland, and Rutland – again received the forest justices in 1208. The sums derived

34 Doris M. Stenton, ed., *Pipe Roll 10 John*, PRS 61 n.s. 23 (London, 1947), pp. xvii–xviii.

35 *Records of the General Eyre*, pp. 68–71.

36 Holt, *The Northerners*, p. 158.

37 *Annales Monastici*, iii, p. 31. No evidence about these events can be found in the pipe roll accounts for the Essex forest eyres of 1208 and 1209: *Pipe Roll 10 John*, pp. 36–7; *Pipe Roll 11 John*, pp. 199–200.

38 A. Mary Kirkus, ed., *Pipe Roll 9 John*, PRS 60 n.s 22 (London, 1946), p. 27.

39 *Wendover*, ii, pp. 49–51.

from two of the counties were paltry in both years, but Northumberland, after being charged £105 in 1207, had £348 of penalties imposed on it in the following year, and a further £197 in 1209. The pipe roll of 1207 includes accounts for eyres in six forest counties, Cornwall, Devon, Hampshire, Northumberland, Rutland, and Surrey: one before Hugh de Neville and Peter de Lyons, three before Hugh de Neville alone, and two without any justices being named.[40]

On 22–3 March 1204 the forest areas of Devon and Cornwall had been reduced by the payment of substantial fines to the king, who needed money to support his unavailing attempt to defend his duchy of Normandy. This had consequences in the next forest eyres in those counties. Most of Devon, excluding Exmoor and Dartmoor, had been disafforested for 5,000 marks, but in the eyre of 1207 Ottery St Mary was charged ten marks for the wild beasts (*feris*) taken before the county had its liberty, while the bishop of Exeter suffered a 500 mark amercement because he and his men had hunted in the forest of Devon and Cornwall and had not informed the knights and other men of the two counties concerning the fine they made for their liberty.[41] In 1209 the men of Devon were charged 300 marks and a palfrey because they would not allow Hugh de Neville to make the regard in Devon or a perambulation between the king's forest and the lands outside it.[42] In 1204 Cornwall had been entirely disafforested for a fine of 220 marks and twenty palfreys, but an eyre was nevertheless held in the county in 1207 and penalties of £325 imposed.[43] It is possible that these were in respect of offences committed between the previous eyre in 1200 and the charter of 1204, although this is nowhere stated, and this did prove to be the last Cornish forest eyre ever held.[44]

A forest heading in the Surrey account is followed only by a fine of £10 for the release of Adam de Tindesle from prison until the forest eyre, and the men of the county fined 500 marks and five palfreys to disafforest the county according to the terms of a charter which they had received; the first payment of a fifth was due at Michaelmas 1207.[45] It cannot be established whether the grant of the charter preceded the intention to hold an eyre in the county or whether it was solicited when the justices had already arrived

---

[40] *Pipe Roll 9 John*, pp. 3, 66, 76, 138, 149, 184. The second tranche of the Surrey penalties, in *Pipe Roll 10 John*, p. 95, names Neville as the justice.

[41] *Rot. Chart.*, p. 132; Doris M. Stenton, ed., *Pipe Roll 6 John*, PRS 56 n.s. 18 (London, 1940), p. 40; *Pipe Roll 9 John*, pp. 184–5, 222.

[42] *Pipe Roll 11 John*, p. 92.

[43] *Rot. Chart.*, p. 122b; *Pipe Roll 6 John*, p. 85.

[44] There were a few extra amercements in 1208: *Pipe Roll 10 John*, p. 182.

[45] *Pipe Roll 9 John*, p. 66. The text of the charter is not available because there is no surviving charter roll for the year.

to hold it, but the charter may have covered only part of the county because further penalties were recorded in the 1208 pipe roll and Surrey forest eyres continued to be held for the remainder of the century.[46]

In 1208 there were further forest eyres in seventeen counties, three of which, Hampshire, Rutland, and Northumberland, had already been visited in 1207.[47] In 1209 seventeen counties had forest eyres, of which only three, Nottinghamshire/Derbyshire, Shropshire and Staffordshire, had not been visited during the previous two years, and two of which, Hampshire and Rutland, were being visited for the third time in the three years.[48] In 1210 there were seven further eyres, all of them in counties that had been visited during the previous three years, two only once, four twice and one, Hampshire, three times.[49] Only eleven counties, Buckinghamshire, Cornwall, Cumberland, Devon, Gloucestershire, Lancaster, Lincolnshire, Oxfordshire, Shropshire, Staffordshire, and Worcestershire, had only a single forest eyre between 1207 and 1210, and Sussex was not visited at all. It can be no coincidence that some of these counties were ones from which the lowest yields might have been expected. However, those from Buckinghamshire, Cornwall, Devon, Gloucestershire, Oxfordshire, and Shropshire were substantial, totalling £1,507; the other five realized only £252 among them. The total impositions of 1207–10 amounted to £8,738, far in excess of the £3,727 in the eyres of 1198–1201. As before, much the largest contributor was Yorkshire, with a total figure of £1,329 from two eyres. Northamptonshire was second, with £830 from two eyres; it was one of many counties visited more than once where there were substantial differences between the amounts levied in one eyre and the other, in this case £161 and £669. Hampshire was visited every year between 1207 and 1210, but the amount imposed in the last year, £359, was much greater than the total of £169 for the other three years. Yorkshire, on the other hand, was subjected to two severe eyres in the successive years 1208 and 1209, yielding £605 and £724 respectively. The overall increase in anticipated income from that of the eyres of 1198–1201, far more than double, can be interpreted

[46] *Pipe Roll 10 John*, p. 95. A fine for the disafforestation of a defined part of Surrey had been made to King Richard by the knights of the county in 1189: *Pipe Roll 2 Richard I*, p. 155. It was probably for the confirmation of the resulting charter that the county offered 300 marks in 1201: Doris M. Stenton, ed., *Pipe Roll 3 John*, PRS 52 n.s. 14 (London, 1936), p. 229.

[47] *Pipe Roll 10 John*, pp. 22, 36, 41, 45, 49, 55 (extra Northumberland material from the eyre of the previous year), 58–9 (the second session small, perhaps just for pannage), 75, 110, 125, 133, 138, 156, 164, 179, 188, 192, 200.

[48] *Pipe Roll 11 John*, pp. 9, 23, 76, 87, 95, 102, 107, 118, 122, 143, 150, 159, 169, 186, 189, 199.

[49] C. F. Slade, ed., *Pipe Roll 12 John*, PRS 64 n.s. 26 (London, 1951), pp. 15, 41, 57, 82, 105, 190.

as indicating increased financial pressure which prompted use of the forest laws to raise income to enable John's government to better cope with its growing problems. The particularly heavy total penalties imposed on Northumberland and Yorkshire in these years presage the development of the overt opposition to King John in those counties, and on the issue of the forest in particular, a few years later.[50]

A forest pleas heading appears in the account for Kent, a non-forest county, in 1209. Of the two entries, one for twenty marks from Roger de Crammaville for having dogs contrary to the assize was paid through the sheriff of Essex, which suggests that the offence was committed in that county, where he had another debt; the other, owed by William of Ifield for carrying venison in the forest without warrant, is not so easy to explain.[51] There is also a forest pleas heading in the Norfolk and Suffolk account for 1207, neither county containing any forest. Two men from 'Moleford' were amerced for unspecified forest offences, and Gilbert de Bailleul for carrying a bow in the forest.[52] It is possible that these offences were committed in the forest of Essex by Suffolk men; if 'Moleford' can be identified as Long Melford, the two men lived not far from the forest of Essex, while Bailleul held a sub-tenancy of a fraction of a fee of the honour of Boulogne at a number of places in Essex.[53]

The absence of any Sussex forest eyre between 1207 and 1210 can be accounted for. For a few years after 1221 there were attempts to buy off forest eyres, probably because the men of the counties concerned did not want them to be held before the forest boundaries had been reviewed under the terms of the Charter of the Forest. Nothing like that happened during John's reign, but in 1206 the barons, knights, and free tenants of the rape of Hastings in Sussex offered sixty marks and a palfrey 'to be quit of the common summons of the pleas of the forest when the justices to hold the pleas of the forest came to Sussex'; all those in the rape who would benefit from this were to be participants in the fine, for which the constable would answer at the Exchequer.[54] The effect was confirmed when, on 5 November 1207, the barons, knights, free tenants, and all men of Hastings rape in Sussex received a charter from the king granting them quittance in perpetuity 'from suits and summonses of pleas of the forest and all things

---

[50]　Holt, *The Northerners*, p. 158.

[51]　*Pipe Roll 11 John*, p. 14; *Pipe Roll 12 John*, pp. 35–6.

[52]　*Pipe Roll 9 John*, p. 165.

[53]　H. C. Maxwell-Lyte, ed., *Book of Fees*, 3 vols (London, 1920–31), pp. 237, 241, 1430; index p. 252.

[54]　Doris M. Stenton, ed., *Pipe Roll 8 John*, PRS 58 n.s. 20 (London, 1942), p. 64; *Rotuli de Oblatis et Finibus*, pp. 364. The fine was paid off in 1208: *Pipe Roll 8 John*, p. 72.

which pertain to suits of pleas of the forest'.[55] At the time of the 1198 eyre in the county almost the total of the penalties imposed consisted of the twenty marks charged to Hastings rape 'pro superassisa', for an unspecified default.[56] It remained unpaid until after the charter was issued, but was finally almost cleared in 1209 by the constable of Hastings mainly by setting it off against expenses for works on Hastings Castle.[57] It may be surmised that this was a procedural default on a large scale, perhaps a mass failure by the leading men of the rape to answer the summons to the eyre; and that the fine and subsequent charter resulted from their determination to avoid a repetition. The eyres of 1198 and 1200 in Sussex had produced paltry yields of £15 and £4 respectively, the bulk of the former consisting of the Hastings rape 'superassisa'.[58] No Sussex eyre was held in 1207–10, and at the one held in 1212 all the identifiable penalties were imposed on places in Chichester and Arundel rapes, much further along the coast in western Sussex.[59] The eyre of 1212 was the last in the county for forest pleas, and the final disafforestation of the western part of the county came about as a result of the implementation of the Charter of the Forest in 1225 and 1227.[60]

The eyres from 1207–10 were nearly all held by Hugh de Neville as chief forest justice, named a total of thirty-eight times in the pipe rolls. In nine eyres he is said to have been accompanied by Peter de Lyons, once in 1207 and eight times in 1208, but not at all in 1209. In 1210 the Berkshire eyre was held by Thomas de Sandford and Lyons, and the Hampshire eyre by Sandford, Robert de Tattershall, and Lyons. For a total of six eyres in these years no justices are named, with the accounts being headed simply 'Pleas of the forest'; that heading is also given for the Norfolk and Suffolk and Kent 'eyres'.

❡ The forest eyres of 1212

In 1212 a new series of forest eyres was held, and the justices certainly reached all forest counties, including Sussex for the last time, except Lancaster, Northumberland, Westmorland, and Rutland, before the pipe roll for the fourteenth year of the reign was compiled.[61] Of those four, only

---

55 *Rot. Chart.*, p. 173b; *Rotuli de Oblatis et Finibus*, p. 420.

56 *Pipe Roll 10 Richard I*, p. 227.

57 *Pipe Roll 11 John*, p. 2.

58 *Pipe Roll 10 Richard I*, p. 227; *Pipe Roll 2 John*, p. 248.

59 *Pipe Roll 14 John*, pp. 85–6.

60 *Rot. Litt. Claus.*, ii, p. 80b; *Calendar of Charter Rolls*, 6 vols (London, 1903–27), i, p. 8.

61 *Pipe Roll 14 John*, pp. 16, 22, 38, 57, 60, 63, 67, 70, 75, 81, 85, 90, 98, 101, 110, 119, 127, 134, 140, 145, 152, 156, 160, 165.

Rutland had an account, very short, in the roll for 14 John. In that roll, and again in the next surviving roll, for 16 John, Lancaster had no account, and the Northumberland account in 16 John shows no sign of forest pleas.[62] Westmorland, for which there was no account in either 14 John or 16 John, should nevertheless probably be added to the list of counties visited in 1212. No Westmorland entries are visible in the few details given in the account for the Cumberland forest eyre, but its yield was very high, most included in a lump sum of £359, which might in itself suggest that Westmorland was included in its figures. It seems that by the time the eyres were brought to an end for political reasons they were already effectively complete, although the potential yield from Northumberland may mean that an eyre was intended there.

For the first time in the reign, the country was divided into circuits, long the normal practice with common pleas eyres, with the result that the work was carried through very quickly.[63] One group was led by Hugh de Neville (eleven counties), another by John fitz Hugh (five counties), a third by Philip of Oldcotes (Yorkshire and Nottinghamshire/Derbyshire), while Fulk de Cantelupe and Peter de Lyons were involved in Shropshire and Staffordshire respectively, Lyons with his own heading in the former and Cantelupe in the latter, suggesting that there were two eyres in each of those counties in a single year. The amount of detail given in the pipe rolls about individual amercements and fines was far less than that in 1207–10. Entries in a section of the pipe roll separate from the main forest eyre account, with no justices named, show that Yorkshire's main towns and two districts were particularly severely treated, with huge fines *pro transgressione* imposed on the county (300 marks), York (also 300 marks), Scarborough (£100), Doncaster (60 marks), Tickhill (20 marks), Beverley (300 marks), Ripon (30 marks), the soke of Snaith (£100) and Ainsty wapentake (200 marks), although Scarborough was pardoned 50 marks and Beverley the full 300 marks.[64]

If the imposts on the Yorkshire towns are included in the figures, the penalties imposed by the eyres amounted to £5,504, over half of what the 1207–10 eyres produced in four years, and a high proportion of them were

---

[62] Patricia M. Barnes, ed., *Pipe Roll 16 John*, PRS 73 n.s. 35 (London, 1962), pp. 65–6. The Lancaster account in R. A. Brown, ed., *Pipe Roll 17 John*, PRS 75 n.s. 37 (London, 1964), which covers the years 16 and 17 John (p. 55), has a forest pleas heading and entries (p. 57), which may represent the second year's account for a Lancaster forest eyre in 1212, because the first entry, a lump sum, refers back to the roll for 15 John, which is missing. The account for the eyre, if such it was, would therefore have been entered in the roll for 1213.

[63] *Pipe Roll 14 John*, pp. xxiii–xxiv.

[64] *Pipe Roll 14 John*, pp. 38–9.

paid in the first account.[65] Five counties suffered very heavily and between them accounted for over half this sum. Yorkshire, of course, headed the list with £1,498, followed by Nottinghamshire/Derbyshire (£544), Cumberland (£415), and Staffordshire and Shropshire (£387 and £321 respectively).[66] The area north of the Trent thus bore the brunt, with most more southerly counties suffering far less. It seems clear that much of the impetus which led to the holding of eyres in 1212 must have been financial. The crisis which broke around the king when a plot against his life was discovered in mid-August may have led rapidly to the ending of the eyres if they were still in progress. The plot led to John's modification of the severity of his forest policy, and his command to his senior foresters to swear to demand only that which was customary in the time of Henry II, recorded by the Barnwell annalist.[67] Although no precise date can be ascertained for this decision, the chronology of the Barnwell writer's account suggests that it followed immediately after the flight of the two main plotters; and the investigation into the state of the northern forests by Alexander of Pointon and John of Birkin was initiated on 25 September,[68] only a few days before the Exchequer began its Michaelmas session and the auditing of the forest eyre accounts. The potential for a rebellion in the north again increased, especially with the huge imposts on the Yorkshire towns. Nevertheless, one significant Yorkshireman, Hugh Malebisse, former forester of Galtres, received a pardon for his own debt.[69] The appointment of the commissioners on 25 September makes it clear that the king was well aware of the significance of the north and its forests as a source of opposition to his rule.

The number of claims for the pardoning of forest offences on the basis of the charters of liberties held by different religious institutions (other than those regularly given to the Templars and Hospitallers) that were allowed in 1212 greatly exceeded those of 1207–10, when there were only four.[70] In 1212 such claims were allowed in respect of Battle Abbey in Berkshire and Hampshire, Ramsey Abbey and the bishop of Ely (twice) in Huntingdonshire, St Albans Abbey in Sussex, Merton Priory in Surrey, Sempringham Priory in Lincolnshire, Oseney Abbey in Oxfordshire,

[65] *Pipe Roll 14 John*, p. xxiv.

[66] *Pipe Roll 14 John*, pp. 16, 63, 90, 156, 165.

[67] *Walter of Coventry*, ii, p. 207: Nam cum novis exactionibus forestarii totam fere Angliam plurimum vexassent, rex sortem miseratus afflictorum, eas omnino remisit. Insuper et forestariorum capitaneos jurare compulit, ut ea tantum exigerent, quae in diebus patris sui exigere consueverant.

[68] *Rot. Litt. Pat.*, p. 97; Holt, *The Northerners*, pp. 85–6.

[69] Holt, *The Northerners*, pp. 159, 161.

[70] *Pipe Roll 10 John*, pp. 157(Sempringham Priory), 179 (Pipewell Abbey); *Pipe Roll 11 John*, p. 200 (Waltham Abbey); *Pipe Roll 12 John*, p. 105 (Battle Abbey).

Pipewell Abbey in Northamptonshire, and Lenton and Thurgarton priories in Nottinghamshire.[71] It may be suggested that this generosity in the interpretation of charters was another consequence of John's greater liberality on forest matters after the summer of 1212, especially since in several cases the pipe roll entry mentioning the allowance was completed at a time later than the original section of the entry, and two of the allowances were to clear debts remaining unpaid from previous forest eyres. In Derbyshire the dean of Lincoln received a pardon because he did not owe suit, while elsewhere William Brewer and John de St John received pardons because it was their privilege for their service at the king's Exchequer.[72]

ℭ Conclusion

The incidence of forest eyres during the reign of King John owed much to the needs of royal finance, at the beginning of the reign to defend Normandy, in the middle and the end to make possible an attempt at its recovery. From records of receipts at the Exchequer, Nicholas Barratt has made some useful calculations of the proportion of royal revenue raised from the king's forests recorded in the county accounts in the pipe rolls, including that both from forest eyres and fines for forest privileges, over the course of the reign.[73] In the first two years the forest accounted for over £1,000 of income each year, nearly 6 per cent of total royal revenue, as the proceeds of the eyres that began in 1198 came in. For the years 1201 to 1204 the percentage was much lower, at its lowest only half of 1 per cent of total income in 1203. After the loss of Normandy in 1204, forest income began to rise again and then accelerated to reach 5.6 per cent of the total in 1207 and 9.3 per cent in 1208, as a result of the forest eyres of 1207–8. It declined to 5.5 per cent in 1209 and 3.3 per cent in 1210 as the eyres continued, then subsided to only 1.2 per cent in 1211 when no forest eyres are recorded, before rising to a new peak of 11.4 per cent following the savage forest eyres of 1212.

The cessation of forest eyres in 1212 was followed by a period of unrest from 1212 to 1215, leading to the issue of Magna Carta. One clause of the Articles of the Barons, which arose from the negotiations that led to the Charter, made the demand that in future those outside the forest should not have to come before the forest justices following the common summons to a forest eyre unless they were involved in a plea themselves or were serving as a pledge. This provision was accepted by John at Runnymede. Clause 44 of Magna Carta consisted of the same provision, in similar terms but with additional words of clarification, principally that it applied to those

---

[71] *Pipe Roll 14 John*, pp. 67, 81–2, 86, 98, 101, 110, 127, 135, 163, 166.

[72] *Pipe Roll 14 John*, pp. 70, 101, 120, 166.

[73] N. Barratt, 'The Revenue of King John', *English Historical Review* 111 (1996), 835–55, at 847.

who *lived* outside the forest, and that the persons whose pledges were to attend were those *attached for forest offences*. The only clear evidence that this had been an issue during the forest eyres earlier in the reign comes from an attempt to define which men of Leicestershire living in a small forest area adjacent to the forest of Rutland were to come to forest eyres. In the Rutland forest eyre of 1209 a verdict by the knights of Rutland stated that at the summons of the justices of the forest all the men of Leicestershire who lived within two leagues of the forest boundary ought to come to attend the eyre.[74] It is possible that similar inquests were made in other counties but no record has survived.

The Charter's short-term failure to provide peace led to civil war from 1215 to 1217, during which King John died. His death was quickly followed by a revised reissue of the Charter in the name of the young Henry III, late in 1216. After peace was concluded in the autumn of 1217 a separate Charter of the Forest was issued in conjunction with a second reissue of Magna Carta. Clause 44 of Magna Carta 1215, retained in the 1216 reissue, became clause 2 of the Forest Charter of 1217 without further modification. The Forest Charter, consisting of seventeen complex clauses, had four main themes. First was the settlement of the forest boundaries, cutting the extent of the forest in each county to the area established at the beginning of the reign of Henry II in 1154. Second, the Charter amplified the rights of those who had private woods in forests. Third, it set limits on the power of the foresters, by defining what they could and could not do, by limiting their numbers, and by prescribing more humane penalties for offenders that they caught, including bringing to an end all corporal punishments. Finally, it gave amnesties for forest-offences committed between 1154 and 1216.

These events were followed by a lengthy royal minority, with an administration trying gradually to strengthen its authority during a period frequently punctuated by serious unrest, some of it affected by unsuccessful attempts to implement the boundary clauses of the Forest Charter. Partly because of these problems, no attempt was made to revive forest eyres until John's former household knight Brian de Lisle was appointed chief justice of the forest in 1221, and his efforts were of limited success because opposition to the holding of forest eyres, notably in Yorkshire and Nottinghamshire/Derbyshire, led to a suspension of all forest eyre activity for a year beginning at midsummer 1222.[75] A regular pattern of forest eyres could not be fully resumed until the late 1220s, by which time the reduction of the size of forest areas proposed in the Charter of the Forest of 1217, and confirmed in a reissue in 1225, had been achieved in many of the most important forest

[74] *Select Pleas of the Forest*, p. 6.

[75] *Rot. Litt. Claus.*, i, p. 507b.

counties. The income from those eyres was much reduced from what it had been under John. Except for the very oppressive forest eyres of Robert Passelewe and Geoffrey de Langley between 1245 and 1252, and occasional heavy ones in individual counties in a few later years, the forest eyre never again approached the level of severity that it had under John. The peak came in 1212, before the forest reforms that the effects of his rule, not least in the forests themselves, produced during the minority of Henry III.

The Managerial Revolution in the English Church

JAMES A. BRUNDAGE

THE CENTURY between the accession of Henry II in 1154 and the provisions of Oxford in 1258 witnessed momentous changes in the governance of the English kingdom, of which the baronial discontent that led to Magna Carta and its reissues were, of course, one part. This paper will address another of those momentous changes, namely the takeover of leadership in the church by lawyers. This managerial revolution, to use Colin Morris's phrase, profoundly altered the way in which the church conducted its business during the centuries that followed.[1]

The lawyers involved in this revolution were not the ones who worked in the common law courts, but rather clerics trained in the two learned laws, Roman and canon, that contemporaries described as *utrumque ius* or *ius commune*.[2] All priests were supposed to know some canon law of course, but for many that knowledge was decidedly elementary.[3] By 1258 formal legal training had become normal, even commonplace, among English bishops and archbishops. Lesser prelates, too, could by that point often boast some legal training and sometimes law degrees as well.

This change was, to be sure, hardly peculiar to England. By the end of the twelfth century the college of cardinals was already dominated by men trained in Roman and canon law. Two of those cardinals became popes before the end of the century, while at least five of the thirteenth-century

---

[1] Colin Morris, 'From Synod to Consistory: The Bishops' Courts in England, 1150–1250', *Journal of Ecclesiastical History* 22 (1971), 115–23 at 117.

[2] Richard H. Helmholz, *The ius commune in England: Four Studies* (Oxford, 2001), p. 10; Pierre Legendre, 'Le Droit romain, modèle et langage: de la signification de l'*Utrumque Ius*', in *Études du droit canonique dédiées à Gabriel Le Bras*, 2 vols (Paris, 1965), ii, pp. 913–30. Manlio Bellomo, *The Common Legal Past of Europe, 1000–1800*, trans. Lydia G. Cochrane (Washington, 1995), pp. 74–7; Ennio Cortese, *Diritto nella storia medievale*, 2 vols (Rome, 1995), ii pp. 244–5; E. J. H. Schrage, '"Utrumque ius": Über das römisch-kanonische ius commune als Grundlage europäischer Rechtseinheit in Vergangenheit und zukunft', *Revue internationale des droits de l'antiquité* 3rd ser. 39 (1992), 383–412.

[3] For the basic requirements, see *Decretum Gratiani* D. 38 c. 4 and c. 7. Canon law texts are cited throughout from Emil Friedberg, ed., *Corpus iuris canonici*, 2 vols (Leipzig, 1879; repr. Graz, 1959). For an explanation of the Romano-canonical citation system, see James Brundage, *Medieval Canon Law* (London, 1995), pp. 190–205.

popes were full-fledged lawyers.[4] Substantial numbers of bishops and archbishops in France and the Low Countries likewise had serious legal credentials.[5]

Although these developments were not uniquely English, nonetheless English churchmen played a central role in what was happening. It is significant, for example that more than half of the 713 decretals of Pope Alexander III (r. 1159–1181) that found their way into the Church's law books were addressed to English recipients.[6] Critics complained that the increasing prominence of jurists among the episcopate detracted from the spiritual life not only of members of the hierarchy, but also among the faithful at large. 'Formerly the Church used to be governed in peace by the canons,'

---

[4] On the college of cardinals, see Ian Robinson, *The Papacy, 1073–1198: Continuity and Innovation* (Cambridge, 1990), pp. 220–2, as well as Werner Maleczek, *Papst und Kardinalskolleg von 1191 bis 1216: Die Kardinäle unter Coelestin III. und Innocenz III.*, Österreichischen Kulturinstitut in Rom, Publikationen des Historischen Instituts, ser. 1 vol. 6 (Vienna, 1984); Rudolf Weigand, 'Frühe Kanonisten und ihre Karriere in der Kirche', *Zeitschrift der Savigny-Stiftung für Rechtsgeschichte*, kanonistische Abteilung 76 (1990), 135–55, repr. in his *Glossatoren des Dekrets Gratians* (Goldbach, 1997), pp. 403*–23*, furnishes numerous examples. The two twelfth-century lawyer-popes were Urban III (r. 1185–7) and his short-lived successor, Gregory VIII (r. 21 October – 17 December 1187). Although Alexander III has often been described as a trained lawyer, it now appears that he was not: John T. Noonan, Jr., 'Who Was Rolandus?', in Kenneth Pennington and Robert Somerville, eds, *Law, Church, and Society: Essays in Honor of Stephan Kuttner* (Philadelphia, 1977), pp. 21–48, and Rudolf Weigand, 'Magister Rolandus und Papst Alexander III.', *Archiv für katholisches Kirchenrecht* 149 (1980), 3–44, also repr. in his *Glossatoren des Dekrets Gratians*, pp. 73*–114*. The thirteenth-century lawyer popes were Gregory IX (1227–41), Innocent IV (1243–54), Clement IV (1265–68), Adrian IV (1268), and Boniface VIII (1294–1303). Innocent III, like Alexander III, has commonly been described as a lawyer, but his legal qualifications were exceedingly slim; see Kenneth Pennington, 'The Legal Education of Pope Innocent III', *Bulletin of Medieval Canon Law* 4 (1974), 70–7, and 'Further Thoughts on Pope Innocent III's Knowledge of Law', *Zeitschrift der Savigny-Stiftung für Rechtsgeschichte*, kanonistische Abteilung 72 (1986), 417–28, both repr. in his *Popes, Canonists and Texts, 1150–1550* (Aldershot, 1993), nos I and II.

[5] Jean Gaudemet, 'Recherches sur l'épiscopat médiéval en France', in Stephan Kuttner and J. Joseph Ryan, eds, *Proceedings of the Second International Congress of Medieval Canon Law* (Boston), Monumenta iuris canonici (hereafter MIC), Subsidia 1 (Vatican City, 1965), pp. 139–54 at pp. 144–6, and the biographical references in Christine Renardy, *Les Maîtres universitaires dans le diocèse de Liège: Répertoire biographique (1140–1350)*, Bibliothèque de la Faculté de philosophie et lettres de l'Université de Liège, fasc. 232 (Paris, 1981).

[6] Charles Duggan, 'Decretals of Alexander III to England', in Filippo Liotta, ed., *Miscellanea Rolando Bandinelli, Papa Alessandro III* (Siena, 1986), pp. 85–151 at p. 107. The prominence of English prelates among Alexander's correspondents was first pointed out by Frederic William Maitland, *Roman Canon Law in the Church of England* (London, 1898), pp. 123–4.

complained an anonymous Paris preacher, 'but now it is ruled by advocates who do more evil than heretics.'[7]

⟨ Teaching of *ius commune* by Englishmen

No one is born a lawyer. Lawyers are formed in law schools, not in their mother's womb. To explain how these developments came about, I must say something about the teaching of the *ius commune* by Englishmen, both in England and on the Continent. Although scattered allusions to Roman law appear among Anglo-Saxon sources and in the *Leges Henrici primi*,[8] there seems to be no evidence for serious study of Roman law in England before about 1150. It apparently began with Vacarius (*c.* 1120–*c.* 1200), a native of Lombardy who studied civil law at Bologna and was brought to Canterbury in the 1140s as a legal advisor to Archbishop Theobald (r. 1139–61). By the late 1150s he was at York working for Archbishop Roger de Pont l'Évêque (r. 1154–81), who rewarded him with the prebend of Norwell in 1164. Where, when, and under what circumstances Vacarius taught law, assuming that he ever did so, remain matters of controversy. Two things are certain: first, he was the author of a textbook known as *The Poor Men's Book* (*Liber pauperum*) – the kind of book that modern lawyers might call Roman law in a nutshell. The *Liber pauperum* in other words was short, relatively cheap, and covered the rudiments of the subject. Second, although Vacarius is principally known for his textbook, he was primarily a practitioner of canon law and the purpose of the *Liber pauperum* was to provide intending canonists with the basic knowledge of the Roman legal terms, concepts, and institutions that canon law texts employed.[9]

7   Venice, San Marco, Fondo antico, MS 92, fol. 193, quoted by Charles Homer Haskins, *Studies in Medieval Culture* (Oxford, 1929; repr. New York, 1965), pp. 47–8 n. 8: 'Quondam ecclesia consuevit regi in pace per canones, modo regitur per advocatos, per quos fiunt plura mala quam per hereticos …' Compare the complaints of St Bernard of Clairvaux in *De consideratione ad Eugenium papam* 1.10.13, in Jean Leclercq, C. H. Talbot, and H. M. Rochais, eds, *Opera*, 8 vols (Rome, 1957–77), iii, pp. 408–9, also in his *Five Books on Consideration: Advice to a Pope*, trans. John D. Anderson and Elizabeth T. Kennan (Kalamazoo, 1976), p. 44.

8   L. J. Downer, ed. and trans., *Leges Henrici primi* 33.4 (Oxford, 1972; repr. 1996), pp. 136–7.

9   Richard H. Helmholz, *Canon Law and Ecclesiastical Jurisdiction from 597 to the 1640s*, Oxford History of the Laws of England 1 (Oxford, 2004), pp. 121–4; Peter Stein, 'Vacarius and the Civil Law', in C. N. L. Brooke *et al.*, eds, *Church and Government in the Middle Ages: Essays Presented to C. R. Cheney on His 70th Birthday* (Cambridge, 1976), pp. 119–37, also repr. in his *Character and Influence of the Roman Civil Law: Historical Essays* (London, 1988), pp. 167–85, and 'The Vacarian School', *Journal of Legal History* 13 (1992), 23–31; Richard W. Southern, 'Master Vacarius and the Beginning of an English Academic Tradition', in J. J. G.

Prior to 1190 or thereabouts, copies of the authoritative texts of Roman and canon law were available in many English cathedral and monastic librar-ies.[10] Still, up to that point there was no place in England where Romano-canonical law was taught to a standard that would prepare a would-be advocate to compete effectively with his counterparts on the Continent. An Englishman who wanted that kind of training needed to go abroad, to the law schools at Paris, Cologne, or perhaps Montpellier, but above all to Bologna, the pre-eminent centre for legal studies in Western Christendom.[11] A good many Englishmen did just that, and several became internationally respected jurists. One of them was Richard de Morins (*c.* 1160–1242), com-monly known as Ricardus Anglicus. Ricardus taught canon law first at Paris in the 1180s, then at Bologna in the 1190s, and wrote numerous books that became much esteemed among professional canonists. In 1198 he returned to England, where he entered the house of Augustinian canons at Merton and was subsequently elected prior of Dunstable, a position he held for the remainder of his life. He became a busy ecclesiastical administrator, served at one point as King John's ambassador to Innocent III, was appointed a crusade preacher in 1212, and sat as a papal judge-delegate in more than forty cases.[12] Other well-known English canon lawyers active in the late twelfth century included Gerard Pucelle, bishop of Coventry († 1184), John of Salisbury († 1180), Alanus Anglicus (*fl. c.* 1190–1210), and Johannes Galensis (*fl. c.* 1210).[13]

Alexander and M. T. Gibson, eds, *Medieval Learning and Literature: Essays Presented to Richard William Hunt* (Oxford, 1976), pp. 257–86; Leonard E. Boyle, 'The Beginnings of Legal Studies at Oxford', *Viator* 14 (1983), 107–31; Stephan Kuttner and Eleanor Rathbone, 'Anglo-Norman Canonists of the Twelfth Century: An Introductory Study', *Traditio* 7 (1949/51), 279–358 at 287–8, repr. with *Retractationes* in Stephan Kuttner, *Gratian and the Schools of Law, 1140–1234* (London, 1983), no. VIII.

[10]   Ralph V. Turner, 'Roman Law in England before the Time of Bracton', *Journal of British Studies* 15 (1975), 1–25 at 8.

[11]   Southern, 'Master Vacarius', p. 266

[12]   Kuttner and Rathbone, 'Anglo-Norman Canonists', 338–9; Christopher R. Cheney, 'The Making of the Dunstable Annals, A.D. 33 to 1242', in his *Medieval Texts and Studies* (Oxford, 1973), pp. 209–30 at pp. 220–30; Jane E. Sayers, *Papal Judges Delegate in the Province of Canterbury, 1198–1254: A Study in Ecclesiastical Jurisdiction and Administration*, Oxford Historical Monographs (London, 1971), pp. 114–18, 296–301; Robert C. Figuiera, 'Ricardus de Mores and his *Casus decre-talium*: The Birth of a Canonistic Genre', in Stanley Chodorow, ed., *Proceedings of the Eighth International Congress of Medieval Canon Law* (San Diego), MIC, Subsidia 9 (Vatican City, 1992), pp. 169–87, and 'Morins, Richard', in *ODNB* online www.oxforddnb.com/view/article/23518.

[13]   On Gerard Pucelle, see Kuttner and Rathbone, 'Anglo-Norman Canonists', 296–303; Johannes Fried, 'Gerard Pucelle und Köln', *Zeitschrift der Savigny-Stiftung für Rechtsgeschichte*, kanonistische Abteilung 68 (1982), 125–35; Charles

While scattered evidence suggests that law may have been studied during the second half of the twelfth century at cathedral schools in Exeter and Lincoln and at the Abbey of St Albans, the information is insufficient to determine how substantial this may have been.[14] The first clear indication that advanced legal training had become available in England comes from Oxford, beginning in the 1180s. A decision handed down at Oxford by a panel of papal judges-delegate around 1180 notes that they had heard advice from 'many honest, wise men learned in the law'. The witnesses to their decision included Master John of Cornwall, Master Gilbert of Northampton, Master Godfrey of Lardaria, and Master Osbert of Arundel, all of whom were described by contemporaries as able lawyers.[15] The presence in Oxford of law courts and high-calibre lawyers began to attract students to the city.[16] Neither teachers nor students were very plentiful at Oxford at the beginning; however, for around 1186 Gerald of Wales was able to entertain all the Oxford teachers and their chief pupils at a dinner party, and a decade later Abbot Samson of Bury St Edmunds could fit all the resident masters around a single table in his lodgings.[17]

By the 1190s solid evidence shows that sophisticated law teaching was available at Oxford. This was the work of a few law teachers clustered around John of Tynemouth († *c.* 1221) and included Master Honorius († *c.* 1213), Master Simon of Sywell († after 1209), and Master Nicholas de

Donahue, Jr., 'Gerard Pucelle as a Canon Lawyer: Life and the Battle Abbey Case', in Richard H. Helmholz *et al.*, eds, *Grundlagen des Rechts: Festschrift für Peter Landau zum 65. Geburtstag* (Paderborn, 2000), pp. 333–48, and 'Pucelle, Gerard', in *ODNB* online www.oxforddnb.com/view/article/49666. Although one does not usually think of John of Salisbury as a canon lawyer, the law was his principal occupation for most of his career, although where and when he studied law is a matter of speculation: Christopher N. L. Brooke, 'John of Salisbury and his World', in Michael Wilkes, ed., *The World of John of Salisbury*, Studies in Church History, Subsidia 3 (Oxford, 1994), pp. 1–20 at pp. 7–8, and Max Kerner, 'Römisches und kirchliches Recht im Policraticus', also in *The World of John of Salisbury*, pp. 365–79. On Alanus Anglicus and Johannes Galensis, see the articles on them by Joseph Canning and F. Donald Logan in *ODNB* online www. oxforddnb.com/view/article/53478 and www.oxforddnb.com/view/article/28551.

14 Kuttner and Rathbone, 'Anglo-Norman Canonists', 321–9.

15 H. Mayr-Harting, ed., *Acta of the Bishops of Chichester, 1075–1207*, Canterbury & York Society 56 (Torquay, 1964), no. 64 at pp. 125–7.

16 Richard W. Southern, 'From Schools to University', in J. I. Catto, ed., *The History of the University of Oxford*, vol. 1: *The Early Oxford Schools* (Oxford, 1984), pp. 1–36 at pp. 16–17.

17 Giraldus Cambrensis, *Opera*, i: *De rebus a se gestis*, pp. 72–3; H. E. Butler, ed. and trans., *The Chronicle of Jocelin of Brakelond Concerning the Acts of Samson, Abbot of the Monastery of St. Edmund*, Medieval Classics (New York, 1949), pp. 94–5; Southern, 'Master Vacarius', pp. 270–1; H. G. Richardson, 'The Oxford Law School under John', *Law Quarterly Review* 57 (1941), 319–38 at 324.

l'Aigle († 1216).[18] We not only know their names and something about their careers, but, more important, records of their teaching survive in two manuscripts. The *Quaestiones Londonenses* (now in the British Library, hence the title) consist of *reportationes* of fifty-eight academic disputations by John of Tynemouth and his associates in the Oxford law schools during the late 1190s.[19] The other manuscript (now in the library of Gonville and Caius College, Cambridge) contains a copy of Gratian's *Decretum* with glosses that bear the *sigla* of John of Tynemouth and his colleagues.[20] The sophistication of the arguments in the London *quaestiones* and the Caius glosses, coupled with their broad range of references not only to authoritative texts of both Roman and canon law, but also to the work of leading contemporary canonists on the Continent, demonstrates that shortly before 1200 the schools of Oxford could provide legal training in both laws on a level comparable with that available at Paris or Bologna.[21]

At that point the Oxford schools of grammar, the other liberal arts,

[18] Kuttner and Rathbone, 'Anglo-Norman Canonists', 304–21, 334–9; Rudolf Weigand, 'Die Anglo-Normannische Kanonistik in den letzten Jahrzehnten des 12. Jahrhunderts', in Peter Linehan, ed., *Proceedings of the Seventh International Congress of Medieval Canon Law* (Cambridge), MIC, Subsidia 8 (Vatican City, 1988), pp. 249–63; Rudolf Weigand, Peter Landau, and Waltrud Kozur, eds, *Magistri Honorii Summa 'De iure canonico tractaturus'*, MIC, Corpus glossatorum 5 (Vatican City, 2004–); A. B. Emden, *Biographical Register of the University of Oxford to A.D. 1500*, 3 vols (Oxford, 1957; repr. 1989), i, p. 560; ii, pp. 956–7; iii, pp. 1704, 1923; Charles Duggan, 'Honorius', in *ODNB* online www.oxforddnb.com/view/article/50350.

[19] BL MS Royal 9.E.VII, fol. 191ra–198vb; Stephan Kuttner, *Repertorium der Kanonistik (1140–1234)*, Studi e testi 71 (Vatican City, 1937), pp. 251–2, as well as Kuttner and Rathbone, 'Anglo-Norman Canonists', 319–21; James A. Brundage, 'The Crusade of Richard I: Two Canonical *Quaestiones*', *Speculum* 38 (1963), 443–52, and 'A Twelfth-Century Disputation Concerning the Privileges of the Knights Hospitallers', *Mediaeval Studies* 24 (1962), 153–60, both reprinted in *Crusades, Holy War and Canon Law* (Aldershot, 1991), nos. III and XII, and also 'The Treatment of Marriage in the *Questiones Londinenses*', *Manuscripta* 19 (1975), 86–97, repr. in *Law, Sex and Marriage in the Middle Ages* (Aldershot, 1993), no. XII.

[20] MS 283/676; Kuttner, *Repertorium der Kanonistik*, pp. 251–2; Kuttner and Rathbone, 'Anglo-Norman Canonists', 317–19; Charles Duggan, 'The Reception of Canon Law in England in the Later-Twelfth Century', in Kuttner and Ryan, *Proceedings of the Second International Congress of Medieval Canon Law*, pp. 359–90 at pp. 371–7, 388–90.

[21] Southern, 'From Schools to University', p. 21; Boyle, 'Beginnings of Legal Studies', 110–14. John of Tynemouth and the other masters mentioned in the *Quaestiones Londonenses* and the Caius glosses had all left Oxford before 1200 to enter the service of Archbishop Hubert Walter and other bishops as ecclesiastical administrators, a career that provided far more lucrative opportunities for advancement than teaching did: Thomas of Marlborough, *History of the Abbey of Evesham*, ed. and trans. Jane Sayers and Leslie Watkiss, Oxford Medieval Texts (Oxford, 2003)

theology, and law seem to have been separate enterprises operated by individual masters who were not affiliated, formally at least, with one another. Shortly after 1200, however, this apparently began to change. Innocent III referred in a letter dated 2 January 1201 to one John Grim, doctor of theology, under the title Master of the Scholars of Oxford (*magister scholarium Oxonie*). This is the earliest explicit indication that the Oxford masters had begun to acquire a corporate identity of some sort, although just how that happened is uncertain.[22] The schools of individual Oxford law teachers seemingly coalesced into a single school in which both Roman and canon law was taught (*schola utriusque iuris*). Although the split into separate faculties of civil and canon law occurred at some unknown date after 1234, the distinction between them was in practice more apparent than real. Unlike other faculties at Oxford, civil and canon law shared bedels, for example, and sometimes voted as a single faculty in Congregation. The civil law faculty was primarily a preparatory school for students of canon law.[23]

At Cambridge canon law seems to have been taught as soon as organized schools appeared there, shortly after 1209. Exactly when teachers of civil and canon law organized a formal faculty of canon law at Cambridge is not clear, but it was certainly in existence by 1250 and probably had been for some decades before then. A separate civil law faculty appeared by 1256, but as at Oxford it was largely a preparatory course for students who went on to study canon law.[24]

❡ Transformation of church courts

While systematic law teaching was beginning to take shape, church courts were also undergoing a transformation in response to the ever-growing volume of litigation that bishops and other prelates had to deal with.[25] One of

---

§§230, 233, pp. 232–4, 236; Christopher R. Cheney, *Hubert Walter* (London, 1967), pp. 164–6.

[22] C. R. Cheney and Mary G. Cheney, eds, *The Letters of Pope Innocent III (1198–1216) concerning England and Wales: A Calendar with an Appendix of Texts* (Oxford, 1967), no. 279, pp. 46, 220–1; M. B. Hackett, 'The University as a Corporate Body', in *History of the University of Oxford*, i, pp. 37–95 at pp. 38–9.

[23] Boyle, 'Beginning of Legal Studies', at 130–1, and Leonard E. Boyle, 'Canon Law before 1380', in *History of the University of Oxford*, i, pp. 531–64 at pp. 533–42.

[24] M. B. Hackett, *The Original Statutes of Cambridge University: The Text and its History* (Cambridge, 1970), pp. 29, 32, 130–1; James A. Brundage, 'The Cambridge Faculty of Canon Law and the Ecclesiastical Courts of Ely', in Patrick Zutshi, ed., *Medieval Cambridge: Essays on the Pre-Reformation University* (Woodbridge, 1993), pp. 21–45.

[25] Martin Brett, 'Canon Law and Litigation: The Century before Gratian', in M. J. Franklin and Christopher Harper-Bill, eds, *Medieval Ecclesiastical Studies in Honour of Dorothy Owen*, Studies in the History of Medieval Religion 7

a bishop's most time-consuming tasks from the outset of Christian history was to settle quarrels and disputes within his community. St Bernard of Clairvaux (1090–1153) declared that the pope and other bishops were morally obliged to settle disputes among Christians: 'We cannot abandon the downtrodden; we cannot refuse judgment to those who suffer injustice. If cases are not tried and litigants heard, how can judgment be passed?'[26]

Prior to the mid-twelfth century bishops were generally able to deal with their judicial business in person. When faced with a perplexing controversy, they might bring the matter before their diocesan synod, the customary forum for the adjudication of especially sensitive and troublesome ecclesiastical disputes.[27]

When a problem was straightforward and a quick decision was needed, of course, a bishop could usually deal with it himself, and this was typically his first choice. Bishops and other prelates were expected to know some law and their official duties required them to become practical men of affairs.[28] During the last quarter of the twelfth century, as canon law grew more complex and its procedural technicalities became more numerous and arcane, however, bishops began to find it not so much advisable as essential to have trained legal advisors available on a regular basis.[29] They usually rewarded their legal experts with prebends in their cathedral chapters and other ecclesiastical posts, which made these positions attractive to clever and ambitious men. Thus, for example, Bishop Seffrid II of Chichester (r. 1180–1204), whose own legal learning was not insignificant, employed Master Ralph

---

(Woodbridge, 1995), pp. 21–40 at pp. 32, 40; Charles Duggan, 'Papal Judges Delegate and the Making of the "New Law" in the Twelfth Century', in Thomas N. Bisson, ed., *Cultures of Power: Lordship, Status, and Process in Twelfth-Century Europe* (Philadelphia, 1995), pp. 172–99 at p. 195.

[26] *De consideratione* 1.10.13 in his *Opera* 3:308, trans. Anderson and Kennan, p. 43.

[27] English bishops in the twelfth century typically held diocesan synods once or twice a year; Council of Windsor (1070) c. 4, in Dorothy Whitelock, Martin Brett, and Christopher N. L. Brooke, eds, *Councils and Synods with Other Documents Relating to the English Church*, vol. 1: *A.D. 871–1204*, 2 pts (Oxford, 1981) pt 2, p. 580; Martin Brett, *The English Church under Henry I* (London, 1975), pp. 155–61; Morris, 'From Synod to Consistory', 116. On synodal procedure, see Christopher R. Cheney, *English Synodalia of the Thirteenth Century* (London, 1941; repr. 1968), pp. 8, 26–31.

[28] On prelates' need to know law, see e.g. Gratian's *Decretum*, D. 10 c. 3–4, d.p.c. 6, D. 38 c. 4, and c. 7, D. 39 c. 1, and c. 11 q. 1 d.p.c. 30. Prelates whose legal learning was minimal might come to regret it, as did Abbot Odo of Battle (r. 1175–1200), recounted in Eleanor Searle, ed. and trans., *Chronicle of Battle Abbey*, Oxford Medieval Texts (Oxford, 1980), pp. 324–5.

[29] Paul Fournier, *Les Officialités au moyen âge: Étude sur l'organisation, la compétence et la procédure des tribunaux ecclésiastiques ordinaires en France de 1180 à 1328* (Paris, 1880; repr. Aalen, 1984), pp. 7–8.

of Ford to assist him in dealing with legal problems. Archbishop Hubert Walter (r. 1193–1205), for another, induced three distinguished Oxford law teachers, John of Tynemouth, Simon of Sywell, and Master Honorius, to desert their students and join his staff.[30]

As bishops and archbishops started to become overtaxed by an unrelenting increase in judicial business, they responded by delegating more and more of the burden of hearing and deciding cases to the legal experts on their staffs. Starting around 1170 in the triangular region bounded on the north and west by the British Isles, on the south by Normandy, and on the east by the Rhineland, documents from one diocese after another show that the legal experts on the bishop's administrative team were commencing to preside as judges in all save the most sensitive cases that came to the bishop for adjudication. Contemporary documents usually describe these judges as the bishops' officials.[31] In the technical terminology that canonists borrowed from Roman law, these officials exercised their bishop's ordinary jurisdiction.[32] The vast majority of these officials, not surprisingly, were men who had studied law, and from the mid-thirteenth century onward they increasingly held the doctorate in canon law, Roman civil law, or sometimes in both laws.

During the first half of the thirteenth century the nature of the jurisdiction of bishops' officials gradually changed. At the beginning of the century officials exercised the bishop's ordinary jurisdiction as his delegate and their decisions could be appealed to the bishop. By mid-century, however, custom had so enhanced their position that they had secured a near-monopoly on the exercise of ordinary jurisdiction within the diocese. Pope Innocent IV (r. 1243–54) ruled in 1246 that a disappointed litigant could not appeal from the decision of the official to the bishop. Instead he must take his complaint to a higher court, such as that of the archbishop or the pope.[33] The official

[30] Mayr-Harting, introduction to the *Acta of the Bishops of Chichester*, pp. 13–21; Cheney, *Hubert Walter*, pp. 164–6.

[31] Morris, 'From Synod to Consistory', 120–1; David M. Smith, 'The "Officialis" of the Bishop in Twelfth- and Thirteenth-Century England: Problems of Terminology', in Franklin and Harper-Bill, *Medieval Ecclesiastical Studies*, pp. 201–20.

[32] Bernard of Pavia, *Summa decretalium* 1.21.1, ed. E. A. T. Laspeyres (Regensburg, 1860; repr. Graz, 1956), p. 16, defined the term: 'Ordinarius iudex est qui in ecclesiasticis ab Apostolico, in secularibus ab Imperatore totalem quandam habet iurisdictionem.' For the Roman roots of the term, see Max Kaser, *Das römische Zivilprozessrecht*, 2nd edn, ed. Karl Hackl, Handbuch der Altertumswissenschaft Abt. 10, Rechtsgeschichte des Altertums, Teil 3 Bd. 4 (Munich, 1996), pp. 529–30.

[33] VI 2.15.3 *Romana ecclesia* (Innocent IV, 21 April 1246); August Potthast, *Regesta pontificum Romanorum inde ab A. post Christum natum MCXCVIII ad A. MCCCIV*, 2 vols (Berlin, 1874–5), no. 12062; Morris, 'From Synod to Consistory', 119, 121; Wilfried Trusen, 'Die Gelehrte Gerichtsbarkeit der Kirche', in Helmut Coing, ed.,

now *was* the bishop so far as ordinary jurisdiction was concerned, except for the relatively few cases that the bishop reserved for judgment in his court of audience.[34]

The courts that bishops' officials headed gradually grew into permanent episcopal consistory courts (often called officialities on the Continent) with a supporting staff to assist the official-principal. These courts dealt with a broad range of matters that touched the lives of ordinary Christians in numerous ways. Litigation over marriages was a mainstay of English consistory courts, as was the punishment of fornication, adultery, concubinage, and other sexual offences. Beyond that they handled complaints about infractions of other disciplinary rules, such as those against usury or working on Sundays or holy days; ruled on transactions involving church property; and dealt with disputes over benefices, the collection of tithes and other church revenues, the probate of wills, and the administration of decedents' estates.[35] It would have been difficult for almost any Christian to go through life without coming into contact with these courts at some point.

❡ The ascendancy of lawyers

Men with advanced training in the *ius commune* began to hold positions of power and authority in the English church from the 1140s onward.[36] Thus Jocelin de Bohun, who had studied law at Bologna during the 1130s, became bishop of Salisbury in 1142; Robert de Chesney, a skilled lawyer, after serving as archdeacon of Leicester was elected bishop of Lincoln in 1148, the same year that Gilbert Foliot became bishop of Hereford, before being translated to London in 1163; and Hilary, a former advocate at the Roman curia, became bishop of Chichester in 1147.[37] Even Thomas Becket

---

Handbuch der Quellen und Literatur der neueren europäischen Privatrechtsgeschichte, vol. 1: *Mittelalter (1100–1500): Die gelehrten Rechte und die Gesetzgebung* (Munich, 1973), pp. 467–504 at pp. 474–5; Fournier, *Officialités*, p. 13.

[34] Irene Josephine Churchill, *Canterbury Administration: The Administrative Machinery of the Archbishopric of Canterbury Illustrated from Original Records*, 2 vols (London, 1933), i, pp. 470–99.

[35] Charles Donahue, Jr., *Law, Marriage, and Society in the Later Middle Ages: Arguments about Marriage in Five Courts* (Cambridge, 2007), esp. chapters 2–6 and 10–12; Richard H. Helmholz, *Marriage Litigation in Medieval England*, Cambridge Studies in English Legal History (Cambridge, 1974) and *Canon Law and Ecclesiastical Jurisdiction*, pp. 206–36; as well as Brundage, *Medieval Canon Law*, esp. chs 4, 5, and 8.

[36] Mary G. Cheney, 'The Compromise of Avranches of 1172 and the Spread of Canon Law in England', *English Historical Review* 56 (1941), 177–97 at 195–7.

[37] Turner, 'Roman Law in England', 9–10; Emden, *Biographical Register*, i, p. 406; Dorothy M. Owen, 'Chesney, Robert de', in *ODNB* online www.oxforddnb.com/

had spent a year studying civil and canon law at Bologna and Auxerre in his youth, surrounded himself with lawyers while he was archbishop of Canterbury (r. 1162–70), and resumed his legal studies during his exile.[38] This pattern continued and gradually grew more common in subsequent generations.[39] Over the whole period from 1216 to 1499, 57 per cent of English bishops were Oxford men and 45 per cent of them had studied law at the university. Similarly, among the smaller number of Cambridge men appointed to English sees 55 per cent were lawyers.[40]

Likewise appointments to lesser ecclesiastical positions, such as cathedral deans, archdeacons, prebendaries, and (predictably enough) the officials-principal of bishops, strongly favoured law-trained men. Master Honorius, for example, wound up as archdeacon of Richmond, while his former colleague, John of Tynemouth, returned to Oxford in 1225, this time as its archdeacon; Peter of Blois became archdeacon of Bath; Ivo of Cornwall secured the archdeaconry of Derby, and so on. Statistical analyses of the alumni records of Oxford and Cambridge during the high and later Middle Ages further attest that men who had studied law by and large enjoyed significantly greater success in securing mid-level church positions than theologians, physicians, or those in the arts faculties.[41]

Medieval students were acutely aware of all of this. Theology was, of course, the queen of the sciences – at least in theory. But to the chagrin of teachers of the liberal arts and theology, students and those who supported them gave priority to vocational studies, such as law.[42] As Dante (1265–1321) observed, 'Lawyers and physicians – and for that matter most religious

view/article/5232; Christopher Brooke, Introduction to W. J. Millor, H. E. Butler, and C. N. L. Brooke, eds, *The Letters of John of Salisbury*, 2 vols (Edinburgh and Oxford, 1955–1979) i, p. xxxvi.

[38] William FitzStephen, *Vita Sancti Thomae*, §7; Herbert of Bosham, *Vita Sancti Thomae* §§3.12, 7.1; and John of Salisbury, *Vita Sancti Thomae* §5, all in James Cragie Robertson, ed., *Materials for the History of Thomas Becket, Archbishop of Canterbury*, 7 vols, Rolls Series 67 (London, 1875–85) ii, p. 304; iii, pp. 17, 207, and 523–7; John of Salisbury, *Letters*, no. 279 at ii, pp. 602–8.

[39] Among many others, Gerard Pucelle became bishop of Coventry in 1183; Bartholomew of Ford was named bishop of Worcester in 1180 and archbishop of Canterbury in 1184; and Simon of Apulia secured the see of Exeter in 1214, where the canonist Bartholomew of Exeter († 1184) was one of his predecessors.

[40] T. H. Aston, 'Oxford's Medieval Alumni', *Past & Present* 74 (1977), 3–40 at 27–8, as well as T. H. Aston, G. D. Duncan, and T. A. R. Evans, 'The Medieval Alumni of the University of Cambridge', *Past & Present* 86 (1980) 9–86 at 70.

[41] Aston, 'Oxford's Medieval Alumni', 28; Aston, Duncan, and Evans, 'Medieval Alumni of Cambridge', 71–5.

[42] Alan B. Cobban, *The Medieval Universities: Their Development and Organization* (London, 1975), pp. 8, 18, 165; Richard W. Southern, *Scholastic Humanism and the Unification of Europe*, 2 vols (Oxford, 1995–2001), i, p. 8.

– study, not in order to acquire knowledge, but rather to secure money or high position.'[43] Theologians, philosophers, and church authorities tried to fight back. They stigmatized law and medicine as grubby lucrative sciences and forbade monks, friars, and regular canons to study them.[44] Teachers of grammar and rhetoric denounced the vainglorious lust for power and the greed for wealth that led students to desert their classrooms to take up the study of the *Decretals* and the *Digest*.[45] Knowledge, preachers thundered, is a gift of God and hence cannot be sold.[46]

Fulminations of this sort failed to lure medieval Englishmen away from studying Roman and canon law, as the evidence of enrolments in the higher faculties at Oxford and Cambridge makes plain.[47] An anonymous twelfth-century student expressed what were clearly the feelings of many:

> Galen makes you rich, and so does Justinian's law,
> From these you gather grain, from the others only straw.
>
> …
>
> Socrates and Plato produce a scanty yield,
> I'll go for the money with assets as my shield.
> An abundant harvest demands a fertile field.[48]

---

43 Dante, *Convivio* 3.11.10 in *Tutte le opere*, ed. Fredi Chiapelli (Milan, 1965), p. 569: '[S]ì come sono li legisti, [li] medici e quasi tutti li religiosi, chi non per sapere studiano ma per acquistare moneta o dignitade.'

44 Second Lateran Council (1139) c. 9, in G. Alberigo *et al.*, eds, *Decrees of the Ecumenical Councils*, trans. Norman P. Tanner *et al.*, 2 vols (London and Washington, 1990), i, p. 198; Charles Homer Haskins, *The Renaissance of the Twelfth Century* (Cambridge, MA, 1927; repr. New York, 1958), p. 216; Manlio Bellomo, *Saggio sull'università dell'età del diritto comune* (Rome, 1992), pp. 17–18.

45 Peter of Blois, *Epist.* 140 in *Opera omnia*, ed. J. A. Giles, 4 vols (Oxford, 1847), ii, p. 37; Dante, *Paradiso* 9.133–5 and 12.82–5, ed. Chiapelli, pp. 276, 285, as well as Richard Kay, ed. and trans., *Monarchia* 3.9, Studies and Texts 131 (Toronto, 1998), pp. 210–12.

46 Gaines Post, Kimon Giocarinis, and Richard Kay, 'The Medieval Heritage of a Humanistic Ideal: "Scientia donum Dei est, unde vendi non potest"', *Traditio* 11 (1955), 195–234.

47 Aston, 'Oxford's Medieval Alumni', 9–11; Aston, Duncan, and Evans, 'Medieval Alumni of Cambridge', 57–63.

48 Stephan Kuttner, 'Dat Galienus opes et sanctio Justiniana', in A. S. Crisafulli, ed., *Linguistic and Literary Studies in Honor of Helmut A. Hatzfeld* (Washington, 1964), pp. 237–46 at p. 243, repr. in Kuttner's *History of Ideas and Doctrines of Canon Law in the Middle Ages*, 2nd edn (Aldershot, 1992), no. x: 'Dat Galienus opes et sanctio Justiniana / Ex aliis paleas, ex ista collige grana / … Quid Plato, quid Sortes, quid friuola gentis egene? / Preferem uberes: luo sumptibus otia pene / Pinguis aratur ager, spem messis concipe plene.' I owe the translation of the first distich to Beryl Smalley, *The Becket Conflict and the Schools: A Study of Intellectuals in Politics in the Twelfth Century* (Oxford, 1973), p. 19.

❦ *Ius commune*, Magna Carta, and church governance

By way of conclusion let me briefly address two further questions: first what role did the developments that I have just been discussing play in shaping Magna Carta? And second, how did those developments impinge on the governance of the English church in the later Middle Ages?

Professor Helmholz has recently scoured Magna Carta and compared the contents of each clause with the *ius commune* legal doctrines on that topic current in the early thirteenth century, as John Hudson points out in his essay. Helmholz found a substantial number of resemblances, and I shall summarize a few of them.[49] In brief, Helmholz discovered that while some clauses of Magna Carta (such as 2–6, 9, 13, 15–19, 32–5, and 61) show little or no similarity to the teachings then current among Roman and canon jurists, many more clauses either restate *ius commune* rules in different language (e.g. 12, 14, 36, 40) or closely track teachings then current among the jurists of the *ius commune* (e.g. 1, 28, 30, 31, 41, 42, 52, 54, 57, 63).

Given these resemblances—and the detailed argument that Helmholz presents strongly suggests that they are not simply random—how do we account for them? It seems highly likely that one or more of those involved in drafting Magna Carta was familiar enough with the texts of the *ius commune* not only to employ terms such as *delictum* (ch. 20), *testes* (c. 38), *damnum* (ch. 41), *consuetudines* (ch. 41), or *inquisitio* (ch. 52), but, far more telling, to use them properly in a technical legal sense. Let me say something further about the term *delictum* that Professor Hudson uses as an example in order to illustrate what I mean. If you turn to this word in a standard Latin dictionary, such as Lewis and Short or the *Oxford Latin Dictionary*, you will find a list of meanings such as transgression, fault, offence, crime, or wrong, fortified by a string of quotations from Plautus, Caesar, Sallust or Horace, to support them. For a lawyer, however, a delict is a fundamental element in the law of obligations.[50] In law *delictum* means an act, or a failure to act, that gives rise to a civil liability to compensate the person or persons harmed by that act or failure to act. Beyond that, things become extremely complicated, but my point here is that whoever drafted the twentieth clause of Magna Carta used the term as a lawyer would. That person or persons was almost certainly aware of the relevant texts of the *ius commune*.

Who that person was cannot be determined. Archbishop Stephen

[49] R. H. Helmholz, 'Magna Carta and the *ius commune*', *University of Chicago Law Review* 66 (1999), 297–371.

[50] Reinhard Zimmermann, *The Law of Obligations: Roman Foundations of the Civilian Tradition* (Oxford, 1996), pp. 1–3, 902–6, 913–18; Bruce W. Frier, *A Casebook on the Roman Law of Delict*, American Philological Association, Classical Resources Series no. 2 (Atlanta, 1989), pp. 1–2.

Langton (r. 1207–28) has long been the usual suspect.[51] Langton himself was trained as a theologian and had taught theology at Paris in the 1180s. At that point canon law and theology were only beginning to diverge from one another and had not yet become distinct disciplines, although by 1215 their separation was already well advanced.[52] However much, or little, Langton may have absorbed of the legal side of theology, he certainly had legal experts at his side during the negotiations that led to Magna Carta. They included Adam of Tilney († 1219) and William of Bardney, in addition to his official, Thomas of Frackenham († 1238) and possibly also John of Kent.[53] Even King John had at least one man learned in the *ius commune* with him at Runnymede. This was Benedict of Sawston (later bishop of Rochester), who, ironically, is thought to have studied with Stephen Langton at Paris.[54] What role advisors such as these may have played in hammering out the document we simply do not know, and perhaps never will.

Lastly, I come to the long-term results of the process that I have dealt with in this paper, a process that I might call juridification—at least if the standard dictionaries recognized such a word. A minority of the lawyers who played leading roles in that process, including for example Gerard Pucelle, Bartholomew of Exeter, Gilbert Foliot, Baldwin of Ford, Benedict of Sawston, Roger de Pont l'Évêque, and Hilary of Chichester, ended up as bishops or archbishops. Indeed, one of them, Thomas Cantilupe, not only became bishop of Hereford but was also canonized a saint—a decidedly

---

[51] J. C. Holt, *Magna Carta*, 2nd edn (Cambridge, 1992; repr. 1997), pp. 269–71.

[52] Joseph de Ghellinck, *Le mouvement théologique du XIIᵉ siècle: Sa préparation lointaine avant et autour de Pierre Lombard, ses rapports avec les initiatives des canonistes*, 2nd edn, Museum Lessianum, section historique no. 10 (Bruges, 1948; repr. Brussels, 1969), pp. 203–13, 416–510; Herbert Kalb, 'Juristischer und theologischer Diskurs und die Entstehung der Kanonistik als Rechtswissenschaft', *Österreichisches Archiv für Recht und Religion* 47 (2000), 1–33, and 'Rechtskraft und ihre Durchbrechungen im Spannungsfeld von kanonistischen und theologischen Diskurs', in Helmholz, *Grundlagen des Rechts*, pp. 405–19.

[53] Kathleen Major, 'The "Familia" of Archbishop Stephen Langton', *English Historical Review* 48 (1933), 529–53 at 529–31, 533, 537–40; Kuttner and Rathbone, 'Anglo-Norman Canonists', 320. John of Kent had been a member of the circle around John of Tynemouth at Oxford in the late 1190s; his *siglum* appears in the *Quaestiones Londonenses*, fols 194vb–ra, 195rb, and 196ra. See also Joseph Goering, 'The "Summa de penitentia" of John of Kent', *Bulletin of Medieval Canon Law* 18 (1988), 13–31.

[54] Sayers, *Papal Judges Delegate*, pp. 130, 208, and Jane E. Sayers, *Papal Government and England during the Pontificate of Honorius III (1216–1227)*, Cambridge Studies in Medieval Life and Thought 3rd ser. 21 (Cambridge, 1984), p. 176; Marion E. Gibbs and Jane Lang, *Bishops and Reform 1215–1272, with Special Reference to the Lateran Council of 1215* (Oxford, 1934; repr. London, 1962), p. 167; M. N. Blount, 'Sawston, Benedict of', in ODNB online www.oxforddnb.com/view/article/24660.

uncommon distinction for a lawyer.[55] By 1250 men with a legal education
and background had already become numerous among the English episcopate and would dominate it for much of the later Middle Ages. Many
more law-trained men occupied lesser but still influential posts as cathedral deans, prebendaries, bishops' officials, archdeacons, and rural deans,
which gave them authority over clergy and laity alike. Many of these men
also served in high offices in the royal as well as the ecclesiastical administration of England – as chancellor, keeper of the king's seal, justices in the
common law courts, and with notable frequency as diplomats, a position
in which their legal training made them exceptionally effective.[56] Their
legal skills enabled them to exercise influence across territorial and political boundaries. They could and did work easily and effectively, not only as
lawyers and judges, but also as negotiators with the papal curia and with
their counterparts in the service of foreign monarchs, merchants, and
moneylenders.

Men trained in Roman and canon law constituted a new class of medieval intellectuals. The study of the *ius commune* attracted large numbers of
the most talented and ambitious men with agile minds in each generation
during the closing centuries of the Middle Ages. These were men of learning. They almost invariably collected books and many of them amassed
impressive libraries that included not only legal texts and treatises, but also
volumes of the classics, current literature both in Latin and the vernaculars,
philosophy, theology, medicine, and the sciences.[57] Skilled lawyers exercised
an intellectual and political influence in late medieval society out of all proportion to their numbers.[58]

The downside to all of this was that the church in late medieval England

---

[55] R. G. Griffiths and W. W. Capes, eds, *The Register of Thomas de Cantilupe, Bishop of Hereford* (A.D. 1275–1282), Canterbury and York Society 2 (London, 1906–7), Introduction, pp. ix–xi; Emden, *Biographical Register*, i, pp. 347–9; Ronald C. Finucane, 'Cantilupe, Thomas de', in *ODNB* online www.oxforddnb.com/view/article/4570.

[56] Donald E. Queller, *The Office of Ambassador in the Middle Ages* (Princeton, 1967), pp. 26–30, 68, 154–6; Garrett Mattingly, *Renaissance Diplomacy* (Boston, 1955; repr. Baltimore, 1964), pp. 18, 20–5.

[57] Brundage, 'Tools of the Trade: Medieval Lawyers' Libraries', forthcoming in Kjell Modéer, ed., *To Collect the Minds of the Law*, and the literature cited therein.

[58] Manlio Bellomo, 'Una nuova figura di intellettuale: Il giurista', in Cinzio Violante and Johannes Fried, eds, *Il secolo XI: Una svolta?* (Bologna, 1993), pp. 237–56; Alain Boureau, 'How Law Came to the Monks: The Use of Law in English Society at the Beginning of the Thirteenth Century', *Past & Present* 167 (2000), 29–74 at 41; William J. Bouwsma, 'Lawyers and Early Modern Culture', *American Historical Review* 78 (1973), 303–27.

became conspicuously legalistic.[59] Church courts and officials flourished and multiplied. Their jurisdiction reached ever deeper into the personal lives of ordinary Christians, and their intrusiveness led to widespread resentment. As an anonymous poet complained:

> Theire frauds, theire snares, their filthinesses bold,
> Which no great margins of a book can hold.
> These are the men that all the world affright,
> Whose very face for feare makes the earth looke white.
>
> ...
>
> How much by inbred mischeefe they intend,
> Or by their office how they may offend,
> What pen of swiftest scribe can thoroughly write?[60]

As worldly and ambitious men trained as lawyers took control of the church's upper management levels, abuses of power also increased. In the words of Christopher Cheney: 'The reign of law was never established. What prevailed was the reign of lawyers.'[61]

---

[59] Alan B. Cobban, 'Theology and Law in the Medieval Colleges of Oxford and Cambridge', *Bulletin of the John Rylands University Library of Manchester* 65 (1982), 57–77 at 72.

[60] An Elizabethan translation of the *Apocalypsis Goliae episcopi*, lines 221–31; the text appears in Thomas Wright, ed., *Latin Poems Commonly Attributed to Walter Mapes*, Camden Society o.s. 16 (London, 1841), at pp. 11–12 with the translation at p. 287.

[61] Christopher R. Cheney, *From Becket to Langton: English Church Government, 1170–1213* (Manchester, 1956; repr. 1965), p. 75.

Magna Carta, the *ius commune,* and English Common Law

JOHN HUDSON

THE IMPORTANCE of the Angevin period to the development of a characteristically English common law is widely recognized. Less well known, but also of considerable significance, was the Anglo-Norman contribution to the *ius commune,* the Roman and canon law studied and practised in Europe during this period.[1] However, the question of influence from the *ius commune* to English common law remains very problematic. One method of tackling the issue is to take a single legally important text and investigate the possibility of *ius commune* influence upon it, or indeed the possibility of the continuing effect of some earlier influence of canon law upon English law. An obvious text for such examination is Magna Carta: how far was the legal background to the great charter purely English, how far was it that of broader developments in European learned law?

❆ State of the issue

The maximalist position concerning the influence of *ius commune* is best made by Professor Helmholz, in his article 'Magna Carta and the *ius commune',* published in the *University of Chicago Law Review* in 1999. The article makes the argument that the *ius commune,* the amalgam of the Roman and canon laws that governed legal education in European universities and influenced legal practice in Europe from the twelfth century forward, played a role in the drafting of a significant number of the Charter's provisions.[2]

The contrary view is best presented in J. C. Holt's magisterial book, *Magna Carta,* first published in 1965 and reissued in 1992 with a substantial new chapter on 'Justice and Jurisdiction'. Holt states that

---

[1] See e.g. Charles Duggan, *Twelfth-Century Decretal Collections and their Importance in English History* (London, 1963); James A. Brundage, *The Medieval Origins of the Legal Profession* (Chicago, 2008), pp. 110–14; Eleanor Rathbone, 'Roman Law in the Anglo-Norman Realm', *Studia Gratiana* 11 (1967), 253–71; Stephan G. Kuttner and Eleanor Rathbone, 'Anglo-Norman Canonists of the Twelfth Century: An Introductory Survey', *Traditio* 7 (1949/1951), 279–358.

[2] R. H. Helmholz, 'Magna Carta and the *ius commune',* *University of Chicago Law Review* 66 (1999), 297–371, 300–1. I would like to thank Dick Helmholz and Rob Bartlett for their helpful and good-spirited comments on an earlier draft of this article, and David d'Avray for his help on Langton's biblical commentaries.

the extent and quality of ecclesiastical influence on the Charter are not easy to determine. ... Some clauses reveal an immediate canonical influence ... However, canonical influence was sometimes narrower and ecclesiastical intervention more restricted than laymen would have liked. The clearest and most certain evidence on the attitude of Langton [the archbishop of Canterbury] and his colleagues is not to be found in the chronicles, or even in contemporary canon law, but in the Articles [of the Barons] and the Charter. In these they acted throughout with a proper regard for the distinctions between the spiritual and the temporal, refusing to permit secular interference in the former, and intruding themselves as little as possible into the latter.[3]

The debate is of interest for various reasons. It is relevant to histories of liberty or the constitution. Thus Helmholz writes: 'The sum of the argument being made here is that, in this most basic statement of English customary law and constitutional principle, it requires no giant stretch of the imagination to think that the resources of the *ius commune* played a part.'[4] More specifically, it is relevant to the events of the last years of John's reign and to the making of the Charter. In particular it raises the issue of the influence that the archbishop of Canterbury, Stephen Langton, had both upon the events of 1215 and upon the content or phraseology of the Charter.[5] This in turn relates to interpretation of lay ideals for reform in 1215, both in the moral terms in which the question used to be posed – for example, how far were the barons of 1215 self-interested, how far altruistic – and in terms of the nature of political thinking amongst the lay elite.

A further issue, as already suggested, is the extent of the influence of the *ius commune* on the development of the common law. Helmholz's view of Magna Carta is linked to his wider arguments for the importance of the *ius commune* in English legal development.[6] Like others, he points out that there were plenty of channels through which influence might flow; for example, a significant although decreasing proportion of Angevin royal

---

[3] J. C. Holt, *Magna Carta*, 2nd edn (Cambridge, 1992), pp. 284–6.

[4] Helmholz, 'Magna Carta', 371.

[5] On the archbishop's possible influence, see esp. F. M. Powicke, *Stephen Langton* (Oxford, 1928), pp. 112–14; J. Baldwin, 'Master Stephen Langton, Future Archbishop of Canterbury: The Paris Schools and Magna Carta', *English Historical Review* 123 (2008), 811–46; see also Holt, *Magna Carta*, pp. 268–71, 280–7. For the influence of Langton's *familia* or of other bishops, see Helmholz, 'Magna Carta', 361. For Langton's knowledge of canon law, see Helmholz, 'Magna Carta', 360–1.

[6] See e.g. R. H. Helmholz, 'The Early History of the Grand Jury and the Canon Law', *University of Chicago Law Review* 50 (1983), 613–27. Note also e.g. Alain Boureau, *La Loi du royaume* (Paris, 2001).

justices were ecclesiastics.[7] He also notes that the copying of ideas from other legal systems is a common lawyerly habit, implying perhaps that the balance of proof may rest on those who wish to play down the influence of the *ius commune* on English legal development.[8]

In assessing that influence we have to distinguish various possibilities and recognize various difficulties of interpretation. Similar solutions to similar problems, and therefore similar legal norms, may exist in different legal systems without requiring influence on one from the other. Secondly, there might be influence from *ius commune* with regard to vocabulary rather than practice, or practice rather than vocabulary; distinguishing the two may be hard. A third complexity concerns the chronology of influence. *Ius commune*, or indeed earlier canon law, might already have had an influence on English legal practice or vocabulary, so that Magna Carta is presenting us with contemporary English law rather than the immediate influence of *ius commune* in 1215.[9]

The issue of the chronology also needs to be borne in mind when dealing with 1215 and the production of the Charter. Did the *ius commune* influence the barons and their demands as rebellion was breaking out? Or was any influence rather on the process of the drafting of a Charter, elements of which process can be deduced from comparing the Charter with its precursors, the Unknown Charter and the Articles of the Barons?[10] Associated with the timing and nature of influence is another problem; how does the Latin of the Charter relate to the French in which at least the barons, and arguably the churchmen, thought? We are helped here by having a translation of the Charter, and also Anglo-Norman vernacular texts of the coronation charters of Henry I, Stephen, and Henry II that may also be associated with the events of 1215.[11] However, we simply know very little

---

[7] Helmholz, 'Magna Carta', 359, gives the proportion as 'something like half'. This estimate derives from Ralph V. Turner, *The English Judiciary in the Age of Glanvill and Bracton, c. 1176–1239* (Cambridge, 1985), pp. 88–90, where Turner is discussing Richard I's judiciary. At p. 149 Turner gives the proportion in John's judiciary as five out of seventeen.

[8] Helmholz, 'Magna Carta', 367. Helmholz does speculate that some of the drafters may have been deliberately seeking to advance the fortunes of the *ius commune* in England, seizing upon the events of 1215 as an opportunity: Helmholz, 'Magna Carta', 367–8.

[9] Note similarly Helmholz, 'Magna Carta', 304–5, on the Roman and canon law influence on the English coronation oath.

[10] See esp. J. C. Holt, 'Magna Carta and the Origins of Statute Law', in *Magna Carta and Medieval Government* (London, 1985), pp. 293–8, for changes between the Articles of the Barons and Magna Carta.

[11] Holt, *Magna Carta*, pp. 475–6, on the Anglo-Norman version of Magna Carta. Of course, the Anglo-Norman vocabulary of this translation need not be precisely the vocabulary of the discussions. For an edition of the text of Henry I's charter,

about the process of drafting whereby French thoughts were turned into Latin text.[12]

❧ The case for learned influence

Even the strongest proponents of the influence of *ius commune* do not suggest that it was all-pervading within Magna Carta. Some clauses were concerned only with local or immediate problems.[13] Others claim explicitly to assert long-standing custom, for example with regard to reliefs.[14] Custom could be acceptable to those trained in the *ius commune*, as is apparent, for example, from the common addition of the *Libri Feudorum* to the *Corpus Iuris Civilis*; the former were a set of texts concerned with fief-holding compiled in Bologna in the mid-twelfth century.[15]

As for clauses where learned law was of consequence, in some the influence was general. The most obvious example is clause 1, stating that the Church was to be free. Here the influence was of long standing and need not be on the specific wording of the Charter.[16] Rather, the general ideas, derived from Church reform and canon law of a period rather earlier than the *ius commune*, had already been present, for example, in Henry I's coronation charter: 'First of all, I make the holy Church of God free.'[17] King Stephen's 'second' charter of liberties, in 1136, had stated that 'I grant the holy Church to be free.'[18] Then King John, in a clause of Magna Carta with no model in the Articles of the Barons, granted 'that the English Church be free', a clause translated into French as 'que les yglises d'Engleterre seront franches', 'that the churches of England be free'.[19]

see Felix Liebermann, 'The Text of Henry I's Coronation Charter', *Transactions of the Royal Historical Society* n.s. 8 (1894), pp. 46–8.

[12] Note also the caution of Helmholz, 'Magna Carta', 310.

[13] E.g. c. 33, mandating the removal of fish-weirs from the Thames and Medway and throughout England except on the sea coast.

[14] C. 2, setting out sums to be paid as *per antiquum relevium*.

[15] See Helmholz, 'Magna Carta', 309. He points out at 309–10 that, despite the shared presence in the *Libri Feudorum* and Magna Carta of various points, for example judgment by peers, he does not wish to argue for the influence of the former on the latter.

[16] Helmholz, 'Magna Carta', 311–14. The inclusion of 'in perpetuum' need not be a sign of any direct *ius commune* influence, as the phrase had often appeared in English charters both before and after 1066. Note e.g. its presence in the charter of liberties granted by Peter de Brus to his knights and free tenants of Cleveland between 1207 and 1209: W[illiam] Brown, ed., *Cartularium prioratus de Gyseburne*, 2 vols, Surtees Society vols 86, 89 (Durham, 1889, 1894), i, pp. 92–4.

[17] Stubbs, *Select Charters*, p. 117.

[18] Stubbs, *Select Charters*, p. 143.

[19] Magna Carta, c. 1.

Next there are some clauses where influence from learned law can be quite well established.[20] Clause 22 lays down that 'No cleric is to be amerced concerning his lay tenement, except according to the measure of the others aforesaid [that is, according to his offence], and not according to the amount of his ecclesiastical benefice.' Amongst the principles underlying this clause was the canonical one that ecclesiastical benefices were not the cleric's personal possessions. Clerical offences should therefore not harm Church property.[21]

Clause 27 states that 'if any free man dies intestate, his chattels are to be distributed by his nearest relations and friends, under the supervision of the Church, saving to everyone the debts which the deceased owed to him.'[22] In contrast, the lawbook of the late 1180s known as *Glanvill* states that 'When anyone dies intestate, all his chattels are understood to be his lord's.'[23] Magna Carta may be looking back to a provision in Henry I's coronation charter, that if one of the king's barons or men 'prevented by arms or sickness, will not have given or have disposed to give [his chattels], his wife or children or relatives, or his lawful men, are to divide it for his soul, as seems best to them.'[24] Alternatively Magna Carta may be influenced by the *ius commune*, and here the specification of ecclesiastical supervision is notable.[25]

There are also other clauses where *ius commune* influence on procedure can be suggested with some plausibility.[26] Clause 55 deals with unjust fines and amercements, placing them before the twenty-five barons mentioned in the security clause of the Charter, together with Archbishop Langton, if he could be present, and others whom he wished to summon. If Langton could not be present,

> the business shall nevertheless proceed without him, provided that
> if any one or more of the aforesaid twenty-five barons are in such
> a suit they shall stand down in this particular judgment, and shall

[20] See also n. 61 below, on Magna Carta, c. 52, and its model in the Articles of the Barons, c. 25.

[21] Helmholz, 'Magna Carta', 329–31.

[22] This clause was omitted from the 1216 reissue of the Charter.

[23] *Glanvill*, bk vii. c. 16, p. 89; see also Sir Frederick Pollock and F. W. Maitland, *The History of English Law before the Time of Edward I*, 2nd edn with intro by S. F. C. Milsom, 2 vols (Cambridge, 1968), ii, p. 356 n.

[24] Henry I, Coronation Charter, ch. 7, in Stubbs, *Select Charters*, p. 118.

[25] See Helmholz, 'Magna Carta', 332–3.

[26] Further instances that appear plausible include c. 41 on merchants, on which see Helmholz, 'Magna Carta', 342–4, although note the Charter's provision concerning reciprocal action.

be replaced by others chosen and sworn in by the rest of the same twenty-five, for this case only.

Such arrangements resemble those for papal judges-delegate.[27]

Another instance of possible influence, although perhaps only on vocabulary, is clause 20:

> A free man shall not be amerced for a small offence except according to the extent of the offence, and for a great offence he shall be amerced according to the greatness of the offence, yet saving always his livelihood (*contenemento suo*); and a merchant likewise, saving his merchandise (*mercandisa sua*); in the same way a villein shall be amerced, saving his waynage (*waynagio suo*).

Significant here may be use of *delictum* to indicate an offence. This is not a word commonly used in English law at the time, for example not being employed by *Glanvill*, whereas it is one familiar in Roman and Canon Law, including in statements concerning the proportionality of punishment.[28] In Magna Carta it replaces the word *forisfactum* that is used in the equivalent clause of Henry I's coronation charter. Whilst use of *ius commune* words is not very common in Magna Carta, instances such as this may suggest 'a drafter who felt himself at home with Continental law'.[29]

Beyond instances of general or specific influence on ideas, procedures, or vocabulary, there are some other clauses where parallel concerns of Magna Carta and of the *ius commune* might suggest influence of the latter upon the former. These might include the rights of widows or the insistence that the king should 'appoint as justices, constables, sheriffs or bailiffs only those who know the law of the realm and mean to observe it well'.[30] Parallels between Magna Carta and concessions made in other European countries, where the influence of the *ius commune* is accepted, might also be taken to confirm that *ius commune* was an influence on the Charter.[31]

In addition to such possible instances of direct influence of *ius commune* upon clauses of the Charter, there were areas of English secular practice where learned law had probably been influential already before 1215. Clause 9 of the Charter lays down that 'the sureties of a debtor shall not be distrained so long as the principal debtor is able to satisfy the debt.'[32] One of

---

[27] Helmholz, 'Magna Carta', 357–8; Jane E. Sayers, *Papal Judges Delegate in the Province of Canterbury, 1198–1254* (Oxford, 1971), pp. 135–43.

[28] See Appendix: Magna Carta c. 20; see Helmholz, 'Magna Carta', 328.

[29] Helmholz, 'Magna Carta', 368.

[30] Magna Carta cc. 7, 8, 45, on which see Helmholz, 'Magna Carta', 314–7, 345–7.

[31] Helmholz, 'Magna Carta', 365.

[32] On this, see Helmholz, 'Magna Carta', 317–19.

Justinian's laws likewise allowed sureties to be sued only after the assets of the principal debtor had been exhausted.[33] The lawbook *Glanvill* states that 'when a loan is accompanied by the giving of sureties only, if the principal debtor defaults and is not able to pay, recourse is to be had to the sureties.'[34] It seems that *Glanvill's* treatment of debt itself was influenced by the *ius commune*. In this instance, therefore, the influence of *ius commune* on Magna Carta is not a direct one upon drafting, but indirect, on the English law that is recorded in the Charter.

ℭ The case against the influence of the *ius commune*

The main elements of the case limiting the influence of the *ius commune* can be summarized as follows. First, both sides in the debate accept that some clauses of the Charter concern English custom, uninfluenced by the *ius commune*. Second, it can be argued that some suggestions of *ius commune* influence on other clauses are flawed, either in exaggerating similarities or in indicating only parallels, not necessarily influence. The burden of proof is thus placed back on those arguing for *ius commune* influence; in the absence of proof, it may be considered simply not necessary to add the *ius commune* into the equation.

Let us take a selection of clauses where *ius commune* influence has been suggested but where it may be unnecessary. Clause 40 of Magna Carta states that 'To no one will we sell, to no one will we deny or delay right or justice.' In this instance Holt, too, suggests the possibility of the influence of ecclesiastical legislation in England going back to 1186.[35] However, it seems likely that the question of the sale of justice was a common concern, as is clear from the discussion in the *Dialogue of the Exchequer*. Richard fitz Nigel recognized that payments to the king were likely to arouse strong emotions. The Master addresses the Pupil in the *Dialogue*, stating that

> offerings are said to be made for future benefits ... when someone offers the king a certain amount for justice concerning some estate or revenue of his, not to ensure that justice is done – lest you flare up and say that we sell justice for money – but rather to have it done without delay.[36]

Of course, it could be argued that Richard here is influenced by the *ius commune*, but such an argument seems unnecessary.

---

[33] Nov. 4.3.1.

[34] *Glanvill*, bk x. c. 3, p. 118; note also bk x. c. 5, p. 119.

[35] Holt, *Magna Carta*, p. 285; see also Helmholz, 'Magna Carta', 340–2; John T. Noonan, *Bribes* (New York, 1984), ch. 7.

[36] Fitz Nigel, *Dialogue*, bk ii. c. 23, pp. 178–80.

Clause 20, as we saw earlier, concerns the proportionality of amercement to the seriousness of the offence [*delictum*], and the exclusion of certain property from amercements even for great offences.[37] Concerning this
clause, Helmholz concludes that 'It looks very much as though the drafters
of the Charter, seeking to put a stop to what they regarded as King John's
high-handed use of legal institutions to enrich himself, found in contemporary canon and Roman laws the principle, and even some of the words, they
hoped would curb his actions.'[38] There are difficulties with this conclusion.
The opening of the clause is surely based on Henry I's coronation charter:

> If any of my barons or men does wrong he will not give a gage in
> mercy of his goods, as he did in the time of my father or my brother;
> but according to the extent of the wrong, he will make amends thus
> just as he would have made amends previous to the time of my father,
> in the time of my other ancestors.[39]

A similar principle appears in town charters, from the time of Henry I
onwards.[40] On a second point, that the *ius commune* gave protection to the
necessities of livelihood, Helmholz may have a stronger point, but again
earlier English practice is significant. Richard fitz Nigel wrote the following
of the sale of debtors' goods:

> If an insolvent debtor has already achieved the belt of knighthood,
> his other goods may be sold, but he will be allowed to keep a horse
> (not any horse, but the one he normally uses), so that someone who
> has become a knight in rank will not be forced to travel on foot. But
> if he is the kind of knight who delights in the glory of arms and in
> using them, and has earned the right to be called an active knight, all
> the armour of his body, along with all the horses he needs to carry it,
> will be exempted from being sold, so that he may fight for the king
> and the kingdom when he is needed, equipped with arms and horses
> ... Moreover, the sheriff must warn his agents to follow this order in
> selling things: each debtor's moveable goods are sold first; but the
> plough animals, with which he is accustomed to cultivate the fields,
> are spared as far as possible, so that the debtor will not be forced fur-
> ther into poverty by their loss.[41]

---

[37] See above, p. 104.

[38] Helmholz, 'Magna Carta', 329.

[39] See Appendix: Henry I, Coronation Charter, c. 8, in Stubbs, *Select Charters*, p. 119.

[40] Adolphus Ballard, ed., *British Borough Charters, 1042–1216* (Cambridge, 1913),
pp. 151–7.

[41] Fitz Nigel, *Dialogue*, bk ii. c. 14, pp. 164–6.

Likewise *Glanvill* states of a man amerced for purpresture that he should not lose anything 'de suo honorabili tenemento',[42] and that aids should only be exacted in moderation according to the size and wealth of a man's fiefs, lest the man 'be seen to lose his *continementum*'.[43] *Contenementum* is the word used in the Charter for the property that a free man should retain even when amerced for a major offence.[44] It is, of course, again possible that *Glanvill* and fitz Nigel were influenced by the *ius commune*, but another possibility is that both they and Magna Carta were using some general principle of fair treatment, or that Magna Carta was extending a principle that once had applied only to men of a certain honourable status, such as knights.

Similarly the provision of clause 35, standardizing across the realm measures of wine, ale, corn, and cloth, and likewise weights, has parallels in the *ius commune* treatment of weights and measures.[45] However, regulation of weights and measures stretches back through the Angevin assizes to Anglo-Saxon England, via William of Malmesbury's story of Henry I standardizing the measure of an 'ell' of cloth to the length of his forearm.[46] A clause stating that 'no one shall be taken or imprisoned upon the appeal of a woman for the death of anyone except her husband' appears in Magna Carta, although not in the Articles of the Barons. A similar provision appears in *Glanvill*, and again there seems no need to suggest any more than common concern between English law and the *ius commune* which also restricted women's initiation of criminal proceedings to cases involving direct harm to themselves or relatives.[47] Clause 38 of the Charter states that 'Henceforth no bailiff shall put anyone on trial by his own unsupported allegation, without bringing credible witnesses [*testibus fidelibus*] to the charge.' Unsupported accusations by officials seem to have been a concern at least as early as the first part of Henry II's reign. Such developments may have been

---

[42] *Glanvill*, bk ix. c. 11, p. 114; Hall notes that 'contenemento' appears as an alternative reading in two manuscripts.

[43] *Glanvill*, bk ix, c. 8, p. 112. Note also E.-J. Tardif, ed., *Le Très Ancien Coutumier de Normandie*, ii. 3, lvi. 4 (Rouen, 1881), pp. 2, 46; like *Glanvill*, the *Très Ancien Coutumier* rested on customary practice and royal/ducal legislation, rather than *ius commune*.

[44] See above, p. 104.

[45] Helmholz, 'Magna Carta', 335–7

[46] See *III Edgar*, 8. 1–2, *V Æthelred*, 24, *VI Æthelred*, 32. 2, in Felix Liebermann, ed., *Die Gesetze der Angelsachsen*, 3 vols (Halle, 1903–16), i, pp. 204, 242, 254; William of Malmesbury, *Gesta regum Anglorum*, ed. and trans. R. A. B. Mynors, R. M. Thomson, and M. Winterbottom, bk v. c. 411, 2 vols (Oxford, 1998–9), i, p. 742; *Howden*, iv, pp. 33–4.

[47] Magna Carta c. 54 and see Appendix, Magna Carta c. 20: *Glanvill*, bk xiv. c. 3, p. 174. See Helmholz, 'Magna Carta', 350–2.

related to concerns about unsupported official accusations in ecclesiastical cases, notably by archdeacons. It may indeed have been in reaction to concerns about unsupported *ex officio* accusations that Henry II and his advisors introduced the standardized use of the jury of presentment.[48] Whilst concerns were expressed in canon law concerning unsupported accusations, again the need for *ius commune* influence on Magna Carta seems unnecessary.[49]

One can also raise questions about the significance of vocabulary as an indicator of *ius commune* influence on Magna Carta.[50] Re-examination of the use of *delictum* in clauses 20 and 21 of the Charter reveals the difficulties of working from vocabulary to influence on thought or practice. *Delictum* is used in the *ius commune* but also in other possible sources for the drafters of Magna Carta. In particular it appears in the Bible, frequently in the Book of Leviticus, and also, for example, in I Kings [I Samuel], a book upon which Langton wrote a commentary.[51] Given its use in the Bible, it is therefore not surprising that *delictum* appears in earlier texts from England in the general sense of sin or offence.[52]

Furthermore, whilst *Glanvill* does not use *delictum* in his treatment of crime, preferring the terms *crimen* or *felonia*, the *Dialogue of the Exchequer* does use the word in a fashion resembling that of Magna Carta:

> For whoever is convicted of having offended against the king's majesty, is condemned in one of three ways according to the quality of his offence to the king; for either the culprit is judged answerable in all his moveables for minor wrongdoings; or in all immoveables, that

[48] See R. C. van Caenegem, 'Public Prosecution of Crime in Twelfth Century England', *Legal History: A European Perspective* (London, 1991), pp. 1–36; Helmholz, 'Early History of the Grand Jury'.

[49] Helmholz, 'Magna Carta', 337, 368, sees the use of the word *testis* here as further evidence of *ius commune* influence; it is a word which fits 'the world of the *ius commune* better than … [that of] the common law in 1215'. A problem here is that *Glanvill* does not deal with *ex officio* prosecutions. He does, however, use the word *testis* with some frequency, for example in the context of trial by battle concerning land where a claimant must have his case fought by a champion who was a suitable witness concerning the matter: *Glanvill*, bk ii. c. 3, pp. 24–5. Note also e.g. *Glanvill*, bk. ii c. 21, p. 37, on *testis* being used with reference to the knights of the Grand Assize. Note also the use of *testis* in the *Très Ancien Coutumier*, xl. 3, lxii. 3, pp. 34, 54.

[50] Note also the comments of Helmholz, 'Magna Carta', 368–9.

[51] Note also e.g. Psalm 18.14: 'emundabor a delicto maximo.' David d'Avray (personal communication) shows that Langton's commentaties do not treat 'delictum' here in any technical legal fashion. For quotations relevant to the argument that follows, see Appendix.

[52] See *Dictionary of Medieval Latin from British Sources*, ed R. E. Latham *et al.* (London, 1975–), s.v. 'delinquere'.

is estates and rents, so that he is disinherited of them, which is for greater wrongdoings; or for any of the greatest or heinous offences, in his life and members.[53]

Once again it seems unnecessary to argue that Richard's vocabulary was influenced by the *ius commune*.[54] For example, *delictum* is also used with reference to the proportionality of amercement in Peter de Brus's charter of liberties for his knights and free tenants of Cleveland, issued between 1207 and 1209. This document surely cannot have had direct influence from Langton or his circle, and its vocabulary and provisions do not otherwise suggest *ius commune* influence.[55]

It is also worth bringing into consideration another feature of clause 20. The terms that it uses for the items supporting the livelihood of those amerced, *contenementum*, *mercandisa*, and *waynagium*, are Old French words given Latin form. This reminds us that at least most of those discussing the provisions of the Charter would have thought more readily in French than in Latin.[56] Let us turn then to the translation of the Charter, and there we do indeed find *contenement*, *marchandise*, *gaagnage*. It would have been pleasing also to find one of the Anglo-Norman words meaning offence, *delit*. One might then have argued that *delictum* is derived from the vernacular, not from *ius commune*. In fact the word used is *forfait*, the vernacular equivalent of *forisfactum* as used in Henry I's coronation charter, but not in this clause of Magna Carta.[57] The translation of Henry's charter also uses *forfait* in the relevant clause. What may have happened is that

---

[53] See Appendix, Fitz Nigel, *Dialogue*, bk ii. c. 16, p. 168. See *Dictionary of Medieval Latin from British Sources*, s.v. 'delinquere', for some uses in the early plea rolls.

[54] Note also *Leges Willelmi*, 40, Liebermann, *Gesetze*, i, p. 515: 'Ne quis pro paruo delicto adiudicetur.'

[55] See Brown, *Cartularium prioratus de Gyseburne*, Appendix, i, p. 93. Note also the use of *delictum* in *Pseudo-Cnut de Foresta*, Prol., Liebermann, *Gesetze*, i, p. 620: 'ut omnis delinquens rite secundum modum delicti et delinquentis fortunam patiatur.' Note further the use of *delictum* in c. 1 of the 1215 Magna Carta of Cheshire, Geoffrey Barraclough, ed., *Charters of the Anglo-Norman Earls of Chester*, Record Society of Lancashire and Cheshire 126 (Gloucester, 1988), no. 394, and in charters for Corbridge and Eynsham in the years close to Magna Carta: Ballard, *British Borough Charters*, p. 157. Note also the use of *delictum* in the *Très Ancien Coutumier de Normandie*, lxxix. 12, lxxx. 7, lxxxviii. 1–2, pp. 83, 85, 98–9; here *delictum* refers to serious offences.

[56] James Tait, 'Studies in Magna Carta: waynagium and contenementum', *English Historical Review* 27 (1912), 720–8; see also Austin Lane Poole, *Obligations of Society in the XII and XIII Centuries: Ford Lectures delivered at Oxford in 1944* (Oxford, 1946), pp. 89–90.

[57] Note also the use of *forfeit* in the *Leis Willelme*, e.g. 1.1, 2.1, 2.2a, 3.3; Liebermann, *Gesetze*, i, pp. 492, 494, 496. In the French version of the *Articuli Willelmi*, c. 10, Liebermann, *Gesetze*, i, p. 489, it is used to translate *culpa*. See further, e.g. the

discussions in French used the word *forfait* but for some reason this was put into Latin in Magna Carta as *delictum*. The only other use of *delictum* in the Charter is in clause 61, with reference to breach of the terms of the 1215 settlement; there the French translation uses *mesfaiz*, another common vernacular word for offence or misdeed.[58] I remain unclear as to why *forisfactum* was avoided in clauses 20 to 21, but strongly suspect it was deliberate. The choice of *delictum* presumably was in part because *felonia* and perhaps *crimen* were too specific. It seems plausible then that *delictum* was used for the lack of specificity of its sense, as illustrated by its biblical usage, rather than as a term derived from the *ius commune*.[59] Even advocates of the influence of the *ius commune* note the problems of proving their case:

> The existence of so many parallels between the *ius commune* and Magna Carta's chapters at the very least raises the possibility of influence. But is it really likely? There is no 'smoking gun' to prove it, and not all the parallels show the distinct footprints of emulation. They simply prove that a similar path was trod.[60]

For many clauses, proposed links to *ius commune* may seem unnecessary. The most compelling arguments regarding *ius commune* influence relate to those clauses where it might be expected, notably those involving the Church, be they general, such as clause 1, or specific, as with clause 22 concerning amercement of clerics.[61] There are also instances where *ius commune* may have had an earlier influence on English law, for example regarding debt.[62] In other clauses there may have been additions or vocabulary selections in the process of drafting that reflect the influence of those trained in the *ius commune*. Thus clause 5 of the Unknown Charter follows

use of *forfait* and related words in G. J. Brault, ed., *The Song of Roland*, 2 vols (University Park, 1978), lines 608, 1393, 2029, 3758, 3827.

[58] 'Mesfaiz' is used, for example, in an Old French gloss of the story of Cain and Abel; see M. Quereuil, *La Bible française du XIIIᵉ siècle: edition critique de la Genèse* (Geneva, 1988), pp. 122, 123. I would like to thank Dr Clive Sneddon for his help on this point.

[59] For the specific meaning of *delictum* in Roman Law, and the contrast with crime, see e.g. Barry Nicholas, *An Introduction to Roman Law* (Oxford, 1962), pp. 207–27.

[60] Helmholz, 'Magna Carta', 359.

[61] Note also the inclusion in c. 25 of the Articles of the Barons of the phrase 'appellatione remota', a phrase taken from canon law in the context of the papal appointment of judges-delegate; see Helmholz, 'Magna Carta', 307–8. In the Articles it is used with reference to a judgment being made by Langton and the bishops, in the context of King John's claim to have a Crusader's respite from answering cases. Again, therefore, the context is very much ecclesiastical. On this clause and its equivalent in the Charter, see also Holt, *Magna Carta*, pp. 251, 286; Helmholz, 'Magna Carta', 347–51.

[62] See above, p. 105.

the model of Henry I's coronation charter in dealing with intestate succession: 'If [the king's baron or man] is snatched by arms or by unforeseen illness his wife or children or relatives and closest friends are to make a division [of his chattels] for his soul.' By the time of the Articles of the Barons, this has been reformulated with more technical vocabulary, and mentions the supervision of the Church: 'If any free man dies intestate, let his goods [*bona*] be distributed through the hand of his closest relatives and friends and through the view of the Church.'[63] Such reformulation may involve *ius commune* influence. However, this is to allow the *ius commune* only a decidedly more restricted influence than is presented in the maximalist case.

❴ Magna Carta and English common law

Rather than needing influence from learned law, many of the general ideas, specific concerns, ancient customs, and legal practices mentioned in Magna Carta can be traced to earlier English practice and circumstance. Key concerns of the Charter are prefigured in Howden's report of an agreement between John and William de Longchamps in 1191:

> It is conceded that bishops and abbots, earls and barons, vavassours and those holding freely, shall not be disseised of their lands or chattels at the will of the justiciars or officials of the lord king, but they are to be treated by judgment of the court of the lord king according to the lawful customs and assizes of the realm, or through the mandate of the lord king.[64]

Urban privileges also dealt with matters such as rights of marriage and wardship, amercement, and debt.[65] More general principles, similar to those of Magna Carta, were included in a London legal collection of the first decade of the thirteenth century.[66] The charter of Peter de Brus for the knights and free tenants of Cleveland and their men included provisions such as that 'If anyone falls into forfeiture it will be measured according to his chattels and according to the offence [*delicti*] through which he fell [into it].'[67]

---

[63] Articles of the Barons, c. 16; Magna Carta, c. 27 interestingly replaced the word *bona* with *catalla*, and added 'saving to everyone the debts which the deceased owed them.'

[64] *Howden*, iii, p. 136; see the comments of Holt, *Magna Carta*, pp. 120–1.

[65] Holt, *Magna Carta*, pp. 58–9, 299; see above, p. 65, on the proportionality of amercement.

[66] Holt, *Magna Carta*, pp. 93–5; Liebermann, *Gesetze*, i, p. 635–40, 655–60, 664.

[67] Holt, *Magna Carta*, pp. 67–8; Brown, *Cartularium prioratus de Gyseburne*, i, pp. 92–4.

In addition, we have seen that Magna Carta's provisions concerning appeals by women and concerning weights and measures reflect existing law.[68] Other provisions too contain what was considered good custom, although good custom that had been abused by John.[69] Clause 32 lays down that 'We will not hold lands of those who are convicted of felony except for a year and a day, and then the lands are to be given back to the lords of the fees.' *Glanvill* had stated that the land of an outlaw or convicted felon should 'remain in the hand of the lord king for a year, but when the year is up it shall revert to the right lord, that is to him of whose fee it is, save the pulling down of houses and the rooting up of trees.'[70] Other clauses sought to increase the provision of royal justice with regard to remedies that were clearly welcomed by the rebels, as when clause 18 laid down, unrealistically as it turned out, that assizes of novel disseisin, mort d'ancestor, and darrein presentment be held four times a year in the county courts.

Magna Carta, therefore, was in part a statement of existing law, and a demand for its observance. The areas of judicial practice that appear to have been most popular with the rebels were those that protected sub-tenants, such as the assizes of novel disseisin and mort d'ancestor.[71] Many of the protests concerned either the treatment of criminal offences or, in particular, the treatment of land holding and associated practices with regards tenants in chief. Whereas the sub-tenant enjoyed protection from his lord as offered by the king through the routine judicial processes introduced by the Angevins, the tenant in chief did not enjoy such protection against his own lord, the king. In some matters, for example the pattern of inheritance, there were customary norms, but the king's position as lordless lord still allowed him to exercise a discretion not enjoyed by other lords. In other aspects the evidence for customary norms is limited, but one response in Magna Carta was to present its provisions as if they were ancient custom.[72] This was true, for example, with respect to the occasions on which a lord might take an aid and in particular with respect to reliefs. Henry I's coronation charter refers to 'lawful and just relief', the Unknown Charter to a 'just [*rectum*] relief'. The Articles of the Barons refer to 'the ancient relief, to be expressed in the Charter'. Only in Magna Carta do amounts come to be specified:

---

[68] See above, p. 107.

[69] Note e.g. c. 24 states that 'no sheriff, constable, coroners, or others of our bailiffs shall hold pleas of our Crown'; see William Sharp McKechnie, *Magna Carta*, 2nd edn (Glasgow, 1914), pp. 307–8.

[70] *Glanvill*, bk vii. c. 17, p. 91. See McKechnie, *Magna Carta*, pp. 338–9.

[71] This suggestion is made by Holt, *Magna Carta*, p. 123.

[72] Holt, *Magna Carta*, pp. 298–301; see also p. 102 on the Charter being an *ex parte* statement.

the heir or heirs of an earl concerning the whole barony of an earl through £100; the heir or heirs of a baron concerning a whole barony through £100; the heir or heirs of a knight concerning a whole knight's fee through 100s. at most; and who owes less gives less according to the ancient custom of fees.

There is quite strong evidence for 100s, that is £5, having been 'the reasonable relief concerning one knight's fee according to the custom of the realm', as *Glanvill* says.[73] However, the only evidence for £100 being considered a 'reasonable relief' for a barony comes from a pipe roll of Richard I, recording a proffer that a man be allowed to pay this relief.[74] There are other instances of the amount being paid, but also very different amounts, and both *Glanvill* and the *Dialogue* agree that there was no set sum: 'for baronies there is no certain figure laid down, because the chief baronies in making satisfaction to the lord king for their reliefs are at his mercy and pleasure.'[75]

Thus Magna Carta exaggerates the extent to which it is a statement of existing English law. Contested areas are presented as long settled. However, the concentration on the contested is not surprising. There was little need for the Charter to record unchallenged custom, for example to state the right of the eldest son to inherit land held by military tenure. It was areas of less settled law which allowed the king – and sometimes other lords – to use their discretion in ways which led to grievance, rebellion, and hence Magna Carta.

If Magna Carta was not, then, simply a statement of existing good custom, it gains further significance as a stimulus to legal development. In part this resulted from the symbolic role that Magna Carta acquired following its reissues.[76] It appeared as the first Statute in early Statute Books, providing an English model for written legislation. In addition, some clauses of the 1215 Charter were firmly enforced, for example that concerning the level of reliefs.[77] Other clauses had more complicated and unintended effects. Clause 34 specifies that 'The writ which is called *Praecipe* shall not, in future, be issued to anyone concerning any tenement whereby a free man may lose

---

[73] Holt, *Magna Carta*, p. 304; on reliefs, see more generally ibid., pp. 298–307.

[74] See Holt, *Magna Carta*, p. 52. Note *Très Ancien Coutumier*, lxxxiv. 1, p. 93.

[75] *Glanvill*, bk ix. c. 4, p. 108; Fitz Nigel, *Dialogue*, bk ii. cc. 10, 24, pp. 144, 180.

[76] See also Holt, *Magna Carta*, pp. 392–7, and e.g. J. R. Maddicott, 'Magna Carta and the local community 1215–1259', *Past and Present* 102 (1984), 25–65. D. L. d'Avray, '"Magna carta": its background in Stephen Langton's academic biblical exegesis and its episcopal reception', *Studi Medievali* 3rd ser. 38 (1997), 423–38, discusses the role of Stephen Langton in the reissues.

[77] See Robert C. Stacey, *Politics, Policy, and Finance under Henry III, 1216–1245* (Oxford, 1987), pp. 217–18, and more generally pp. 3–9. Other clauses were dropped from the reissues: e.g. c. 15 on aids, c. 19 on the holding of assizes.

his court.' This prohibition seems to have led very rapidly to the creation of a new writ, known as 'nuper obiit', which gave protection to a deforced parcener claiming a share of an inheritance, against co-parceners.[78] More generally, the termination of the undifferentiated writ *praecipe* may have stimulated the development of sharply defined writs of entry, and thus the further development of the set forms of action that characterized English law even into the nineteenth century.[79]

ℭ Conclusion

I have argued that the direct influence of *ius commune* on the making of Magna Carta in 1215 was limited to a few clauses. It remains possible that ideas derived from the *ius commune* had a different influence, on the conceptions of community, corporation, and conjuration that underlay the ideas of constraining the king through the Charter and associated processes.[80] In addition, consideration of the possible influence of the *ius commune* on Magna Carta re-emphasizes the need to explain the relationship between ecclesiastical and lay, religious and secular both in the events of 1215 and in the development of English common law. For example, even if one rejects the possibility that the rebel barons themselves, rather than churchmen, used canon law to claim the moral high ground, the religious presentation of elements of reform still needs explanation.[81]

Furthermore, the shared interests and ideas and the mutual involvement of clergy and laity are clear. Churchmen were significant tenants in chief, affected by matters such as the raising of scutage. They were also significant in the administration of the realm, as indeed is illustrated by the provisions for the publicizing of Magna Carta recorded in the Dunstable annals: 'the king then restored to many of them [the rebels] their castles and other rights, and charters were completed there concerning the liberties of the realm of England which were deposited in safe-keeping in each bishopric.'[82]

---

[78] S. F. C. Milsom, 'Inheritance by Women in the Twelfth and Thirteenth Centuries', in Morris S. Arnold *et al.*, eds, *On the Laws and Customs of England: Essays in Honour of Samuel E. Thorne* (Chapel Hill, 1981), pp. 74–6.

[79] See S. F. C. Milsom, *The Legal Framework of English Feudalism* (Cambridge, 1976), pp. 92–102, esp. pp. 101–2.

[80] See R. W. Southern, review of J. C. Holt, *Magna Carta*, *English Historical Review* 82 (1967), 342–6, at 343.

[81] Note esp. that when the disaffected were considering replacing John with another king in 1212 their favoured candidate was Simon de Montfort, the leader of the recent Albigensian Crusade: Holt, *Magna Carta*, p. 226 n. 139.

[82] See Holt, *Magna Carta*, p. 259; also pp. 353–4 for some copies of Magna Carta being sent to bishops, although on a shire-by-shire basis; A. J. Collins, 'The Documents of the Great Charter', *Proceedings of the British Academy* 34 (1948), 233–79, at 275–6.

Involvement in royal administration made more likely ecclesiastical influence on at least some administrative procedures.[83] Thus the *Dialogue* states that

> when the account of the county farm is complete, ... the sheriff's oath is administered by the marshal, just once ... and thus he is absolved and dismissed. Some used to believe, though, that the sheriff should take a separate oath for each separate item needing confirmation by oath, so that every time he declared something that could be confirmed by his oath alone, he would also take an oath. But wise men experienced in divine law considered this a dangerous view, since the sheriff has sworn once for all that he has given a true account of everything, to the best of his knowledge. Therefore the former opinion eventually fell into disrepute, along with its author, and the barons contented themselves with a single oath – that is, an oath taken once – just as they are united in the confession of one faith.[84]

The 'divine law' here mentioned may be canonical or it may be more generally biblical or theological, bearing in mind that theology and canon law, whilst still closely related, were growing more distinct at this time.

A further general influence on reform ideas in 1215, indeed, may have been theological. The Parisian scholars associated with Peter the Chanter were very concerned with moral and practical questions, including those relating to rule and kingship.[85] One member of the circle was Stephen Langton.[86] His biblical commentaries show him tackling questions that were of relevance in 1215.[87] Thus he took the following passage, Deuteronomy 17:14:

> When thou art come into the land which the Lord thy God giveth to thee, and shalt possess it, and shalt dwell therein, and shalt say, I will set a king over me, like as all the nations that are about me: thou shalt in any wise set him king over thee, whom the Lord thy

---

[83] Note also the comment of Holt, 'Magna Carta and the Origins of Statute Law', 302, that 'in so far as churchmen influenced the changing content of the Charter, it was not as canonists but as secular administrators experienced in royal government.'

[84] Fitz Nigel, *Dialogue*, bk ii. c. 28, p. 190.

[85] See more generally John W. Baldwin, *Masters, Princes, and Merchants: The Social Views of Peter the Chanter and his Circle*, 2 vols (Paris, 1970); also Philippe Buc, *L'Ambiguité du livre: prince, pouvoir, et peuple dans les commentaires de la bible au moyen âge*, Théologie historique 95 (Paris, 1994).

[86] Note Baldwin, *Masters, Princes, and Merchants*, pp. 25–31.

[87] See d'Avray, 'Magna Carta'; Baldwin, 'Master Stephen Langton'.

God shall choose: one from among thy brethren shalt thou set king over thee: thou mayest not set a stranger over thee, which is not thy brother.

On this he commented that

Here the subject is the making of a king. But what is said here is not a command with respect to the king, but a permission, because he does not give an order here that they should make a king, but that, if they were going to make one, he should at least be of their tribe. It was not so pleasing to the Lord that they should make a king; in fact it displeased him. Hence Osee (13:11): *I gave them a king in my anger.* Again, Samuel, rebuking them because they had desired a king, told them of the tyrannical exactions by the king which lay in store, not as being licit, but as being permitted as a punishment for them.

Such ideas give a further context for at least some churchmen's thinking in 1215.

However, to return finally to the more narrowly legal, a more general problem remains. Given the importance of the study of particularly canon but also Roman law by clerics of England and Normandy in the late twelfth and early thirteenth centuries, why does it appear that learned law had only limited influence on the development of English law? As with Magna Carta, any influence generally seems to have been on underlying thinking or on discussion of parallel problems, rather than through the adoption of procedures from the *ius commune*.[88] Part of the explanation may have been conscious antagonism to the *ius commune*, expressed even by such a critic of Henry II as Ralph Niger.[89] Another may be the strength and degree of standardization of English custom, backed by royal enforcement, even during the reign of Henry II.[90] Yet given the number of ecclesiastics amongst royal justices, ecclesiastics who happily applied canon law in ecclesiastical courts, and given that a royal servant such as William de Longchamps could not only administer royal law but also produce a treatise on canon law procedure, an essential explanation seems to be the capacity

---

[88] See e.g. Mary G. Cheney, '*Possessio/proprietas* in Ecclesiastical Courts in Mid-Twelfth-Century England', in George Garnett and John Hudson, eds, *Law and Government in Medieval England and Normandy: Essays in Honour of Sir James Holt* (Cambridge, 1994), pp. 245–54; also Helmholz, 'Early History of the Grand Jury' and Rathbone, 'Roman Law', 266. Note further *Glanvill*, bk. ii. c. 12, p. 32, for attention being drawn to a parallel with ecclesiastical court procedure, bk ii. c. 19, for an echo of Roman terminology in an inappropriate place.

[89] Rathbone, 'Roman Law', 256–7, 269.

[90] See e.g. Holt, *Magna Carta*, pp. 92–3, 96, 111; J. G. H. Hudson, 'F. W. Maitland and the Englishness of English Law', Selden Society Lecture 2006 (London, 2009).

of such administrators consciously to operate in two separate legal spheres.[91] However, the exploration of why these men performed such a feat of hat swapping must be left for another occasion.

---

[91] See *Glanvill*, bk vii. c. 15, p. 88, on English and Roman/canon law's different treatment of the son born before his parents married. Note also the comments of Fitz Nigel, *Dialogue*, Prologue, p. 2.

APPENDIX

❰ Magna Carta, Clause 20: delictum, forfait, forisfactum

(i) Magna Carta 1215, clause 20:

Latin text

Liber homo non amercietur pro parvo **delicto**, nisi secundum modum **delicti**; et pro magno **delicto** amercietur secundum magnitudinem **delicti** ...

A free man shall not be amerced for a small offence except according to the extent of the offence, and for a great offence he shall be amerced according to the greatness of the offence ...

Anglo-Norman text

Frans hom ne set amerciez por petit **forfait** fors solon la maniere del **forfait**, e por le grant **forfait** seit amerciez solonc la grandesce del **forfait** ...

A free man shall not be amerced for a small wrong except according to the manner of the wrong, and for a great wrong he shall be amerced according to the greatness of the wrong ...

(ii) Henry I Coronation Charter, c. 8.

Latin text

Si quis baronum vel hominum meorum **forisfecerit**, non dabit vadium in misericordia pecunie sue, sicut faciebat tempore patris mei vel fratris mei, sed secundum modum **forisfacti**, ita emendabit, sicut emendasset retro a tempore patris mei, in tempore aliorum antecessorum meorum.

If any of my barons or men does wrong he will not give a gage in mercy of his goods, as he did in the time of my father or my brother; but according to the extent of the wrong, he will make amends thus just as he would have made amends previous to the time of my father, in the time of my other ancestors.

Anglo-Norman text

Se nul de mes hummes u de mes barons eit **forfait**, il ne dura puint de gage en merci de sun aveir, sicum al tens mun pere u mun frere, mes sulunc la maniere del **forfait** essint l'amenderat, sicum il l'eust amende avant le tens mun pere al tens mes ancesurs ...

If any of my men or of my barons does wrong he will not give a gage in mercy of his goods, as he did in the time of my father or my brother; but according to the manner of the wrong, he will make amends thus just as he would have made amends previous to the time of my father, in the time of my other ancestors ...

(iii) I Kings [I Samuel], 6:8

8. tolletisque arcam Domini et ponetis in plaustro et vasa aurea, quae exsolvistis ei **pro delicto**, ponetis in capsella ad latus eius ...

And take the ark of the Lord and place it in a cart, and place the gold vessels, which you have paid to him for the offence, in a chest at its side ...

(King James version: and take the ark of the Lord, and lay it upon a cart; and put the jewels of gold, which ye return to him for a trespass offering, in a coffer by the side thereof …)

See also verses 4 and 17 for similar uses of 'pro delicto'.

(iv) Richard fitz Nigel, *Dialogus de Scaccario*, Bk. ii c. xvi

Quisquis enim in regiam maiestatem **deliquisse** deprehenditur, uno trium modorum iuxta qualitatem **delicti** sui regi condempnatur, aut enim in uniuerso mobili suo reus iudicatur pro minoribus culpis, aut in omnibus immobilibus, fundis scilicet et redditibus, ut eis exheredetur, quod fit pro maioribus culpis, aut pro maximis quibuscumque uel enormibus **delictis** in uitam suam uel membra.

For whoever is convicted of having offended against the king's majesty is condemned in one of three ways according to the quality of his offence to the king; for either the culprit is judged answerable in all his moveables for minor wrongdoings; or in all immoveables, that is estates and rents, so that he is disinherited of them, which is for greater wrongdoings; or for any of the greatest or heinous offences, in his life and members.

(v) Charter of Peter de Brus for his knights and free tenants of Cleveland, 1207×9

Et si aliquis in forisfacturam ceciderit, amensurabitur secundum catella sua, et secundum **delictum** per quod ceciderit.

And if anyone falls into forfeiture, it will be measured according to his chattels and according to the offence through which he fell.

vi) *Leges Willelmi*, 40, cf. II Cnut, 2. 1

Ne quis pro paruo **delicto** adiudicetur:

Prohibemus ne pro paruo **forisfacto** adiudicetur aliquis homo morti; sed ad plebis castigationem alia pena secundum qualitatem et quantitatem **delicti** plectatur.

That no one be adjudged for a small offence.

We forbid that any man be adjudged to death for a small wrong; but for the chastisement of the people, let another punishment be imposed according to the quality and quantity of the offence.

vii) *Pseudo-Cnut de Foresta*, Prologue

He sunt sanctiones de foresta, quas ego Canutus rex, cum consilio primariorum hominum meorum de foresta, condo et facio, ut cunctis regni nostri Anglie ecclesiis et pax et iustitia fiat, et ut omnis **delinquens** rite secundum modum **delicti** et **delinquentis** fortunam patiatur.

These are the sanctions concerning the forest, which I king Cnut, with the counsel of my foremost men of the forest, establish and make, so that there may be both peace and justice for all the churches of our kingdom of England, and so that every offender may suffer duly according to the measure of the offence and the fortune of the offender.

Justice without Judgment:
Criminal Prosecution before Magna Carta

BARBARA HANAWALT

R EADING the criminal cases in the early Lincolnshire assize rolls of 1202, one might conclude that the judicial system was woefully inadequate. Few cases were prosecuted to the extent of the law, and more often than not, the person who appealed the alleged criminal did not bother to appear in court. Cases came before the assize justices either through appeal by the person wronged or their nearest kin or through the process of community action, that is, hue and cry or the opinion of the men of the four neighbouring vills who made presentments of wrongdoing. Not all criminal actions can be represented in these cases, for if they are, we must conclude that English society in the early years of the thirteenth century was relatively peaceful. The cases involve, for the most part, personal violence. Robbery, burglary, homicide, and rape are the meat of the criminal side of the assize cases. Simple thefts did not come before the king's justices, and wounding appeared only when the appellor, the party bringing the accusation, said that the action had broken the king's peace. In this period before Magna Carta and before the Fourth Lateran Council, both of which would dictate a change in the way that criminal cases were tried, the justices could call upon the litigants to undergo the ordeal by water or hot iron or go to trial by battle. But use of these modes of proof was rare. Instead, the parties did not appear in court, or the judges dismissed the cases because there was a flaw in the pleading, or the parties were willing to pay a fine to have the king excuse them.

Using the Lincolnshire assize of 1202,[1] this paper explores the issue of justice without judgment and suggests that people were using the courts as a negotiating tool either to produce a showdown with their adversary or to force the other party into an out-of-court settlement. The drastic modes of proof, in themselves, might have encouraged evasion of trial or out-of-court settlements. While the lack of convictions and the large number of people who did not appear at the trial might strike a modern reader as an indication of irresponsibility in the administration of justice, to the people using the courts apparently it was an adequate system of maintaining order.

---

[1] Doris Mary Stenton, ed., *Lincolnshire Assize Rolls*, A.D. 1202–1209, Lincolnshire Record Society 22 (Lincoln, 1926). This roll has been selected since it contains the most cases (434).

As Maitland has argued, the law, the judicial system, and the general population did not accept rampant self-help as the norm.[2] They did not want
to simply fight each other to gain their ends. Instead, they sought to reach
negotiated settlements that would not leave the community rent asunder
over private disputes. Courts, even if they did not adjudicate disputes, were
valuable tools for resolving them. The late-twelfth- and thirteenth-century
assize and eyre rolls have been studied extensively by legal historians, but
these scholars have concentrated on procedure and its evolution as well as
on the presumed goals of kings and justices. I, as a social historian, will try
to discern the advantages that people using the courts found in taking their
fights and perceived wrongs into an official setting even if they did not seek
official judgment.

Glanvill, the treatise on the laws and customs of England written perhaps less than twenty years before the Lincolnshire assize, included a brief
section on criminal pleas at the end of a general discussion of the workings
of the assize and of writs dealing with the wide range of property disputes.
In the introductory comments the author states that 'pleas are either civil or
criminal'. Some of the criminal pleas belong to the crown and some to the
sheriffs of the county. Those matters which belong to the king are various
forms of treason and breaking of the king's peace including homicide, arson,
robbery, and rape: felonies punishable by death or 'cutting off of limbs'. All
other thefts are the matter for the sheriffs and these are determined in
county courts rather than the king's court.[3]

Criminal cases came within the purview of the king's court through
either a specific accuser (a private prosecutor), or an accusation based on
'public notoriety'. In other words, those accused came to court either by
appeal or by presentment because they were suspected of the crime and
the presentment jury had good reason to believe that they might be guilty.
Glanvill is clear that 'the truth of the matter shall be investigated by many
and varied inquests and interrogations before the justices, and arrived at by
considering the probable facts and possible conjectures both for and against
the accused, who must as a result be either absolved entirely or made to
purge himself by ordeal'.[4]

Even the process that Glanvill outlines leaves room for considerable community opinion and also puts the burden of proof on the person making
the appeal.[5] The accuser must have sureties for prosecuting his or her suit.

[2] Frederick Pollock and Frederic William Maitland, *The History of English Law
before the Time of Edward I*, 2nd edn intro. by S. F. C. Milsom, 2 vols (Cambridge,
1968), ii, p. 574.

[3] *Glanvill*, bk. ii, c. 2, pp. 3–4.

[4] *Glanvill*, bk. xiv, c. 1, p. 171.

[5] Margaret H. Kerr, 'Angevin Reform of the Appeal of Felony', *Law and History*

That is, he or she must have community approval and find people in the community who have a reasonable belief that the appeal is justified and will have the prosecuting party present at the trial. But even *Glanvill*, and presumably the justices, realized that the sureties would undertake a great burden in supporting an appellor, so that it was sufficient that the person making an appeal do so on solemn oath.[6] The persons making the appeal put themselves at considerable risk. If they made a false appeal or did not appear in court to pursue their appeal, they would be taken and fined.[7] In cases where there was not an appeal, the community was charged with raising the hue and cry if the culprit was caught red-handed – that is, with the bloody weapon or with stolen goods. In the case of the four vills making a presentment, they had to secure the alleged felon and notify the sheriff or his bailiffs.[8] Imprisonment was to be used in the case of homicide, but mostly the suspects were released to pledges or mainpernours. The pledges would be liable to fines if they did not produce the person for trial and the vills would be fined as well. If the suspect did not appear and had fled, he would be outlawed.[9] Persuasive means in the way of fines could be used to bring the appealed or indicted suspect to court.[10] The whole system put a considerable burden on individuals and local communities to bring suspected criminals to justice, but it also gave them immediate access to manipulating the courts and other individuals in the community to their own advantage.

The crimes appearing in the Lincolnshire assize rolls amount to approximately 430 cases. It is often difficult to establish exactly what the crimes were and often the charge was simply breaking of the king's peace. The cases include 114 cases of homicide, eighty-nine of robbery with violence, sixty-five of wounding, forty-nine of rape, and a number of less serious breaches

Review 13 (1995), 351–91, 352, 354. The use of appeals for crimes was introduced by the Normans. Private appeals were introduced in the Assize of Clarendon. Henry II and his successors worked toward changing private appeals into a tool for public prosecution.

[6] *Glanvill*, bk. xiv, c. 1, pp. 171–2.

[7] Kerr, 'Angevin Reform', 359–64. Kerr notes that the Angevin kings tried to stop the practice of abandonment of appeals by fining those who did not follow up their appeal. The concern was real, because between 1194 and 1256 50 per cent of the appeals were abandoned.

[8] Roger D. Groot, 'The Jury of Presentment before 1215', *American Journal of Legal History* 26 (1982), 1–24. Groot argues that the juries of presentment were already making judgments about the validity of cases before 1215. He argues that the jurors and the vills gained substantial credence on guilt or innocence, but it was only after 1215 that they emerged as something like the modern petit jury.

[9] Pollock and Maitland, *History of English Law*, ii, pp. 578–582; Kerr, 'Angevin Reform', 366–368.

[10] Kerr, 'Angevin Reform', 360–6.

of the peace. Austin Lane Poole argued that the number of crimes was high, considering that the justices had visited Lincolnshire in the two preceding years. Thus all the alleged crimes would have been committed during that year.[11] Lincolnshire, however, was one of the most populous counties in England, with 83,384 people, according to the figures in the Domesday Book.[12] By 1202 the population of Lincolnshire would have increased considerably from the 1086 figure. The number of crimes, therefore, is not particularly high given the population.

The majority of these cases, 353, came into court by appeal of the victim or a relative. Only seventy-seven were brought by jury presentment.[13] *Glanvill* provided brief descriptions of the types of crime, dividing homicide into two types. Murder was done secretly, 'out of sight of all by the killer and his accomplices'. It could not be followed by the hue and cry. No one could make an accusation of murder except the nearest blood relative. The same rule applied to simple homicide.[14] In any appeal, *Glanvill* explained that when both parties are present in court, the accuser must allege 'that he saw or that, in some manner approved by the court, he knew with certainty that the accused' had committed the crime. All free men and villeins could make appeals. A woman could make appeals only in the case of homicide of her husband if she saw the deed, 'because husband and wife are one flesh', and in the case of the rape of her body.[15] Of the appeals in the rolls, seventy-two were made by women. Forty-six of these appeals were for rape.

Glanvill was specific about the way in which rape must be appealed. 'In the crime of rape a woman charges a man with violating her by force in the peace of the lord king. A woman who suffers in this way must go, soon after the deed is done, to the nearest vill and there show to trustworthy men the injury done to her, and any effusion of blood there may be and any tearing of her clothes'. Her public prosecution was not over. She then had to do the same before the reeve of the hundred and afterwards proclaim it publicly to the next county court. A woman could not go to battle to prove this, so that the accused would either undergo the ordeal or try to disprove the woman's accusation. The option of agreeing to marry the victim was not

---

[11] Austin Lane Poole, *Obligations of Society in the XII and XIII Centuries: Ford Lectures Delivered at Oxford in 1944* (Oxford, 1945), pp. 82–8. Figures are from Irwin L. Langbein, 'The Jury of Presentment and the Coroner', *Columbia Law Review* 33 (1933), 1329–65, at 1337 n. 24.

[12] Josiah Cox Russell, *British Medieval Population* (Albuquerque, 1948), p. 53.

[13] Poole, *Obligations of Society*, p. 87.

[14] *Glanvill*, bk xiv, c. 3, p. 174.

[15] *Glanvill*, bk xiv, c. 1, p. 172. He speaks of treason only in the procedure, but it is the same as is used for crimes, as he states on p. 174. For a discussion of women bringing appeals, see Daniel Klerman, 'Women Prosecutors in Thirteenth-Century England', *Yale Journal of Law and the Humanities* 14 (2002), 271–320.

permitted, because it could lead to marriage between persons of different estates to the disgrace of the woman and 'the fair repute of their families' whose name 'would be unworthily blackened'.[16] Most of the appeals of rape were quashed either because the appeal was not made in the proper language or, more likely, the woman did not appear in court.[17] *Glanvill* was concerned that the rape might be a prelude to marriages of misalliance, but the evidence of concords involving marriage is rare. In a Cornish case, Malot Crawe appealed Robert, son of Godfrey of rape. He denied it, but the jurors attested that 'she was seen bleeding'. The victim and accused purchased a licence from the justices to marry.[18] More common, perhaps, was an out-of-court settlement, but again, the evidence is slim. Leviva daughter of Siwat appealed the son of Agge and made her appeal in the proper way, but 'they are brought into agreement by half a mark, which Simon ought to pay next Sunday'.[19]

Women who prosecuted the homicide of a husband (ten cases) either did not appear or the accused fled and was outlawed. In two cases women appealed the death of a son, but again other factors led to the dismissal of the case. In one of the cases in which a woman appealed the death of her father, the justices ruled that since she was married and her husband was alive, she could not make an appeal. She paid a fine, and the suspect was acquitted.[20]

The outcome of the appeals by women in court was not different from the general pattern of appeals. In the vast majority of cases, the appeals were not prosecuted; in other words, the appellor did not come to court. In 164 cases the appellor did not prosecute, and in thirteen of these cases the appealed did not appear either. In the late-twelfth and thirteenth centuries those appealed by prosecutors who did not appear were usually acquitted.[21] During the reign of Henry II an attempt was made to hold prosecutors

---

[16] *Glanvill*, bk xiv, c. 6, pp. 175–6.

[17] For a discussion of the problems of making an appeal and the success in doing so see Barbara A. Hanawalt, 'Whose Story Is This? Rape Narratives in Medieval English Courts', in *Of Good and Ill Repute: Gender and Social Control in Medieval England* (Oxford, 1998), pp. 124–41.

[18] F. W. Maitland, ed., *Select Pleas of the Crown*, AD 1200–1225, Selden Society I (London, 1888), no. 7, p. 3.

[19] *Lincolnshire Assize Rolls*, no. 916.

[20] *Lincolnshire Assize Rolls*, no. 690; Daniel Klerman, 'Settlement and the Decline of Private Prosecution in Thirteenth-Century England', *Law and History Review* 19 (2001), 1–65, at 10. He found that in the thirteenth century women brought a third of all appeals, including two-thirds of the homicide appeals.

[21] Klerman, 'Settlement and the Decline of Private Prosecution', 13.

in private appeals to more account by having them find sureties for their appeal and by fining them for failure to pursue it.[22]

In thirty cases the appellor did prosecute, but the judges dismissed the pleas.[23] The usual reasons for an appeal to be dismissed were that the person did not repeat the appeal as it was originally made, the hue and cry had not been raised, or no wound appeared on the victim. The justices also made distinctions about what they would consider a valid appeal. When Hugh de Ruperes appealed John of Haceby of 'wickedly' coming into his fields with his plough animals and destroying his meadows and beating his men, he changed his plea at the trial and left out the beating. Because he changed the plea so that the action did not involve personal violence, the appeal was null. Trespass was not yet an action and the justices judged his appeal as invalid.[24] Likewise the justices took a dim view both of people who frequently made spurious appeals and of those who had been appealed several times. For instance, a man appealed of rape more than once, but who was not prosecuted, fell under suspicion. Such people were taken into custody as being of ill repute.[25] The cases show that the justices were aware of the manipulations to which the courts could be subjected. Innocent people could be harassed by false appeals, but guilty people could get away with repeated offences because of the difficulty of making a successful appeal.

To protect against malicious appeals, the law permitted the purchase of the writ *de odio et atia*, a plea alleged to be made 'in spite and hatred'.[26] The writ was not purchased cheaply, and perhaps for that reason it was rarely used. Andrew of Edlington paid ten marks to have his case tried speedily and before a jury and to have inquiry whether this appeal was made for just cause or for hatred and malice, but another man paid only one-half mark for the writ.[27] Magna Carta established that no payment had to be made for the writ, but even before that, if the jurors cited hatred on the part of the appellor, it was grounds for dismissal of the case.[28] Gilbert of Willingham appealed Gilbert son of Geoffrey of arson in the burning of his

[22] Kerr, 'Angevin Reform', 360–2.

[23] Stenton, 'Introduction', *Lincolnshire Assize Rolls*, pp. lix, lx; Kerr, 'Angevin Reform', 359–60. She found that about 50 per cent of the appeals between 1194 and 1256 were withdrawn. From 1218–19 on the abandoned appeals were referred to a jury. Klerman, 'Settlement and the Decline of Private Prosecution', 12, found that in the thirteenth century 57 per cent of the prosecutors dropped their appeals.

[24] *Lincolnshire Assize Rolls*, no. 765; Stenton, 'Introduction', pp. lvi, lviii.

[25] Stenton, 'Introduction', p. lix.

[26] Pollock and Maitland, *History of English Law*, i, pp. 587–9.

[27] *Lincolnshire Assize Rolls*, nos. 594, 841, 909, 938.

[28] Kerr, 'Angevin Reform', 270, cites a rise in cases brought to a jury in cases of 'spite and hatred'.

house. He claimed that after the fire was extinguished, he raised the hue and cry. He pointed out Gilbert son of Geoffrey, and the neighbours followed in pursuit. Gilbert, the accused, denied the story and the villagers of Willingham said that they never saw him fleeing and that the appellor never pointed him out to them. They concluded that he had made the appeal out of hatred and the case was dismissed.[29]

Another common outcome was for the parties to put themselves on the king's mercy. This option, of course, cost money, usually a half mark. The records do not explain why some of the prosecutors would pay to withdraw the case when it appeared that they would win. Geoffrey of Holtham appealed two men of his son's murder and the evidence seemed to indicate strongly that they did commit the crime. But he withdrew his appeal.[30] Perhaps most of these cases were withdrawn because of a technicality in pleading, but they might also represent an out-of-court concord.

An agreement to settle between the two parties appeared in twenty-five of the cases in Lincolnshire.[31] Before 1218 justices would often give a licence for a concord in exchange for a monetary payment. Those concluding a concord without permission were fined if the justices knew about the settlements. In the eyre rolls between 1194 and 1208, eighty-two concords are recorded, and only two were stated to have been made without permission.[32] Daniel Klerman estimates that perhaps 40 per cent of the appeals ended in settlement.[33] In a Cornish case of what sounds like extraordinary violence, the parties paid for a concord. Anger of Penhale in Ladock appealed Andrew of Trendeal, saying that in the king's peace and in felony he attacked him and 'so wounded him that 4 bones were extracted from his head'. This assault was part of a robbery in which Andrew of Trendeal took a cloak. Anger of Penhale appealed him as a maimed man (more of this plea later). The wounds were shown and were still fresh in the shire court. But Andrew of Trendeal denied the whole charge, word for word. The two got a licence from the king to agree. Andrew gave Anger one mark and the king got one-half mark for the licence. In a second, separate appeal involving the maimed Anger, William le Vernur appealed Roland de Penworth of robbing him of not just the cloak but also a hoe. William wanted judgment of the court. Roland denied the whole matter word for word. Anger was asked whether Roland struck him or not and Roland replied that only Andrew had done so. William had made a false claim, but Roland had to make a fine of 10s.

[29] *Lincolnshire Assize Rolls*, no. 616; Stenton, 'Introduction', p. lvii.

[30] *Lincolnshire Assize*, no. 650; Stenton, 'Introduction', p. lviii.

[31] Stenton, 'Introduction', p. lix.

[32] Kerr, 'Angevin Reform', 368, 374.

[33] Klerman, 'Settlement and the Decline of Private Prosecution', 16.

and in addition he gave 40d. to Anger.[34] The concord is duly recorded, but one wonders what was behind the assault, why William le Vernur made a separate appeal, and why Anger was willing to settle for a concord after losing four bones from his skull. The court records do not tell the whole story.

If the person making the appeal pursued the accusations and appeared in court or if the charges against the accused were made by presenting juries, then, according to the law, the accused was to undergo either an ordeal or a trial by battle. Only four cases in the 1202 roll called for a proof by ordeal of hot iron and three by water. The water ordeals are actually recorded as having taken place, but none of hot iron are. In one case the person failed the water ordeal and in the other two cases the person succeeded. In the case of the man who failed the ordeal, his goods were confiscated, but the record does not state what happened to him.[35] Lincolnshire was not unusual in the low number of ordeals. A diligent search of the records before 1215 by Margaret Kerr turned up only seventeen cases of ordeal by water and three of hot iron where there was some evidence that these actually occurred.[36]

The tradition of proof by ordeal was very ancient. The idea was that a person who was innocent could carry the hot iron and recover from the wounds easily and that the pure water would accept the innocent person, who would sink, but the guilty would be rejected by the water and would float. The process had undergone Christianization, in that a priest would bless the iron or the water and it would, therefore, be up to God to determine guilt or innocence. The Fourth Lateran Council of 1215 disallowed priests a role in the ordeal and as a consequence, England switched to a trial or petit jury. The early assize records show that the justices were already moving away from judgment by ordeal. When the ordeal was recommended, the person was already suspected by the jurors or was of ill repute and the ordeal was a way of proving their initial suspicions. Even those who succeeded in passing the test of the ordeal were either forced to leave the kingdom and had their goods confiscated or paid for permission to stay.[37] Letitia of Clixby appealed Hugh Shakespeare of coming to her mother's

34 Doris Mary Stenton, ed., *Pleas before the King or His Justices, 1198–1202*, 2 vols, Selden Society vols 67, 68 (London, 1953, 1949), ii, nos. 289, 290, pp. 62–3.

35 *Lincolnshire Assize Rolls*, nos. 595, 843, 844, 1004 (hot iron), 544, 693a, 857 (water); Stenton, 'Introduction', pp. li–lii.

36 Margaret H. Kerr, Richard E. Forsyth, and Michael J. Plyeley, 'Cold Water and Hot Iron: Trial by Ordeal in England', *Journal of Interdisciplinary History* 22 (1992), 573–95, at 578.

37 For a complete discussion of the ordeals, see Kerr, Forsyth, and Plyeley, 'Cold Water and Hot Iron'. This article includes not only the history of ordeal and the use of it prior to Magna Carta, but also physiological descriptions of the effects and the reason so many people passed the test. A detailed case of the ordeal by water can be found on p. 582 and of hot iron on p. 588.

house where he bound both her and her mother and robbed them. The jurors and the men of the four neighbouring vills suspected him and said that he was 'of evil repute'. He made his law by water and was saved, but he had to give the king two marks to avoid abjuring the realm and had to find pledges for his faith.[38]

The ordeal of hot iron was more serious as an ordeal and was, to modern thinking, unfairly administered. The person appealed had the right to choose whether he or the accuser had to undergo the ordeal. A case, probably typical, shows the reluctance of the justices to carry out this ordeal. Astin of Wispington appealed Simon of Edlington of assaulting him in his meadows and 'thrust[ing] out his eye, so that he is maimed in that eye'. He appeared in court and showed the recent wound. Simon came and denied that he had done the deed. The appeal was attested to by the coroners and the county at large. Astin's wife had first made the appeal before he was able to do so. 'Judgement: Let the law be made, and let it be the choice of the appealed whether he or Astin carry the iron.' Needless to say, Simon chose to have Astin carry the iron. 'And afterwards they both came and put themselves in mercy.' In another case in which the evidence of a broken arm and wounds in the head were well attested, the accused opted for the victim to carry the iron, but the victim withdrew himself and the accused was acquitted.[39]

Trial by battle was another form of proof found in *Glanvill*'s treatise,[40] but it is even more uncommon than the ordeal by hot iron, with only two cases appearing in the assize at Lincoln. The appellor had to offer to prove his appeal with his body. Both parties were to come armed and to fight until the death of one or until one cried craven. It was a vicious fight so that it is no wonder that people opted out of it. Ralph the blacksmith, for instance, appealed Ralph, son of Jordan of assaulting Agnes his wife and robbing her of five shillings, three rings and two silver brooches. In addition, he gave her a wound on her head and broke a window in her house. The blacksmith offered to prove it with his body. Because the jury said that all the correct procedures had been followed, hue had been raised, and Agnes had a little wound on her head, the justices recommended a duel. Both parties came armed for the fight, but afterwards, they put themselves in mercy.[41]

The law permitted a man to refuse the duel if he was sixty or older or if he was maimed and could not fight. Adam son of Gladwin appealed William of Nettleham for killing his son in Bicker market. He offered to prove his words 'as the court shall consider as of his sight and hearing as

---

[38] *Lincolnshire Assize Rolls*, no. 855.

[39] *Lincolnshire Assize Rolls*, nos. 595, 851, 843; Stenton, 'Introduction', p. lii.

[40] *Glanvill*, bk xiv, c. 1, p. 172.

[41] *Lncolnshire Assize Rolls*, no. 638; Stenton, 'Introduction', pp. lii–liii.

a man who has passed his fighting age'. Since he was over sixty, the duel did not take place.[42] Men who were wounded sometimes included in their appeal that they were maimed, perhaps as a precaution against having to fight.

To a modern reader, the record of the court appears to be a dismal failure in bringing the guilty to judgment. In Lincolnshire in 1202, two men were hanged; sixteen men fled, escaped capture, and were outlawed; eleven took sanctuary in a church and abjured the realm; and nine were members of the clergy and claimed benefit of clergy. Again, Lincolnshire appears not to be unusual since this was a general pattern in other counties.[43] Maitland observed that if John's reign 'may have been a bad time for honest folk; it seems to have been a holiday for robbers and murderers.'[44]

Poole argued that perhaps the crown was less interested in judgments in the early assizes than in the substantial profit from the criminal side of the assize. A roll of amercements and other profits from the assize are included for Lincolnshire in 1202. Money accruing to the crown from the criminal procedures alone amounted to £527 12s. The fine of *murdrum*, perhaps instituted by William the Conqueror to protect his French followers from the English, was charged to the community when a person was found killed violently and it could not be established that his kin were English. The fine only applied to the secret homicide that *Glanvill* described. Since there was only one case in which a secret murder occurred and the victim was established to be English, it is possible that the *murdrum* fine was simply another way of raising money. The amount assessed on the wapentakes of Lincoln for twenty-seven cases of *murdrum* varied from 13s. 4d. to £10. The scribe apparently had strong feelings about particular cases. When a man was found guilty of killing his wife, the scribe wrote *murdrum* in the margins three times. The highest fine of £10 was assessed. But even when he wrote the word more times, the fines were sometimes lower. Since these fines were imposed on the whole wapentake, the amount would not have been excessive.[45]

Other amercements, however, fell more heavily on the community or on individuals. The frankpledge was required to follow the hue and cry and bring the culprit to justice. If they failed to do so they were fined. Once the suspect was caught it was the responsibility of the individual's pledges

---

[42] *Lincolnshire Assize Rolls*, no. 650; Stenton,'Introduction', p. liii.

[43] Klerman,'Settlement and the Decline of Private Prosecution', p. 12, recorded 1,249 cases for the thirteenth century and also found few convictions; Kerr, Forsyth, and Plyley,'Cold Water and Hot Iron', 578. They found only eight cases of people being maimed or hanged in the eyres from 1194–1208.

[44] *Select Pleas of the Crown*,'Introduction', p. xxiv.

[45] Poole, *Obligations of Society*, pp. 84–6.

to insure his appearance in court. If the accused did not appear, then the pledges were in mercy. This raised £95 for the crown in the Lincolnshire assize of 1202. The situation was no better for the person bringing the appeal. Fines were imposed on a person who made an appeal but did not appear in court, or a person who made an appeal with a flaw or with evidence that the justices deemed insufficient or even false. These fines varied from a half mark to a mark. Those parties wishing to purchase a licence for a concord likewise paid. Jurors were fined for failing to make a presentment that they should have known about or for making a false or foolish presentment.[46] It is no wonder that the visitation of the justices was dreaded. It cost the population a considerable amount of money when one considers that an unskilled labourer made 1d. a day.

Considering the expense of justice, one understands better the protection provided in the twentieth clause of Magna Carta: 'a freeman shall not be amerced for a small offence except in accordance with the measure of the offence; and for a serious offence he shall be amerced according to the greatness of the offence.' The villein was to be amerced in the same way and none of the amercements were to be imposed 'except on the oath of honest men of the neighbourhood'. Indeed, fines were excused in the thirteenth century because of poverty.[47]

Even if we accept the argument that the king was perhaps more interested in the considerable money made from the criminal cases in the assizes than in ridding the country of felons, we must investigate the more sanguine argument of Maitland that the king, his justices, and the community did not accept violent self-help as a viable means for settling disputes. As Poole points out, a day in court was expensive in terms of potential fines. In addition, prosecutors had the expense of travelling to the county town, food and lodging. Why, considering the expenses and the likelihood that they would not receive a judgment, did anyone make an appeal? There was, of course, the threat of reprisals from the king, his justices, and the sheriff if crimes were not reported, but it is also possible that the many people who appealed those who attacked them violently gained something themselves. Certainly, they would have known that their chances of gaining a conviction were slim; there had been two assizes in Lincolnshire before that of 1202. In 1202 under 10 per cent of the cases led to some resolution that presumed admission of guilt, such as outlawry, benefit of clergy, sanctuary and admission of guilt with abjuration of the realm.

I argue that conviction was not the goal of their appeals. We seldom know the motivations of those making the appeal or the history of quarrels within the community. Klerman has made the argument that the

---

[46] Poole, *Obligations of Society*, pp. 87–8.

[47] Poole, *Obligations of Society*, pp. 89–91.

courts were a useful tool to those of a lower social status who wanted to achieve some sort of retribution against those with more power. The powerful could use self-help and their might to make right. But the ordinary members of the community probably benefited from going to the king's justices and bringing the weight of public opinion to bear on their case in court.[48] They might not win a judgment, but they could get a concord.

Enough cases indicate that the jurors of the community and even the judges were well aware of ancient and recent fights. In a case already cited, when a man accused another of arson in Willingham, the jurors knew that he only instituted the plea because of his hatred for the person he accused. Perhaps the fire that consumed his home was accidental, but he took the occasion to accuse an old enemy. Because, in *Glanvill's* words, 'The truth of the matter shall be investigated by many and varied inquests and interrogations before the justices, and arrived at by considering the probable facts and possible conjectures both for and against the accused', the justices acquired a good knowledge of local conditions. In one case, Lucy of Morwinstow appealed three boys of robbing her of 20s. 8d. and a cloak worth half a mark. But the jurors said that she was a hireling, and that a man lay with her in a garden. The boys hooted her so that she left her cloak, which they took and pawned for two gallons of wine. The judgment was that one of the accused was to give her 3d. for the wine and went quit. Apparently the value of the cloak was assessed as the equivalent of what the boys paid for the wine. Two boys did not come and their pledges were in mercy.[49] Either Lucy had overvalued her loss or it was impossible for a hireling to get restitution in the king's court.

In an elaborate case, Thomas son of Lefwin appealed Alan the reaper of attacking him on the road. Thomas claimed that Alan had carried him to his house, assaulted him, broken a small bone in his arm, and robbed him. He then carried him back to the road. In his appeal, Thomas said that 'as quickly as he could' he raised the hue and cry and the neighbours came. He then sent for the king's sergeant, 'who came and found the robbery in Alan's house'. Thomas claimed that his knife and cap were stolen, but only the knife was found. No evidence was found that the bone was broken. The inconsistencies in Thomas's story were enough to dismiss the case, but further details showed that revenge might have been the motive for the attack. Thomas had attacked a woman in Alan's family and perhaps the judges were willing to overlook the obvious evidence of the crime and accept the information from the neighbours that it was done to settle an old score.[50]

[48] Klerman, 'Settlement and the Decline of Private Prosecution', 18–20.

[49] *Select Pleas of the Crown*, no. 16, pp. 7–8.

[50] *Lincolnshire Assize Rolls*, no. 733; Stenton, 'Introduction', p. lix.

Bringing a case to the assize may also have had a number of advantages that overrode the costs. For a person of good community standing who was appealed by someone of ill repute, it was possible to purchase the privilege of an enquiry into his own reputation. If the jury found him of good repute, he would go free of the appeal with only the need to find sureties for his good behaviour. The cost of the privilege for an inquiry was worth the investment, because it publicly verified his good reputation and probably made him immune from further frivolous suits.[51]

By invoking the king's peace the case was taken out of the local arena and the sheriff's court and put into the royal courts where the four vills as well as a sworn jury would inquire into the probable facts of the case. Lady Stenton suggested this possibility in her introduction to the Lincolnshire Assize of 1202. 'Gilbert of Ashby appealed Robert nephew of Everard that in the king's peace and wickedly, in despite of the peace given him in two wapentakes he assaulted him and wounded him in the head and gave him other blows, so that he was shamefully treated and almost dead.' Or take the case of Osbert of Lindsey who appealed Alan of Stickney of coming with force to his free tenement in Stickney. Osbert wished to dwell there and had erected a house, but Alan came and cut through the posts so that the house fell down. For good measure he wounded him and robbed him of 11s. Osbert had been to the county court and Alan had pledged him in the king's peace. But after this assurance of peace, Alan came to the house of Margery, Osbert's mother, where she lay dead and in which Osbert was with his niece. The niece was heir to Margery's land but Alan ejected them and their people and wounded Osbert. 'And all these things he did with his force in the peace of the king and wickedly.'[52] When the shire could not enforce a peace, there was a hope that the king's court could do so. The audience for the cases was larger and the solemnity of the proceedings as well as the recording of the case might have ensured a more permanent record.

Bringing the case into the king's court could also force an adversary into settlement. The threat of ordeal or trial by battle might very well persuade the adversary to pay the court costs to settle the matter out of court.

In some cases, the king and his justices tried to mediate personal animosities. In Northampton in 1202 Hugh son of the priest of Grafton was twice outlawed for the death of Richard Rambaud. The shire jurors explained that in the day of King Richard, Hugh had been outlawed by Richard's brother, Robert, but Hugh had come back with a writ to the sheriff in 1198. The writ was read in the full shire court and the sheriff was ordered to help

---

[51] Doris Mary Stenton, ed., *The Earliest Northampton Assize Rolls*, A.D. 1202–1209, Northamptonshire Record Society 5 (London, 1930), p. xxvi.

[52] *Lincolnshire Assize Rolls*, nos. 608, 612; Stenton, 'Introduction', p. l.

make peace between Hugh and the kin of Richard Rambaud. When the kin heard of Hugh's return, Robert Rambaud threatened to bring another appeal. Hugh was ordered to bring sureties, but he did not appear. The sergeant was told to find Hugh and bring him in to court. But he could not find him. Evidently, the fear of reprisals was so great that Hugh could not find sureties and he himself feared for his life. It was a throwback to the old blood vengeance of the Anglo-Saxon period. Hugh was outlawed once again.[53] The king and his justices seemed to understand this old principle when they made an effort to negotiate a settlement.

Lady Stenton speculates that, at least in the twenty-five cases of concord in Lincolnshire, the litigants might have been harkening back to a time less than a hundred year previously when people paid the *wer* to the kin of the slain person, the *bot* in compensation to the lord of the murdered man, and the *wite* as a fine to the king. The invasions and intermarriages tended to destroy these essentially personal actions, but the 'spirit of compromise' of the earlier days may be preserved in the concords and even in out-of-court settlements that we cannot know about.[54] Maitland was probably right that increasingly self-help was not acceptable and that the king's justice was valued if only as a tool toward dispute settlement. We seem to see in the early assizes a range of compromises among the population and among the justices over use of the court not just for judgment, but for regularizing the old systems of compensation. Judicial systems are perennially used by antagonists as one tool among many for winning a point. There can be justice without judgment.

---

[53] *Northampton Assize Rolls*, p. xxv.

[54] *Lincolnshire Assize Rolls*; Stenton, 'Introduction', p. lxi.

What Did Magna Carta Mean to Widows?

JANET S. LOENGARD

THE MEN who put together Magna Carta were concerned, among other things, about their wives and sisters and daughters and other female relatives who would, by a husband or father's death, be made heiresses or widows. Widows – the subject of this essay – appear in clauses 7, 8, and 11 of the 1215 Charter, and in clause 7 of the 1225 version, in the context of their remarriage, maritagium, inheritance, and dower. All those provisions were intended for their protection. As the result, for several generations the reaction to Henry II and his sons moved beyond merely curtailing abuses to creating a climate favourable to women who had lost their husbands. Paul Brand has argued that, by the end of the thirteenth century, attitudes had shifted to make dower, at least, less an automatic entitlement to a valid marriage; in any event, it is certain that in the following century dower became less secure.[1] But that has nothing to do with the world of King John and Magna Carta. The intent here is to discuss the background to the Charter provisions and analyse their practical effects.

The drafters of Magna Carta had reason for their concern. Widows in England had long been the subject of royal intervention. Perhaps it is because they were vulnerable and needed protection – they are classed as *personae miserabilis*, persons to be cared for, at canon law – or perhaps it is because they were potentially disruptors of the orderly transmission of property from generation to generation, or because there was uneasiness about a grown woman free to some extent to make her own marital choices.

Henry I's coronation charter promised that a childless surviving wife should have her dower and maritagium and that she would not be given in marriage except according to her will. If she had children, she would have dower and maritagium so long as she 'kept her body honestly' and again there was the provision on remarriage. Henry's barons were told 'likewise to restrain themselves towards the sons and daughters and wives of their men'.[2] But Henry did not restrain himself; the only pipe roll remaining from his reign shows women making payments for dower and/or maritagium and

---

[1] Paul Brand, 'Earning and Forfeiting Dower in Medieval England', *Journal of Legal History* 22:1 (April 2001), 1–20.

[2] Charter of Liberties, King Henry I, §§3, 4, in Stubbs, *Select Charters*, pp. 117–19 at p. 118.

fining not to take a husband.[3] As women in his gift, they had no choice but to bargain with him.

Henry II's pipe rolls tell the same story. Widowed heiresses, widows of tenants in chief or of mesne tenants whose lands had come into the king's hand, appear and reappear making similar payments as well as occasionally fining for an inheritance. Richard brought the use and abuse of widowhood to a new high – although the numbers may in part reflect the increase in available evidence after 1189.[4]

Nothing changed in 1199. Pipe and plea rolls show that John, like his predecessors, regarded widows in his gift as a source of revenue. He could marry them off for a good price or as a reward for service, or he could accept a good price from women who did not want to be married off. There was no carrot; the stick was financial: the maritagium, dower, and inheritance of a recalcitrant widow would be taken into the king's hand.[5] As Sir James Holt has remarked, a widow who paid to remain unmarried was 'bidding not just for freedom but for power over her inheritance, dower, and marriage portion'.[6] The barons' concern about the extortion of those bids is reflected in clauses 7 and 8 of Magna Carta (1215):

> a widow shall have her marriage portion and her inheritance at once and without any hindrance; nor shall she pay anything for her dower, her marriage portion, or her inheritance … No widow shall be compelled to marry … provided that she gives security that she will not marry without our consent if she holds of us, or without the consent of the lord of whom she holds …[7]

---

[3] Joseph Hunter, ed., *Magnum Rotulum Scaccarii vel Magnum Rotulum Pipae de Anno Tricesimo-Primo Regis Henrici Primi* (Record Commission, 1833). Examples of fines by widows, their fathers, or their new husbands for dower and maritagium, pp. 14, 26, 67, 94, 95, 96, 122, 147; fines to remain unmarried, pp. 96, 110.

[4] See, for example, Doris M. Stenton, ed., *Pipe Roll 6 Richard I*, PRS 43 n.s. 5 (London, 1928), p. 163, with the famous entry concerning the sale of the stock of the countess of Aumale because she was unwilling to marry William de Forz.

[5] For a good example, see CRR vol. 3, p. 257: the reply to a dower claim was that the land assigned as dower was in the king's hand because the widow had refused to marry herself at his will.

[6] 'The Heiress and the Alien', in J. C. Holt, *Colonial England, 1066–1215* (London, 1997), pp. 245–69 at p. 265. See also his *Magna Carta*, 2nd edn (Cambridge, 1992), esp. pp. 53–4, 197–200.

[7] I have used the translation in Holt, *Magna Carta*, pp. 448–73 at p. 453. It has been suggested by Natalie Fryde that the provisions of cc. 7 and 8 were intended to apply to all free women rather than only to the widows of tenants-in-chief of the king: *Why Magna Carta? Angevin England Revisited* (Munster, 2001), p. 149. Perhaps it is more likely that the protection they afforded was extended to the larger group of women by c. 60, quoted in n. 8 below, rather than by the effort of

The 1225 Charter conflated clauses 7 and 8 and terms were made more specific: a widow was to remain in the capital messuage forty days until her dower was assigned, and she was to get a third part of all land her husband had held in life unless she had accepted less in nominated dower at the time of her marriage. She was not to be distrained to marry if she gave the required security not to do so without consent.

However, kings were not the only overlords who dealt in widows. Clause 60 of the 1215 Charter (clause 37 of the 1225 version) attempts to ensure that what the king could not do his barons could not either.[8] There is little evidence of lords' dealings with widows before 1215 unless a matter appears at some point in the royal records,[9] but the provision must have been intended to secure the widows of most free landholding men in their dower, marriage portion, or inheritance while precluding compulsory remarriage.[10]

But even if Magna Carta had been in place at the outset of John's reign, clause 7 might not have affected most early thirteenth century disputes involving dower or maritagium, because the king was directly involved in only a small percentage of them.[11] And had it been in place then, even clause

the barons. Of course both the writ of right of dower and the writ of dower *unde nihil habet*, available for all freehold tenements, predate Magna Carta.

[8] 'All these aforesaid customs and liberties which we have granted … shall be observed by all men of our realm … as far as it pertains to them, towards their own men.' Even before 1215, there were said to be limits. 'If they [heiresses] have once been lawfully married and subsequently become widows, they do not revert into the wardship of their lords, though they must ask their consent to marry.' *Glanvill*, bk vii, c. 12, p. 86. The implication is that the lord has no right to marry off the woman, although he can prevent her from remarrying. Theory, however, did not necessarily correspond with practice.

[9] Hubert Walter's grant of a widow and her manors led to a suit by the heir against her second husband: L. F. Salzmann, ed., *An Abstract of Feet of Fines for the County of Sussex, 2 Richard I to 33 Henry III*, Sussex Record Society 2 (Lewes, 1903), p. 31. Ranulf earl of Chester seems to have overreached, marrying off a widow who claimed that she held nothing from him: Thomas Duffus Hardy, ed., *Rotuli de Oblatis et Finibus … Tempore Regis Johannis* (Record Commission, 1835), p. 81.

[10] Further evidence of the intent to protect widows of freeholders of lesser status might be seen in the provision in c. 7 first found in the 1217 redaction of the Charter, declaring that a widow should have reasonable estovers 'de communi' until her dower was assigned. The passage is somewhat ambiguous – it follows discussion of finding a suitable house for a widow whose husband's capital messuage was a castle and is followed by a rule for measuring dower applicable to all women – but the right to estovers would have been more valuable and indeed necessary to women of lower economic status.

[11] However, he intervened in dower suits which may not have directly involved him, ordering postponements or respites or even mandating termination of the action; examples include CRR vol. 2, pp. 94, 279, 298; CRR vol. 5, p. 72; CRR vol. 6, p. 120; CRR vol. 7, p. 283. See n. 67 below for discussion of the point.

60 might not have been invoked with great frequency; in many dower disputes, a dead husband's lord was not the woman's opponent. A widow certainly did sometimes have to deal with him, especially if the lord was guardian of a minor heir, since most dower claims had to be brought first to the heir's court.[12] But many dower suits involved either people who were a husband's grantees, or who had had some transaction with him, or who simply held land that the widow believed had been his, or else they were relatives of the dead man. Widows faced stepsons, brothers-in-law (the dead husband's brother who had become his heir), fathers-in-law, sons-in-law and their wives, nephews, even sons – although very rarely daughters acting alone.[13] And maritagium quarrels very often involved people who were related. It is to these cases, then, that one must look to understand the ordinary functioning of dower and maritagium, something of a woman's relationships with her birth and marital families, and attitudes towards the widow and her property in the first decades of the thirteenth century.[14]

It is hard to overemphasize the economic importance of both dower and maritagium to women and their families. Given the rules of primogeniture, most women were not heiresses. Any land a widow held would usually have been her endowment at the church door or a marriage portion granted by her family. They might well be her only assets because the rule was rapidly evolving – although in the early thirteenth century it had not yet become firm – that a married woman could own no chattels.[15] Those assets came at the expense of sons, stepsons, sons-in-law, brothers-in-law and other heirs who figure so prominently in litigation. Dower actions far outnumbered litigation over maritagium. A dissertation cited by Ralph Turner followed about 450 dower claims to their conclusion between 1194 and 1216 – but a

---

[12] The exception was a suit brought by the writ of dower *unde nihil habet*, alleging that all dower had been withheld.

[13] For land held in military tenure, the only instance in which a woman alone would bring an action against her daughter alone would seem to be where both women were widows who had not remarried, the daughter being the heiress.

[14] 'Property' here refers to real, not personal, property. There is an excellent discussion of the development of dower in Joseph Biancalana, 'Widows at Common Law: the Development of Common Law Dower', *Irish Jurist* n.s. 23 (1988), 255–329.

[15] Ordinarily any personal possessions she inherited or was given before or after marriage became her husband's outright and remained in his estate if she survived him, although in the thirteenth century she had the right to a third of his chattels: *Glanvill*, bk vii, c. 5, p. 80; *Bracton*, ii, p. 179. For a later period, see Richard H. Helmholz, 'Married Women's Wills in Later Medieval England', in Sue Sheridan Walker, ed., *Wife and Widow in Medieval England* (Ann Arbor, 1993), pp. 165–82; see also Janet S. Loengard, 'Which May Be Said to Be Her Own: Widows and Goods in Late Medieval England', in Maryannne Kowaleski and P. J. P. Goldberg, eds, *Medieval Domesticity* (Cambridge, 2008), pp. 162–76.

high percentage of claims overall would not have been included in the study because they appear only with the appointment of an attorney or they disappear from the plea rolls before a final decision.[16] The number of cases had not diminished at the mid-point of the thirteenth century.[17]

Nonetheless, it is sometimes difficult to know what the litigation means. Is it an attempt to deny or whittle down the widow's claim? To make a record, valuable in case of later lawsuits? Or is it a glimpse at an arrangement of family property, an allocation of assets among family members? Only a few defences seem designed to cut off a claim absolutely. Others seek to delay the resolution; the widow might abandon her efforts – or die. Some are a bargaining ploy; opposition might make a woman more amenable to compromise. Quite a few, especially between mother and son, look as if the purpose of the exercise was to provide an entry in the rolls of the royal court.[18] And some do seem to be part of an elaborate shuffling of interests in property extending even beyond the life of the doweress, again secured as a matter of record.[19]

---

[16] Ralph V. Turner, 'John and Justice', in Stephen D. Church, ed., *King John: New Interpretations* (Woodbridge, 1999), pp. 317–33 at p. 326, referring to Patricia Orr, 'English Women at Law: Actions in the King's Courts of Justice 1194–1222' (PhD diss., Rice University, Houston, 1989), pp. 94–116. G. D. G. Hall commented that a decade after Magna Carta dower actions comprised 'almost 20 per cent of the business' in the rolls for 9–10 Henry III: G. D. G. Hall, review of *Curia Regis Rolls of the Reign of Henry III: 9–10 Henry III (1225–1226)*, CRR vol. 12 (London, 1957), in *English Historical Review* 74 (1959), 107–10, at 108.

[17] For example, the edited rolls for Trinity Term 27 Henry III contain 645 cases; almost 150 involve dower. Paul Brand, ed., *Curia Regis Rolls of the Reign of Henry III: 27–30 Henry III (1243–1245)*, CRR vol. 18 (Woodbridge, 1999).

[18] Typically, the son comes and immediately grants the dower, sometimes apparently part of a larger claim as in a 1212 case where the son is then appointed attorney in another dower suit: CRR vol. 6, p. 266. The absence of any real disagreement is also likely where there is a fine made with the services for the tenement being derisory, e.g. mother and son agree that she will hold a substantial amount of land on which he will pay the outgoings and she will give him a pair of spurs worth fourpence each Easter: *Feet of Fines of the Seventh and Eighth Years of the Reign of King Richard I*, PRS 20 (London, 1896; repr. Vaduz, 1966), p. 82; mother remits dower to son in return for twenty-four acres for a penny a year: *Feet of Fines of the Tenth Year of King Richard I*, PRS 24 (London, 1900, repr. 1929), p. 19; mother receives extensive lands with apparently no services owing in return for remission of further claim: *Feet of Fines for Sussex*, p. 34; mother gives up dower and son grants land for a pound of pepper a year: *Feet of Fines of the Reign of Henry II and the First Seven Years of the Reign of Richard I, A.D. 1182–1196*, PRS 17 (London, 1894; repr. Vaduz, 1966), p. 87; mother quitclaims dower to her son who gives all back to her plus two marks rent a year. Her inherited land will remain to her but when she dies it will go to her son and his heirs, ibid. p. 136. This may be to forestall her from granting it to another child during her lifetime.

[19] E.g. CRR vol. 5, p. 170; CRR vol. 6, p. 172; *Placitorum in Domo Capitulari*

Probably the most hostile reply to a dower claim was that the claimant was not a widow at all, because she had not been canonically married to the man she called her husband. Understandably, stepsons and brothers-in-law – whose legitimacy was not affected by the outcome – seem to have been especially attracted to this allegation.[20] It resulted in a writ to the bishop of the place the woman claimed to have been married, whose ordinary would then inquire and report findings by letters patent to the secular court.[21] A variant of the allegation was that the marriage had been irregular – most commonly clandestine, or only on the husband's deathbed; such marriages did not carry dower.[22]

But three defences which would have been equally decisive did not, or even could not, involve family members. One was that the husband had been a villein, or that the widow was, or that the husband had held the land in question in villeinage.[23] A second was that the widow's husband had

Westmonasteriensi Asservatorum Abbrevatio [hereafter *Abbreviatio Placitorum*] ([London], 1811) p. 35.

[20] Examples: CRR vol. 1, p. 322, and William Paley Baildon, ed., *Select Civil Pleas* [hereafter *SCP*], Selden Society 3 (London, 1890), p. 6; CRR vol. 2, p. 41 and *SCP*, p. 39; CRR vol. 2, pp. 63, 79; CRR vol. 3, p. 150; CRR vol. 4, pp. 2 and 38; CRR vol. 6, pp. 144, 153, 363, 391; CRR vol. 7, pp. 99 and 275, 101; Sir Francis Palgrave, ed., *Rotuli Curiae Regis* [hereafter *RCR*], 2 vols (London, 1834–5), ii, p. 56; TNA:PRO Just 1/80, mem. 15d. Of these, six almost certainly involved relatives and others probably did. Professor S. F. C. Milsom has collected citations to such cases in 'Inheritance by Women in the Twelfth and Early Thirteenth Centuries', in Morris S. Arnold *et al.*, eds, *On the Laws and Customs of England* (Chapel Hill, 1981), pp. 60–89 at p. 75 For a quarrel essentially between two women as to which was the wife of the decedent, see CRR vol. 6, p. 391, and TNA:PRO Just 1/229, mem. 8d (1227).

[21] *Bracton*, fols 302–302B, iii, pp. 372–3.

[22] *Bracton* mentions the necessity for endowment at the church door several times, most extensively at fols 303B–4, iii, pp. 376–7. A good example is the long-running case of Cecilia de Cressy, reported in CRR vol. 1, p. 432; CRR vol. 2, p. 63; *SCP*, p. 45, and *Abbreviatio Placitorum*, p. 34. Another is TNA:PRO Just 1/358 mem. 11d (1227), where the defendant's successful argument was that the woman was not married at the door of 'the monastery' and was endowed only three or four days before her husband's death. Also Alice, widow of Adam de Scaldeford, *RCR*, ii, p. 56; Edith of St Ives, CRR vol. 1, p. 322, and *SCP*, p. 45; Agnes, widow of Philip de Dive, CRR vol. 2, p. 41, and *SCP*, p. 39.

[23] TNA:PRO Just 1/229 mem. 6d (1227): defendant says that widow's husband was a villein who could not marry his daughter without merchet; ibid., mem. 12d, where the allegation is both that the husband was a villein and that the land was held in villeinage. In a 1214 case, the defence was that the widow was a villein; she denied it but had villein relatives and produced no family to prove liberty: CRR vol. 7, p. 148. Answers were not always clear-cut; in one case the husband had performed enumerated services required in villein tenure for some of his holdings. The jurors found that some of the land was held in villein tenure and some freely: CRR vol. 6, p. 192. Issues were apparently sometimes unclear enough that the

been a felon or an outlaw, whose land had escheated to the king.[24] And a third was that the widow was not a widow but a wife, that her husband was still alive. Crusades, pilgrimages, and the king's service overseas meant that men were gone from England for years at a time. How could one prove the death of a man who had simply not come back? In 1200 Maud, the wife of William de Wolseley, was able to produce two men who said they were with William when he died and was buried on the way of his pilgrimage to St James.[25] Not everyone could. A husband who disappeared within England must have been equally difficult to trace if he did not want to be found.[26]

Such allegations were exceptional. A widow was more likely to hear her opponent say that she could not have been endowed as she claimed because for one or another reason her husband was not seised in fee of the land she asked on the day when he married her. Perhaps the land was the inheritance or maritagium of her late husband's first wife which he had held only for life by curtesy and which should now descend to the first wife's heirs[27] – who might, of course, not be the husband's.[28] Or the husband had granted the land in maritagium with a daughter before marriage to his (second) wife; or he had sold it before he married, or had acquired it after the wedding.[29] In the early thirteenth century only land held at the time of the marriage was

---

parties reached agreement rather than litigating to a conclusion, as with a widow who gave up her claim to dower for 20 shillings: CRR vol. 1, p. 313.

[24] D. M. Stenton, ed., *The Earliest Lincolnshire Assize Rolls, 1202–1209*, Lincoln Record Society 22 (n.p., 1926), p. 89; also Frederick [sic] William Maitland, ed., *Three Rolls of the King's Court in the Reign of King Richard the First*, PRS 14 (London, 1891; repr. Vaduz, 1966), p. 43: widow of man convicted of the peace of the lord king was allowed to fine for the land but defaulted. See *Bracton*, fols 311–311B, iii, pp. 395–6 for the rule. A husband's confession and outlawry followed by his abjuring the realm had the same effect: CRR vol. 7, p. 244.

[25] George Wrottesley, ed., *Staffordshire Suits extracted from the Plea Rolls temp. Richard I and John*, William Salt Archaeological Society 3 (London, 1882), pp. 32, 66, and *RCR*, ii, p. 76. But even good witnesses could be challenged: Mabel, widow of Gilbert son of Gelin, produced sufficient witnesses present when Gilbert was killed by a tempest in the Irish Sea. Nonetheless her opponent insisted that Gilbert had been seen within the past fifteen days. He produced no witnesses and lost: CRR vol. 3, p. 302; CRR vol. 4, p. 27.

[26] As was the husband of Maud daughter of William; there was conflicting testimony and the entry ends with the order that sufficient witnesses be produced as to the death. No advice is given as to how: Wrottesley, *Staffordshire Suits*, p. 120.

[27] As in *Earliest Lincolnshire Assize Rolls*, pp. 42 and 74, and in CRR vol. 6, p. 163.

[28] And would not be if he were a woman's second husband and she had a son by the first. The issue could also arise with a second wife whose husband had a legitimate son when they married and another with her; her dower did not descend to her own son. See *Rotuli de Oblatis et Finibus*, p. 91, for an example.

[29] TNA:PRO Just 1/341, mem. 2 (1228); CRR vol. 5, p. 28.

subject to dower, unless there had been a special provision including later acquisitions and inheritance.[30]

Several procedural responses delayed an action but did not end it. The most usual was the response of the tenant – the defendant – that he needed a view, presumably because he held several tenements and needed to know which one was meant. Views were abused, asked only to postpone a decision, and later in the century statute limited their use;[31] but during the reign of John they were routinely granted. Another response was that the woman demandant had a (second) husband not named in the writ or not present in court; in the first case a new writ would be required – in effect the action would have to begin over – and in the second she would be told to produce him in court at the next term.[32]

More serious was the objection that the defendant was not the warrantor of the woman's dower and therefore he refused to answer; the widow would be told to produce her warrantor. But what if the warrantor was overseas? What if he was a son unheard of for so long that his mother did not know whether he was alive? What if he had betaken himself to religion? Or was a minor heir in custody of an uncooperative guardian? Or was a hostile adult stepchild?[33] The justices could offer help in summoning a guardian or hostile relative.[34] They could demand witnesses that a son had become a monk. They could tell a woman who did not know who had custody of her son to find out.[35] But in the case of the really untraceable warrantor, as when a son was overseas and his sister perhaps dead, they might effectively throw up their hands and pass the problem along to the king.[36]

One subset of dower was particularly subject to litigation. Dower *ex assensu patris*, by the assent of the (bridegroom's) father, involved the father granting his son – usually the heir – land with which to endow the bride. It

---

[30] *Bracton* fols 309–10, iii, pp. 390–2. When the dower was constituted, but not thereafter, a husband could specifically include future acquisitions: *Glanvill*, bk vi, c. 2, p. 59; *Bracton*, fols 92b–3, ii, pp. 265, 267–8; fol. 95B, ii, p. 275; CRR vol. 2, p. 137; CRR vol. 4, p. 67; CRR vol. 5, p. 28; CRR vol. 6, pp. 115, 338, 366.

[31] Statute of Westminster II (1285), c. 48, *Statutes of the Realm*, 11 vols (1810–1828) i, p. 95.

[32] E.g. *Abbreviatio Placitorum*, p. 37; and CRR vol. 2, p. 173; CRR vol. 4, p. 294; CRR, vol. 6, p. 221.

[33] Heir beyond seas: *SCP*, no. 156, p. 62; heir in custody: *RCR*, i, p. 360; CRR vol. 2, p. 172; hostile stepchild: CRR vol. 2, p. 289, and possibly CRR vol. 3, p. 239 ('ipsa dicit quod quedam filiastra sua Agnes debet esse warantus, quam non potest habere coram justiciariis sine auxilio curie'); heir became a monk: CRR vol. 6, p. 313; warrantor in Ireland: CRR vol. 7, p. 152.

[34] The writ for summoning an heir/warrantor is given in *Bracton*, fol. 298, iii, p. 361.

[35] CRR vol. 6, p. 257.

[36] CRR vol. 5, p. 179.

should have presented no problem, as the son would presumably otherwise have inherited the land after his father's death. But what if the son, young and childless, died before the father, and his bride was herself young enough that she might live another seventy years, bringing her dower to a second or even third husband and producing children who might attempt to claim the tenements at her death? Fathers did all they could to avoid assigning dower in these cases.[37] They swore that they had not been present at the wedding, as they had to be to make the grant; that the grant was not with their assent and will; that the amount granted differed from the claim. A father might well need the land given a dead son so a second son or a daughter, now the heir, could marry; the bride, after all, had her maritagium and could (and usually did) marry again. But that his bargain had turned out badly was not a defence. Fathers generally lost in cases of dower *ex assensu patris*, certainly when the father of the bride had prudently exacted a charter setting out the endowment.

Despite all the rhetoric, often dower looks like an elaborate and delicate dance within a family. It was an accepted institution, the custom of England; a fine from 1217 refers to it as such.[38] That the barons supported it is clear from the Charter. But that did not mean that a given heir, particularly one with no ties of affection to a given widow, necessarily thought he ought to give *that* amount or *that* tenement to *that* person.

There were protests that the tenement claimed was the chief messuage, which ordinarily was not to be granted as dower,[39] or that the lands claimed were more than a third, or that if the dower were granted there would not be enough left to do the king's service; the court could grant admeasurement to determine the value of the inheritance and of a third. Nor were either heirs or doweresses necessarily content with the bargain made years before; dower nominated then might be far less than a third now. Neither party was above trying to improve his or her position.[40] The result is hundreds

---

[37] As in *RCR*, i, p. 365; *CRR* vol. 2, p. 273; *CRR* vol. 3, p. 203; *CRR* vol. 4, pp. 25, 304, *CRR* vol. 5, pp. 142, 224, and 243; *CRR* vol. 6, pp. 84 and 247, 145, 281; *CRR* vol. 7, pp. 25, 99, 206, 319. In several of the suits, the defendant was the daughter or younger son (and now heir) of the late husband's father. In *CRR* vol. 3, p. 79 he was the lord who had held the husband in custody.

[38] TNA:PRO c 60/8, mem. 2, Fine Roll 1 Henry III, online at http://www.finerollshenry3.org.uk. This is part of the Fine Rolls Project headed by David Carpenter, Department of History, King's College, London, and David Crook, formerly of the National Archives.

[39] *Abbreviatio Placitorum*, p. 31; *CRR* vol. 3, p. 23; *CRR* vol. 7, pp. 41 and 48, 191. There might be an exchange, as when in 1202 a widow accepted four sellions for a moiety of the messuage: William Farrer, ed., *Final Concords for the County of Lancaster*, Part I, Record Society of Lancashire and Cheshire 39 (n.p., 1899), p. 14.

[40] *RCR*, i, p. 439; *CRR* vol. 1, p. 419; *CRR* vol. 2, p. 86; *CRR* vol. 5, pp. 206 and 274; *CRR* vol. 6, p. 123; Wrottesley, *Staffordshire Suits*, p. 72; *CRR* vol. 4, p. 304.

of entries in the plea rolls setting out the amount of dower claimed and the amount offered, and hundreds of feet of fines recording the compromise. Time after time, defendants objected that a widow was not endowed with the specific land she claimed but rather with a third of the land her husband had held at her wedding. Even more often in the early thirteenth century, the objection was the reverse: that the endowment was not of a third of that land as claimed but rather of a specific tenement.[41]

The compromises, often heralded in plea rolls with the note that the parties had licence to come to terms, should be relevant for determining the social context of dower; the terms are sometimes set out in plea roll entries themselves or more often in feet of fines. Frequently a widow remitted her claim for a sum of money or provisions. But in many cases it is almost impossible to judge the adequacy of the amount. Too many factors are involved: the value of the dower land, the terms on which it was held, and, above all, the bargaining position or relationship of the parties. A widow who quitclaimed her claim to a third of a vill and half a mark rent to her daughter and son-in-law for sixty marks silver was probably either getting adequate compensation or willingly making a gift.[42] Sometimes, however, the amount seems very small. Was the quitclaim essentially a gift? Did it represent only a fraction of the dower? Some entries simply say that a widow gives up all she has claimed. The likelihood is an out-of-court settlement whose terms cannot be reclaimed – riskier but probably cheaper than getting leave to agree and taking a cirograph. But some feet of fines and cartulary entries suggest that the bargain may have been neither a gift nor an arms-length transaction; status differential may offer a clue.[43] Sometimes dower was a widow's only bargaining chip, and she could not afford to lose everything by asking too much, as when Maud, the twice-married widow of King John's forest justice Hugh Wake, agreed to pay the king eighty marks within a year not to be forced to remarry. She raised half the sum by quitclaiming her dower to her son and heir, who was not Hugh's heir, in return for payment of the first forty marks.[44] Women under less

---

[41] As in the 1201 case between Richard and Eustachia de Kanvill and Nicholas de Verdun, in which each side produced multiple witnesses who claimed to have seen the endowment at the church door but whose testimony was completely at odds. The parties settled. Wrottesley, *Staffordshire Suits*, pp. 71, 73, 170 (summarizing the fine); CRR vol. 1, p. 260.

[42] Isabella, widow of Walter Waleran, CRR vol. 2, p. 109.

[43] The Beauchamp cartulary shows a number of women yielding dower claims with no compensation specified. Given the dominant position and acquisitive habits of several generations of Beauchamps, one suspects that the terms were not generous: Emma Mason, ed., *The Beauchamp Chartulary*, PRS 81 n.s. 43 (London, 1980).

[44] *Rotuli de Oblatis et Finibus*, p. 99.

pressure could drive a harder bargain, or their fathers or second husbands could,[45] accepting other land for that which they claimed or arranging for a steady income.[46] Sometimes they could even gain benefits for a second husband or other children, and it is here that family arrangements become most obvious. Alice, widow of Andrew de Bavent, having got dower from her stepson or older son, conceded it to his (younger) brother, her son, for her life – a transient benefit, but better than nothing.[47] Agnes, widow of John son of Sigar, asked Matthew son of John for dower of twenty acres; he was probably her stepson, because the compromise was that he conceded six acres to her and her late husband's children – presumably Matthew's half-brothers and sisters – for life and then to the children and their heirs to hold of Matthew for thirteen pence a year.[48] Robert and Agnes de Munegeden brought suit against a man who was probably her brother-in-law. He acknowledged her dower, she gave it to him for half a pound of pepper a year, and he acknowledged her sons by her late husband – presumably his nephews – as his heirs and agreed to support the older boy.[49] Dower had many uses.

An issue which came up intermittently was whether a woman, now deceased, had held land in dower or in maritagium. The answer was crucial; dower carried a life estate in the widow, maritagium was heritable. Second marriages of both men and women made the issue more common. It was fairly easy to know how one's mother acquired an interest in land. But in 1212, when the issue was whether a daughter had held land in maritagium or as dower in the time of King Henry, the answer was less certain.[50] When a woman was one's great-grandmother, the second wife of one's great-grandfather, it was murkier still.[51]

The common practice was for a father or brother – less often, a mother or uncle or grandfather – to grant specified land or rents at the time of a daughter's marriage.[52] Maritagium was a kind of hybrid: was it grant or

---

[45] There must arise a question about a widow's agency in instances where a father or new husband appears to have orchestrated the litigation.

[46] E.g. 5s. 4d. a year for life for remission of claim to dower in one-third of a mill, *Feet of Fines for Sussex*, p. 12; five shillings for life for dower claim: ibid. p. 15.

[47] Barbara Dodwell, ed., *Feet of Fines for the County of Norfolk for the Reign of King John, 1201–1215, for the County of Suffolk, 1199–1214* [hereafter *Feet of Fines for Norfolk … and Suffolk*], PRS 70 n.s. 32 (London, 1958; repr. Nendeln, 1977), p. 266.

[48] *Feet of Fines for Norfolk … and Suffolk*, p. 127.

[49] *Feet of Fines for Norfolk … and Suffolk*, p. 168.

[50] CRR vol. 6, p. 213.

[51] CRR vol. 6, p. 46.

[52] The rents could be quite varied; one included 12 pence and 2,000 eels: *Feet of Fines for Norfolk … and Suffolk*, p. 54.

inheritance? Women in the earlier thirteenth century saw it as their share of the family property.[53] Thus when three sisters asked for land and the tenant objected that a fourth was not named, they replied that she had land in maritagium and could not have more than her share of the inheritance. The sheriff was to ascertain if the land was held in maritagium 'of the inheritance of her father'.[54]

Given a society which practised male primogeniture, maritagium was a necessary development, if only to make that system acceptable. Maritagium could be granted to the prospective husband, or the couple jointly, or to the bride herself, but by the reign of King John it was generally a grant to the couple and the heirs of their bodies, or the heirs of the wife's body. Even where the land was given to the husband, it was understood that he held it in custody for the wife; the phrase appears in the plea rolls.[55] He could not alienate it without her consent, and when he died it remained hers, rather than his heir's. If a wife died childless and her husband remarried and had children, they were not to inherit; the maritagium was to revert to the giver. Because it was intended that the possibility of reversion exist for several generations, the donor did not take homage until the third heir entered, since one could not be both lord and heir. But husbands and wives in 1200 and thereafter interpreted the language to mean that if there was a living child resulting from the marriage, the land was theirs absolutely. They were free do with it as they chose, and both couples and widows did. In the early thirteenth century, the widow's maritagium was probably as close as a woman came to having land she could call her own. And as such it gave rise to litigation.

The majority of arguments did not spring up during the original donee's lifetime,[56] although a surprising number of brothers sued or even disseised their sisters after their father's death. Brothers complained that they had been disinherited by the size of the maritagium; or that the land had been given to a sister while the brother was in the grantor's wardship; or that the land had been the maritagium of their dead mother (presumably given by the father after her death, hence without her consent).[57] Or they simply

---

[53] *Feet of Fines for Norfolk … and Suffolk*, 114: maritagium as a sister's share.

[54] F. W. Maitland, ed., *Bracton's Note Book*, 3 vols (London, 1887; repr. Littleton, Colorado, 1963; Buffalo, 1998), iii, no. 1018, p. 56. See Milsom, 'Inheritance by Women', pp. 80–2 for a discussion of the point.

[55] As where husband was said to hold nothing 'nisi per custodiam' through his wife whose maritagium it is. *RCR*, i, p. 393; also *Bracton*, fol. 28b, ii, p. 96.

[56] See, for example, the 1208 action for warranty of charter brought by the son of the donee against the son of the donor, *Final Concords … Lancaster*, p. 26.

[57] CRR vol. 1, p. 87; CRR vol. 4, p. 207; CRR vol. 6, pp. 201 and 208; CRR vol. 2, 180; CRR vol. 3, pp. 85 and 277; CRR vol. 5, p. 92; CRR vol. 1, p. 330.

denied the grant altogether.[58] A prudent father took steps to prevent challenges by having his heir assent to the maritagium in writing, but in at least one instance that did not stop the heir's son from attacking the grant.[59]

In fact, a woman's maritagium was frequently used to provide a maritagium for *her* daughter, or dower for a younger son to give his bride and in this way it was an integral part of family arrangements. Sometime between 1180 and 1182 Thomas Basset granted his younger son a vill, the maritagia of Thomas's mother and his wife – presumably with their consent – and with his wife and other witnesses he watched as his heir took homage for it. Both his grant and the heir's acquiescence were recorded in charters.[60] The multiple successive marriages so common in medieval England also played a role, as when in 1205 a remarried widow came to terms with her son by her first husband, remitting her dower claim for his acquiescence in her grant of her maritagium to a younger son by the second husband.[61]

If dower was a bargaining chip, maritagium was a better one if only because it was given by charter. It was used in negotiations to settle lawsuits, end quarrels, and ally families. Arrangements could be intricate and dispassionate. Thomas and William, litigating about a half hide of land, agreed that it was William's right and William granted Thomas a virgate to give his sister in maritagium with William's son, both of them not yet of marriageable age. If one died, another of William's sons would marry another of Thomas's sisters; meanwhile, son and sister would be in William's wardship – with the maritagium.[62] Thirteenth-century landholders tried to cover all possibilities, but still, the circumstances for litigation were so many. Did a second husband have curtesy, a life interest, in his wife's maritagium? Yes, in the early thirteenth century.[63] What happened to maritagium in the case of a church-mandated divorce? The former wife kept it.[64] Could a widow quit-

---

[58] This must have been the position of the brother of Alicia, daughter of Elias de Amundeville, who asked a recognition of whether she had been seised of land given her *ad se maritand'* until her brother disseised her after their father's death: *Rotuli de Oblatis et Finibus*, p. 63.

[59] CRR vol. 2, p. 268.

[60] William T. Reedy, ed., *Basset Charters*, PRS 88 n.s. 50 (London, 1995), pp. 115, 118.

[61] *Feet of Fines for Norfolk … and Suffolk*, p. 214.

[62] Doris Mary Stenton, ed., *Pleas Before the King or his Justices 1198–1212*, vol. 3, Selden Society 83 (London, 1967), p. 151. See CP 25/1/203/3 no. 14 for a 1206 fine with similar arrangements: Feet of Fines abstracted by Katharine Hanna, at http://www.medievalgenealogy.org.uk/fines/abstracts/CP_25_1_203_3.shtml.

[63] CRR vol. 1, p. 330; CRR vol. 2, p. 309; CRR vol. 3, p. 161; CRR vol. 6, p. 333. It was specifically denied him by the Statute of Westminster II, c. 1.

[64] CRR vol. 5, p. 250; *Bracton* fol. 92B, ii, p. 267.

claim her maritagium while her heir was underage? Apparently so, judging from one case on the point.[65]

Litigants called on the memory of extended family genealogies and juries of lawful men of the neighbourhood and people who had stood at the church door on the wedding day and charters which were so often forged that without witnesses they were of little value. And when the king was present in this, it was most often in the background: the justices wished to speak with him about a difficult case, or he had sent a notice to them postponing or terminating an action to which he was not a party.[66]

Then what difference did Magna Carta make in the short run? For the years between the 1215 Charter and its 1225 reissue, that depends on the provision under consideration. I have not investigated the forced remarriage of widows, but Susanna Annesley, a student of David Carpenter at King's College, London, has done a paper on the subject, using the fine rolls as a source and has indeed found several entries in the years of Henry III's minority where widows appear to be pressured into remarrying; there are several well-known later ones.[67] Certainly records for the reign even as late as 1230 still show money owing on widows' fines not to remarry made during John's reign.[68]

As far as dower and maritagium, the pipe rolls suggest that the young king or those acting in his name went on pursuing payment of proffers for dower dating from his father's reign; the rolls for 3 Henry III and later frequently list the years in which many of them originated.[69] A 1218 entry under

---

[65] CRR vol. 6, p. 17.

[66] Occasionally he was more intrusive: he ordered the justices to give Richard de Beaumont [Bello Monte] the record and reasonable judgment in a matter concerning Rohesia de Beaumont's dower: CRR vol. 2, p. 94; he ordered Geoffrey fitz Peter to assign Agnes, widow of Gilbert de Walton, a third of the dower owed her (rather than all of it) from the land of a single tenant of the fee – she was recorded as being unwilling to contradict a mandate of the lord king and asked a writ against other tenants: CRR vol. 2, p. 279; a jury was in respite because he ordered one made up of six men from each of two counties: CRR 2, p. 298. More extraordinarily, he ordered the justices to inquire 'by sufficient proof' whether one Cristiana had been married to the man she claimed was her husband as she had come to the king prepared to prove the marriage: CRR vol. 4, pp. 2, 38. One entry says simply that a dower suit was not to be heard because the king did not want the plea to be held: CRR vol. 5, p. 72.

[67] Susanna Annesley, 'The Impact of Magna Carta on Widows: Evidence from the Fine Rolls, 1216–1225', the November, 2007 'Fine of the Month' on the Fine Roll Project website.

[68] E.g. the entries on Amabilia de Limesey in TNA:PRO E 372/70 rot. 6d (1225–6) and Chalfont Robinson, ed., *Pipe Roll 14 Henry III*, PRS 42 n.s. 4 (1927), p. 214 (1230).

[69] E.g. B. E. Harris, ed., *Pipe Roll 3 Henry III*, PRS 80 n.s. 42 (1976), p. 97, where

New Oblations shows a widow fining for both dower and inheritance,[70] but, as has been pointed out by a pipe roll editor, it is not always clear how new the new oblations were; the rolls for 2 and 3 Henry III include entries dating to John's last years.[71] Certainly the same names reappear from year to year; new ones do not appear and the number of entries dwindles. Magna Carta's strictures on dower were given at least lip service; a Fine Roll entry for 1225 orders that the land of Hugh Bigod be taken into the king's hand, assigning to his widow 'her reasonable dower belonging to her ... according to the law and custom of the realm of England.'[72]

There are at least two relevant pipe roll entries concerning maritagium. One dates from 1218, the roll of 2 Henry III. The heiress Sibilla de Wias [Ewias] rendered account for 800 marks not to be distrained to marry, to marry as she chose, and to have her maritagium and dower of Robert de Tregoz.[73] But Robert de Tregoz died before April, 1215 and a Fine Roll entry for 1218 on the matter refers to 'the money by which she made fine with King John'. In any event, the demand was respited 'until the lord king orders otherwise'.[74] The more significant entry on maritagium is under New Oblations in the roll for Michaelmas, 1224; the widow of Adam le Butillier accounted for five marks for seisin of a carucate of land, her maritagium.[75] But it was not a typical case; she had brought a writ of entry *cui in vita* against her late husband's lessee and the king had ordered an inquisition as to whether the land was indeed her maritagium.[76]

It is harder to know about the outcome if a dower suit ended in the relevant lord's court, where it was brought; there is generally no extant record. Rarely, reference to a sum paid elsewhere for dower appears in the Curia Regis Rolls when a case was transferred to the king's court. In 1221 William Marshall junior seems to have demanded thirty marks for her dower from the widow of Walter Daubernun,[77] and in 1218–19 Alice, widow of Roger

Alina, widow of William son of Walkelin, is shown to owe thirty marks and a palfrey for her dower 'sicut continetur in rotulo xvi R. J.'.

[70] *Pipe Roll 2 Henry III*, PRS 77 n.s. 39 (London, 1972), p. 89.

[71] The comment is in the introduction to *Pipe Roll 3 Henry III*, pp. xvi–xvii. The editor points out that new proffers recorded on the pipe roll for 2 Henry III arose from both the current year and the latter years of John's reign. Outside of Lancashire, 'fines made since the completion of the 1213–14 account were not enrolled in a pipe roll until (in most cases) 2 Henry III.'

[72] Charles Roberts, ed., *Excerpta e Rotulis Finium in Turri Londinensi asservati Henrico Tertio Rege* AD 1216–1272, 2 vols (Record Commission 1835–6), i, p. 125.

[73] *Pipe Roll 2 Henry III*, p. 93 (Herefordshire).

[74] *Excerpta e Rotulis Finium* i, p. 8.

[75] *Pipe Roll 8 Henry III* (Oxfordshire), PRS 92 n.s. 54 (London, 2005), p. 25.

[76] *Excerpta e Rotulis Finium*, i, p. 120.

[77] *Curia Regis Rolls of the Reign of Henry III, 5–6 Henry III (1221–1222)*, CRR vol. 10

[also called Radulph] de Laston, asked dower of a tenant who alleged that she had already sought it from her husband's heir and had given three marks to have it 'sine impedimento'.[78] Other instances probably lie hidden in the compromises recorded in feet of fines.

The Charter does not appear to have had an immediate effect on what lands were subject to dower. The language of the 1225 Charter clause 7 left room for uncertainty: 'Let there be assigned to her for her dower a third part of all the land of her husband which was his in his life, unless she was endowed of less at the church door.' No one suggested that meant all the land a man ever held, even before the marriage. There are plea roll and fine entries suggesting that some people, including those around the king, understood it to mean all the land held at a husband's death, although without referring to Magna Carta.[79] As it evolved, dower was based on all the land a husband held on the day he married or at any time thereafter, even if not at his death. But most people in the years right after the Charter behaved as if the old rule was not altered unless there was specific agreement to the contrary: the defining date was the day of the wedding. *Bracton* repeated it.[80] The wider scope later ascribed to the language of Magna Carta was not the common law rule during the minority of Henry III.

Nonetheless, the Charter seems to have encouraged a climate favourable to dower throughout most of the thirteenth century. The 1236 Provisions of Merton gave women damages for dower withheld and recovered in court when the lands had been in a husband's possession at his death.[81] The 1275 Statute of Westminster I widened the availability of the writ of dower *unde nihil habet*, which allowed a suit to go directly to the king's courts.[82] The 1285 Statute of Westminster II protected women against second husbands' collusion resulting in loss of dower and permitted suit against the purchaser to whom he had alienated it even though her warrantor was underage.[83] And by 1311, it had become the rule that women were entitled to a third of all lands a husband held at any time during the marriage – and the rule was

---

(London, 1949) p. 84.

[78] TNA: PRO Just 1/180 m.2.

[79] See *Excerpta e Rotulis Finium*, i, p. 86: '[lands] quas idem Wills de nobis tenuit in capite in ballias tua et unde seisitus fuit die qua obiit'. The issue is discussed in Janet Senderowitz Loengard, 'Rationabilis Dos: Magna Carta and the Widow's "Fair Share" in the Earlier Thirteenth Century', in Walker, *Wife and Widow in Medieval England*, pp. 59–80 at pp. 66–8.

[80] *Bracton*, fol. 92, ii, p. 265.

[81] Provisions of Merton, 20 Henry III, c. 1, *Statutes of the Realm* i, p. 1.

[82] Statute of Westminster I, 3 Edward I, c. 49, *Statutes of the Realm* i, p. 38. It could be used except when the widow had received part of her dower from that tenant in the same place before she purchased the writ.

[83] Statute of Westminster II, 13 Edward I, cc. 4, 40, *Statutes of the Realm* i, pp. 74, 91.

ascribed to Magna Carta.[84] Yet Paul Brand has posited that even in the second half of the thirteenth century, there was the thought that dower was to be earned, with the earning defined by a woman's being able to perform the sexual duties of a wife.[85] And in the next century the rise of the use undermined the institution; land held to use was not subject to dower, enabling a man to prevent lands being dowable by transferring them to trustees before his marriage or taking only an equitable interest in later acquisitions. Since nominated dower had virtually disappeared, a woman might receive little or nothing at her husband's death. The jointure – land provided by the husband or his family to be held by husband and wife or the survivor of them – was safer, if less generous, and became common. Two-thirds of the Year Book cases involving dower are from before 1350.

As for maritagium, much of Magna Carta's effect was indirect. The Charter provisions might almost be seen as an example of the law of unintended consequences. Couples were treating maritagia as theirs outright following the birth of issue, and widows, confident in their tenure, were selling maritagia or giving them to the church or daughters and younger sons. With no threat of forfeiture for refusal to remarry, a widow's grants were hard to control; she was dealing with her inheritance. Donors did not see it that way. They fretted over the loss of their reversions, with the resultant possibility of their gifts ending up in the hands of collateral relatives or strangers. Their objections did not prevail in the courts, but in 1285 the first chapter of the Statute of Westminster II provided that grants – any grants, although lands given in free marriage are specifically mentioned – to a husband and wife and their heirs begotten between them could not be alienated but must either descend as specified or revert to the grantor.[86] In other words, it created the fee tail.[87] *De Donis* refers to husbands and wives; widows are not specifically mentioned, but their independence surely contributed to the discomfort of the barons who were the movers behind the statute. In any event, the maritagium evolved into the marriage portion in money, paid by the bride's father to the bridegroom. It was a blow to the bride and potential widow's independence, because the money became the husband's absolutely, and if he died first, it went to his heirs, not to her. Magna Carta was not mentioned.

[84] Year Book Michaelmas 5 Edward II (London, 1679; repr. Clark, NJ, 2007), pl. 1.

[85] Brand, 'Earning and Forfeiting Dower', pp. 2–8. He also pointed out that the Statute of Westminster II c. 34 barred a woman who lived with her paramour from demanding dower of the (late) husband she had left, although the frequency of such demand cannot have been high.

[86] *De Donis Conditionalibus*, Statute of Westminster II, c. I, *Statutes of the Realm* i, p. 71.

[87] The most complete discussion of the maritagium is in Joseph Biancalana, *The Fee Tail and the Common Recovery in Medieval England, 1176–1502* (Cambridge, 2001).

The English Economy in the Era of Magna Carta

JAMES MASSCHAELE

INTERPRETATIONS of the English economy in the era of Magna Carta are currently in a state of flux. For a quarter-century, from the mid-1970s to the late 1990s, the field was dominated by the views of Paul Harvey, particularly those articulated in his 1973 article in *Past and Present*, entitled 'The English Inflation of 1180–1220'.[1] Harvey saw escalating wages and prices as inducing a major economic restructuring, one that tended to benefit lords more than other social groups, including the king. Barons successfully met the challenges of inflation by restructuring their landed estates to emphasize direct production of commodities. The Angevin kings, on the other hand, found themselves losing ground to inflation, without a corresponding ability to restructure their estates. They responded by exercising their regalian rights more aggressively, in an effort to compensate for diminishing incomes from land. This policy was bound to have major political consequences. To quote Harvey: 'No landmark in English constitutional history was more clearly brought about by economic change than Magna Carta.'[2]

Over the course of the past decade, however, Harvey's exposition has come in for sustained criticism. Recent work by Paul Latimer and J. L. Bolton, for example, directly confronts several of Harvey's core arguments about inflation and its influence in the early thirteenth century. In a pair of articles published in 1999 and 2001, Latimer argued that the inflation Harvey attributed to a forty-year period was actually compressed into the space of about five years, between 1199 and 1204.[3] In Latimer's view, the short and abrupt nature of the inflationary surge negates the kind of sweeping economic restructuring advocated by Harvey. Bolton has been an even harsher critic. Using Latimer's work on inflation as his point of departure, he constructed a completely different model for the period. In Bolton's view, King John's reign was defined by *deflation* rather than inflation, deflation

---

[1] P. D. A. Harvey, 'The English Inflation of 1180–1220', *Past and Present* 61 (1973), 3–30.

[2] Harvey, 'English Inflation', 14.

[3] Paul Latimer, 'Early Thirteenth-Century Prices', in Stephen D. Church, ed., *King John: New Interpretations* (Woodbridge, 1999), pp. 41–73; Latimer, 'The English Inflation of 1180–1220 Reconsidered', *Past and Present* 171 (2001), 3–29.

caused by the king's excessive taxation and monetary hoarding.[4] He characterized the era in rather gloomy terms. John's reign, Bolton wrote, encompassed 'difficult years for the English economy' in which most levels of society experienced 'some degree of hardship'.[5] Though perhaps not quite a new orthodoxy, the arguments of Latimer and Bolton have clearly gained currency. Richard Britnell, for example, touched on the matter in his 2004 survey of the medieval economy. He noted the influence Harvey's inflationary arguments once had, but stated that they were no longer tenable and could not explain the period's major developments.[6] Britnell stopped short of endorsing the model proposed by Bolton, however, and suggested that the late twelfth and early thirteenth centuries were characterized by mixed economic performance.

Much of the debate to date has centred on the money supply and the causes and consequences of price movements. This is not entirely surprising. For the first time in English history, the reigns of Richard and John provide data about the prices of a wide variety of goods that are reasonably continuous, commensurable, and coherent. The price data can also be correlated, to a limited extent, with direct and independent evidence about the circulating coinage. But while knowledge of price trends allows historians to measure some key economic relationships, it does not provide a particularly helpful overview of the state of the English economy at the time. It cannot really serve as a proxy for general trends or developments, nor does it allow a particularly good diagnosis of the economy's overall health. Even leaving aside the philosophical debate about how extensively monetary factors can shape a pre-modern economy, the evidence about price relationships and coinage is not rich enough to explain the broad sweep of economic activity in the period. It needs to be seen in conjunction with other non-monetary economic factors, which have been curiously understudied in earlier works on the period's economy. Particularly striking is how little the debate has been influenced by recent work in commercial history. The past two decades have produced a considerable body of scholarship about developments in English commercial life in the later twelfth and thirteenth centuries, developments that shed considerable light on the overall performance of the economy.[7] If King John's reign experienced exceptional monetary shocks

[4] J. L. Bolton, 'The English Economy in the Early Thirteenth Century', in Church, *King John: New Interpretations*, pp. 27–40.

[5] Bolton, 'English Economy in the Early Thirteenth Century', p. 30.

[6] Richard Britnell, *Britain and Ireland, 1050–1530: Economy and Society* (Oxford, 2004), esp. pp. 296–7.

[7] Ellen Wedemeyer Moore, *The Fairs of Medieval England: An Introductory Study* (Toronto, 1985); Maryanne Kowaleski, *Local Markets and Regional Trade in Medieval Exeter* (Cambridge, 1995); Richard H. Britnell and Bruce M. S. Campbell, eds, *A Commercialising Economy: England 1086 to c. 1300* (Manchester,

and price uncertainties, one would expect these to be reflected in declining, or at least stagnant, levels of commercial activity.

What one finds, however, is almost exactly the opposite. In the decades leading up to Magna Carta, England experienced a commercial boom accompanied by strong growth and rising prosperity: Magna Carta was promulgated in an era of sustained economic expansion, intimately connected to increasing trade and commerce. There may well have been short-term phases of difficulty or contraction within the rising general trend, but overall the period was defined far more by its opportunities than its difficulties. Substantiating this claim is the primary task of this paper, which seeks to reassess the significance of commercial development taking place in the later twelfth and early thirteenth centuries. Central to this approach is the charting of changes in commercial institutions within a relatively limited chronological framework, which allows for a more direct comparison between the economy and the concurrent history of politics and events. Evidence related to the substantial commercial changes that took place in the half century preceding Magna Carta can be found in many different places, three of which will come in for special scrutiny in the following pages: the founding of new towns and the acquisition of commercial privileges by established towns; the history of markets and fairs; and the history of transportation. In each of these areas, it is possible to find strong evidence for growth, and the synchronicity of their development is especially noteworthy. These three areas were more than merely incidental parts of the period's economic mix; they were leading elements of the period's changing economy. They drove an overall expansion in commercial activity, an expansion that makes sense only in the context of an economy that was being profoundly reoriented toward trade and exchange.

Before situating these three areas of economic growth within the context of the later twelfth and early thirteenth centuries, however, it will be helpful to understand where the period fits within longer-term trajectories of medieval economic development. From the time of Michael Postan, writing in the decades surrounding the Second World War, historians have seen the medieval economy as having two overarching cycles, one of growth and one of decline.[8] The growth cycle is usually said to begin somewhere

---

1995); R. H. Britnell, *The Commercialisation of English Society, 1100–1500*, 2nd edn (Manchester, 1996); James Masschaele, *Peasants, Merchants, and Markets: Inland Trade in Medieval England, 1150–1350* (New York, 1997); James A. Galloway, ed., *Trade, Urban Hinterlands and Market Integration, c. 1300–1600* (London, 2000); Samantha Letters et al., *Gazetteer of Markets and Fairs in England and Wales to 1516*, List and Index Society, Special Series 32 and 33 ([London], 2003).

[8] Postan's theory is most clearly stated in M. M. Postan, 'Medieval Agriculture in its Prime: England', in M. M. Postan, ed., *The Cambridge Economic History of Europe*, vol. 1: *The Agrarian Life of the Middle Ages*, 2nd edn (Cambridge, 1966),

in the eleventh century and end around 1300; the cycle of decline is seen as taking hold at that point and continuing through the remainder of the medieval period. The growth phase is frequently associated with two phenomena: rising levels of population and a great expansion of cereal cultivation. Advocates of this view, notably Postan, have suggested that the cycle of decline was closely linked to the cycle of growth. Population grew faster than food production, and the longer the growth cycle went on, the more difficult it was to sustain. Decline was virtually inevitable, as first dearth and then severe famine set in. The arrival of the Black Death in the middle of the fourteenth century finished what overpopulation had started a half century earlier, but with such savage ferocity that the economy was unable to return to a sound footing before the sixteenth century.

In the past fifty years, numerous historians have offered different explanations for the cycles first posited by Postan. Monetary historians have drawn a sharp contrast between the expanding coinage of the later-twelfth and thirteenth centuries and the so-called 'bullion famine' of the fourteenth and fifteenth centuries.[9] Political and military historians have contrasted the relative peace and stability of the twelfth and thirteenth centuries with the endless war and violence of the later medieval period, invoking such things as war taxation, piracy, and state interventionism to account for the downturn of the later period.[10] More recently, climate has come into vogue as an explanation for the two great medieval cycles.[11] It is widely accepted that the twelfth and thirteenth centuries were part of the relatively warm and benign climate of the so-called 'Medieval Warm Period', whereas the fourteenth and fifteenth centuries saw the onset of the so-called 'Little Ice

pp. 548–70; but see also M. M. Postan, *The Medieval Economy and Society* (Harmondsworth, 1975), ch. 4. A good overview of the literature on medieval economic cycles can be found in John Hatcher and Mark Bailey, *Modelling the Middle Ages: The History and Theory of England's Economic Development* (Oxford, 2001).

[9] Well summarized in Peter Spufford, *Money and its Use in Medieval Europe* (Cambridge, 1988).

[10] J. R. Maddicott, 'The English Peasantry and the Demands of the Crown, 1294–1341', in T. H. Aston, ed., *Landlords, Peasants and Politics in Medieval England* (Cambridge, 1987), pp. 285–359; W. M. Ormrod, 'The Crown and the English Economy, 1290–1348', in Bruce M. S. Campbell, ed., *Before the Black Death: Studies in the 'Crisis' of the Early Fourteenth Century* (Manchester, 1991), pp. 149–83; John H. A. Munro, 'The "New Institutional Economics" and the Changing Fortunes of Fairs in Medieval and Early Modern Europe: the Textile Trades, Warfare, and Transaction Costs', *Vierteljahrschrift für Sozial– und Wirtschaftsgeschichte* 88 (2001), 1–47.

[11] Mark Bailey, '*Per impetum maris*: Natural Disaster and Economic Decline in Eastern England, 1275–1350', in Campbell, *Before the Black Death*, pp. 184–208; William Chester Jordan, *The Great Famine: Northern Europe in the Early Fourteenth Century* (Princeton, 1996), pp. 16–19.

Age', characterized by longer winters, declining mean temperatures, and worst of all in England's case, excessive rainfall.

What is particularly significant about the considerable mass of scholarship that has accumulated over the last half century around the subject of longer-term trends is how much agreement there has been about situating the era of Magna Carta within a cycle of growth and prosperity. Most existing scholarship sees the early thirteenth century as part of a long phase of economic expansion, a period in which the ills of the later period had not yet taken hold. To date, however, works devoted to the growth phase have concentrated more on overall trends and tendencies than on chronological subdivisions. The failure to develop a more precise temporal framework for possible oscillations in the growth cycle has limited historians' ability to link economic changes to developments in other spheres, including the political sphere. The model of a slow but steady expansion stretching over a period of two or more centuries cannot be easily integrated with a history of events occupying much shorter spans of time.

On closer inspection, though, the premise of a long and steady period of growth has some major flaws, flaws that conceal the links between changes occurring in the economy and other forms of change. A model of steady, long-term growth stretching from the eleventh century through to the end of the thirteenth century can easily obscure strong oscillations of shorter duration. The global economy grew at an extraordinary rate in the twentieth century, for example, but the general trend does not negate the hardships and suffering many people endured in the 1930s. Medieval economic data are scarce enough prior to 1300 to make the identification of shorter-term cycles a difficult task, but it is possible to chart at least some of the terrain. This is indeed what both Paul Harvey and J. L. Bolton have sought to do, and their work encourages further probing of the fluctuations that characterized the economy of the twelfth and thirteenth centuries. Such probing suggests that the half-century prior to the issuing of Magna Carta was actually a period of central importance in the entire longer-term phase of growth. For it was in that era that a previously slow-moving economy went through a significant transformation, ushering in an expansion that generated growth at a pace unknown since the time of the Roman settlement, if even then. To understand the nature of this expansion, it is important to be clear about what came before it. Positing a phase of accelerated growth in the decades prior to Magna Carta does not necessarily mean that growth did not occur in earlier periods. Growth was indeed a hallmark of the eleventh century; and there is good reason to accept Christopher Dyer's recent contention that the origins of the long-term growth phase stretch back at least into the tenth century.[12] But it is not necessary to see growth from

---

[12] Christopher Dyer, *Making a Living in the Middle Ages: The People of Britain*

the tenth through the thirteenth century as a constant or uniform process. There were at least two discrete phases to the growth cycle, an early phase of modest growth, stretching from the tenth century well into the twelfth century, and a later phase of robust growth that began at some point in the second half of the twelfth century and continued for about a century. It is difficult to pin-point when this shift occurred, but faster growth had taken hold by the last quarter of the twelfth century and growth was still accelerating at the time of Magna Carta. Magna Carta thus falls in the middle of an exceptional period of overall expansion, an expansion that was fuelled to a great extent by a tremendous surge in commercial activity.

This surge can be seen most directly in the history of England's commercial institutions, including the fortunes of towns. Particularly telling is the enthusiasm for establishing new towns. Maurice Beresford's classic work, *New Towns of the Middle Ages*, provides a good overview of the chronology of medieval urban development, charting the peaks and valleys of urban foundation in England, Wales, and Gascony across the medieval centuries. According to Beresford's evidence, in the period from 1040 to 1400, the three most active decades for town foundation in England – unlike in Wales and Gascony – were the 1190s, the 1210s, and the 1220s.[13] Beresford noted that these decades saw an enthusiasm for founding towns that was 'never to be equalled again'.[14] More than a third of all of the new towns set up in England during Beresford's 360-year period can be dated to the half-century between 1180 and 1230. It is well known that Richard and John were keen to sell charters for new boroughs, but Beresford did not rely solely on charter evidence when creating his chronology, and he rightly pointed out that the two kings profited from selling charters mainly because founders saw new towns as good investments.

The surge in town foundation was part of a larger process of urban expansion in which long-established towns also shared. The growth of older towns is harder to document than the creation of new ones, but there are numerous indications that they too were prospering in the later twelfth and early thirteenth centuries. One measure of their fortunes is their eagerness to acquire toll exemptions, typically conveyed in royal charters granting freedom from tolls throughout the entire kingdom.[15] Some twenty towns

---

850–1520 (New Haven, 2002), pp. 17–26.

[13] Maurice Beresford, *New Towns of the Middle Ages: Town Plantation in England, Wales, and Gascony* (New York, 1967), p. 331.

[14] Beresford, *New Towns of the Middle Ages*, p. 336.

[15] On the development of tolls, see James Masschaele, 'Tolls and Trade in Medieval England', in Lawrin Armstrong, Ivana Elbl, and Martin M. Elbl, eds, *Money, Markets and Trade in Late Medieval Europe: Essays in Honour of John H. A. Munro* (Leiden, 2006), pp. 146–83.

acquired this valuable privilege in John's reign alone, including burgeoning ports like Ipswich, Yarmouth, and Lynn, shire towns like Cambridge and Gloucester, and a number of smaller but regionally important centres such as Barnstaple and Appleby.[16] Exemptions became increasingly valuable at this time because the proliferation of new commercial centres – including towns, markets, and fairs – meant that tolls could be collected at an ever increasing number of places. But the enthusiasm for acquiring exemptions was also related to the widening of trade horizons at the time, as regional and longer-distance trade became increasingly important to the fortunes of towns. The quest for toll exemptions by the town of Beverley is particularly instructive in this regard. Beverley gained borough status from the arch-bishop of York at some point in the 1120s and enjoyed considerable prosper-ity in the twelfth and thirteenth centuries.[17] The foundation charter stipu-lated that the privileges of the new town were to be modelled on those of York and specifically noted that it was to enjoy the same toll privileges as the county town, namely that the residents of Beverley would be free from toll throughout all of Yorkshire.[18] But in 1200 town leaders were no longer satisfied with the privileges that had been granted to their ancestors in 1120. They acquired a new charter of exemption from the king that gave them freedom from toll collectors throughout the entire kingdom. Beverley's bur-gesses had obviously extended the geographical range of their trade over the course of the twelfth century, but what is most remarkable about their situ-ation in 1200 is the fact that they were willing to pay the enormous sum of 500 marks to acquire the toll exemption.[19] Clearly times in Beverley were good as the thirteenth century dawned.

Another indication that towns were flourishing in John's reign is pro-vided by the history of borough farms. In the twelfth and thirteenth cen-turies, many boroughs acquired the right to make an annual payment, or farm, to the king in exchange for royal recognition of their rights to exercise local self-government.[20] It is far from clear how the king and the leaders of towns negotiated the amount at which their fee-farm was set, but the negotiations must have been based at least in part on the revenues the king was accustomed to collecting in each borough before granting the charter.[21]

16 Adolphus Ballard, ed., *British Borough Charters, 1042–1216* (Cambridge, 1913), pp. 180–1.

17 Arthur F. Leach, ed., *Beverley Town Documents*, Selden Society 14 (London, 1900), pp. xvii–xxii.

18 William Farrer, ed., *Early Yorkshire Charters*, 3 vols (Edinburgh, 1914–16), i, pp. 90–2.

19 Leach, *Beverley Town Documents*, p. xviii.

20 James Tait, *The Medieval English Borough* (Manchester, 1936), ch. 7.

21 Susan Reynolds, *An Introduction to the History of Medieval English Towns*

Once agreed, the farm tended to be left at the same level for long stretches of time, a fact that can be readily appreciated by the consistency with which farms are recorded in the pipe rolls. King John followed in the footsteps of his predecessors by agreeing to terms with a number of towns to pay a farm in exchange for rights to self-government, but his treatment of farms sheds some interesting light on the economic well-being of towns in his reign. First of all, he was able to negotiate relatively high farms, including an agreement with York in 1212 that set the farm at £160 and one with Droitwich in 1215 that prescribed an annual payment of £100.[22] That a secondary town like Droitwich could expect to generate revenues of £100 every year at the end of the reign is quite remarkable. Equally striking is that during the economic slump of the early fifteenth century, many towns clamoured for reductions in their fee farms because they could not sustain the high sums that their ancestors had agreed to pay in the more prosperous conditions of the later twelfth and early thirteenth centuries.[23] What had seemed manageable in the expanding economy of King John's reign seemed insupportable two centuries later.

Borough prosperity in the early thirteenth century is suggested not only by the relatively high fee-farms that were negotiated when new boroughs were chartered, but also by the willingness of a number of established boroughs to accept increments to the farms that had been negotiated at an earlier date. Higher payments can be documented for nine towns in John's reign, and an exhaustive search of the pipe rolls would probably turn up still others.[24] Some of the increments were modest: Derby agreed to pay an additional £10 in 1204 and Huntingdon agreed to the same increment a year later. But some were also quite substantial: Scarborough, for example, had its farm raised in 1201 from £43 to £76. In some cases, towns accepted increments relatively soon after they had negotiated their original farms. Thus, Shrewsbury's leaders agreed to pay an increment of five marks in 1205, even though their original farm of forty marks had been fixed only sixteen years earlier. Even more suggestive are the cases of Andover and Newcastle-on-Tyne, both of which agreed to pay a higher farm not just once but twice during King John's reign: Andover's fee-farm went from £80 to £95 in 1201 and then to £105 in 1204; Newcastle's from £50 to £60 in 1201 and then to £100 in 1213. King John also modified the financial terms of some

---

(Oxford, 1977), pp. 95–6.

[22]　Ballard, *British Borough Charters*, pp. 230–1.

[23]　Charles Phythian-Adams, 'Urban Decay in Late Medieval England', in Philip Abrams and E. A. Wrigley, eds, *Towns in Societies* (Cambridge, 1978), pp. 159–86; Lorraine Atreed, *The King's Towns: Identity and Survival in Late Medieval English Boroughs* (New York, 2001), pp. 144–9.

[24]　Ballard, *British Borough Charters*, pp. 220–32.

of the county farms and a royal policy of extracting or extorting resources whenever and wherever possible is a leitmotif of the reign.[25] The high inflation that characterized the early years of the reign also has some bearing on how burdensome these increments must have seemed to contemporaries. But even taking such conditioning factors into account, it is hard to escape the conclusion that towns could take on these increasing burdens because their revenue streams continued to grow throughout the reign. Subsequent English kings continued to extract the higher sums that had been imposed in John's reign, but they typically did not seek to add to them. The principle of respecting 'customary' payments was one of the central features of Magna Carta, and later kings were naturally reluctant to add increments that were sure to antagonize the defenders of custom. But even taking the changed political circumstances into account, it is still possible to suggest that the pattern of stable farms after John's reign was linked to changing economic circumstances. Towns continued to prosper for most of the century after Magna Carta, but they did not experience the same heady growth later in the thirteenth century as they had earlier on.

A similar pattern of commercial vibrancy in the later-twelfth and early-thirteenth centuries can be found in the history of two other pivotal commercial institutions, namely markets and fairs. In the case of markets, the period gave rise to a plethora of new foundations, many of which became integral parts of regional commercial networks in following centuries. Across the country as a whole, many score, perhaps even hundreds, of new markets were set up between the 1170s and the 1220s.[26] The precise chronology of foundation is difficult to reconstruct before the 1210s, but it is clear that there was keen interest in setting up new markets at the time. Indeed, requests for authorization were so plentiful that John felt compelled to formalize the procedure for granting the right to hold a new market. Rather than continue the haphazard licensing procedures used by his father and brother, he required his sheriffs to review proposals for new markets to determine whether they would damage existing markets by diverting trade.[27] New markets were allowed to operate only if they could be shown to augment local and regional trade. Another indication of the high demand for new franchises is the size of investment the founders of markets made to acquire and protect their rights. In 1204, for example, Reginald Turner agreed to pay twenty marks for the right to set up a market

[25] Brian E. Harris, 'King John and the Sheriff's Farms', *English Historical Review* 79 (1964), 532–42.

[26] For foundation dates of markets, see Letters, *Gazetteer of Markets and Fairs*.

[27] R. H. Britnell, 'King John's Early Grants of Markets and Fairs', *English Historical Review* 94 (1979), 90–6; James Masschaele, 'Market Rights in Thirteenth-Century England', *English Historical Review* 107 (1992), 78–89.

in Woodstock, while the Earl of Richmond paid even more for a new market in Kimbolton.[28] These high payments suggest that founders expected business in their new ventures to be brisk. Equally clear is the fact that markets established in this period enjoyed considerable success in the following decades and centuries. Indeed, what is distinctive about the period is not so much the absolute number of new markets as their quality and subsequent prominence. Enthusiasm for founding new markets continued apace through the thirteenth century, actually gaining steam in the third quarter of the century.[29] But if one examines the markets that were the most important in the commercial configurations of the thirteenth and later centuries, one finds a preponderance of early markets, those set up before about 1225.[30] These early markets generally had the best locations relative to existing transportation networks and they were also set up to operate on the days best suited for the weekly marketing cycles of their area. There were still lots of niches to be filled over the course of the thirteenth century, but the core system of markets that functioned in England right up to the time of the Industrial Revolution had come into being within about a decade of the issuing of Magna Carta.

The history of English fairs tells a similar story. The twelfth century has indeed often been described as the great age of the fairs, both in England and on the Continent. A few of the most successful English fairs – notably the fairs of St Giles in Winchester and St Ives in Huntingdonshire – were active trading venues already in the late eleventh or early twelfth centuries, perhaps even earlier. But the real heyday of English fairs is situated in the last decades of the twelfth and the first decades of the thirteenth century. To quote Ellen Wedemeyer Moore, who has written the standard account of the history of English fairs: 'The crucial period in the development of the international fairs [in England] seems to have been around the turn of the thirteenth century.'[31] We still lack detailed knowledge of the chronology of fair creation in the twelfth and early thirteenth centuries, particularly with respect to the many local and regional fairs operating by the middle of the thirteenth century. But at least a dozen new fairs opened for business in John's reign, in such places as Bridgwater, Marlborough, and Droitwich.[32]

---

[28] Doris M. Stenton, ed., *Pipe Roll 6 John*, PRS 56, n.s. 18 (London, 1940), pp. 8, 111 (assuming the standard Exchequer rate of five marks per palfrey).

[29] R. H. Britnell, 'The Proliferation of Markets in England, 1200–1349', *Economic History Review*, 2nd ser. 34:2 (1981), 209–21 at 210.

[30] James Masschaele, 'The Multiplicity of Medieval Markets Reconsidered', *Journal of Historical Geography* 20 (1994), 255–71.

[31] Moore, *Fairs of Medieval England*, p. 22.

[32] Ballard, *British Borough Charters*, pp. 172–5, supplemented by Letters, *Gazetteer of Markets and Fairs*.

These new foundations illustrate the ongoing commercial optimism that characterized the reign, even though none of them was destined to enjoy the success of venues like Boston and St Ives. They failed to reach similar heights because the cycle of established fairs was reaching maturity while they were getting off the ground. All of the fairs that would flourish in the thirteenth century, with the exception of Westminster, were operating by the time of Magna Carta. And not only were they in operation; by that time they had also coalesced into a regular cycle that was designed to facilitate the trade of international merchants travelling from one venue to the next, eager to buy English wool and cloth and sell imported wine and spices.

A few fairs provide quantitative evidence about the nature of the commercial economy in the decades before Magna Carta, in the form of statements of income generated. The pipe rolls record revenues yielded by Boston fair in a number of years between 1172 and 1212, whenever the honour of Richmond happened to be in the king's hands. Revenues fluctuated greatly from year to year, depending on the level of political turmoil, but the general trend was definitely up. At the start of the documented period, the fairs generated revenues in the vicinity of £70; by the end they were bringing in more than £100 per annum.[33] Similarly high figures are encountered for two other fairs in the period. St Giles fair brought in £146 to the bishop of Winchester in 1189 and St Ives brought in £180 to the abbot of Ramsey in 1212.[34] These figures are quite striking. Only a select group of barons could count on their estates to bring in revenue on a scale comparable to St Ives fair in 1212. Knights and lesser nobility had to content themselves with far less. Henry II's Assize of Arms of 1181, for example, suggests that a man with an annual income of £10 was on a par financially with the holder of an entire knight's fee.[35]

The strong commercial growth that lifted the fortunes of towns, markets, and fairs in the era of Magna Carta can also be associated with a series of improvements and innovations in transportation, particularly land transportation. Indeed, the expansion of commercial venues and the development of more efficient methods of delivering goods went hand in hand. Two major changes in land transportation have drawn special attention to date. The first is the transition from oxen to horses, explored by John Langdon.[36] According to Langdon, oxen were generally better suited than horses for ploughing and other farm-based agricultural work. They were stronger, easier to harness, cheaper to maintain, and could end their working days

---

[33] Moore, *Fairs of Medieval England*, pp. 15–16.

[34] Moore, *Fairs of Medieval England*, pp. 14, 18.

[35] Howden, ii, p. 261.

[36] John Langdon, *Horses, Oxen and Technological Innovation: The Use of Draught Animals in English Farming from 1066–1500* (Oxford, 1986).

in somebody's stewpot. Over the course of the twelfth and thirteenth centuries, however, they lost ground to horses, especially among the peasantry. Langdon associated the change with the broadening of commercial opportunity: oxen may have had better qualities on the farm, but horses were better suited to haul goods off the farm, because of their greater speed. As commercial opportunities increased, farmers continued to respond by replacing oxen with horses. By the end of the thirteenth century, horses had become the dominant agricultural animal in most parts of England.

Impressive development can also be found in the area of bridge construction and maintenance, according to David Harrison's recent study of English bridges.[37] Harrison found that the number of bridges in the country was increasing already in the eleventh century, but more importantly that a great boom in construction occurred in the twelfth and thirteenth centuries. Indeed, the boom was so extensive that relatively few new bridges were built after 1300. In its early stages, the building boom simply increased the number of bridges. By the early thirteenth century, however, the emphasis had begun to shift towards improvements in the quality of existing structures. Bridge builders began to make greater use of stone in their projects, and Harrison suggests that there was a conscious symmetry between the techniques introduced in the later twelfth century for the construction of gothic cathedrals and the techniques used to build the arches and piers of stone bridges.

A final aspect of changing transportation technology that merits attention is vehicle design, more specifically the design of carts and cartwheels. Carts were the general freight carriers of the English Middle Ages. They are ubiquitous in agrarian and commercial sources, but the implications of their construction and design have never been thoroughly investigated. Carting technology went through several major changes in the twelfth and thirteenth century, the most important of which involved the design and construction of wheels. Wheel quality is the primary determinant of a cart's speed as well as the primary determinant of its capacity. As the part most exposed to friction and wear, wheels were also the single most expensive component to maintain. As was true well into the twentieth century, they were constructed primarily out of wood in the Middle Ages, but at some point in the later twelfth or early thirteenth century, a new material was introduced into their construction, namely iron. Iron strengthened cartwheels in two key places – on the outside rolling surface and in the hub, where the wheel revolves around the axle. It was far too expensive to consider as a complete substitute for wood, but its expense could be justified to strengthen the critical parts of a wheel that were subjected to the greatest wear.

---

[37] David Harrison, *The Bridges of Medieval England* (Oxford, 2004).

Possibly the earliest reference to the use of metal cartwheels in England occurs in a pipe roll of 1204. In that year, the sheriff of Hampshire spent nearly £3 to purchase an iron cart (*caretta ferrata*) for royal use.[38] A few years later, a sheriff accounted for the purchase of two iron cartwheels (*pro duabus rotis carete ferratis*).[39] Similar expenses are sprinkled through the pipe rolls of the 1210s and 1220s. In an itemized statement of expenditures incurred to refurbish a cart in 1224, for example, a sheriff paid for a cart body (*caretilla*) and for nails used to attach old ironwork (*vetus ferramentum*) to the cart's wheels.[40] References to carts and carting are a commonplace of the early pipe rolls, including regular payments to have the king's possessions hauled around the country as the royal household moved from place to place. They seldom describe the type of cart used, but iron wheels were clearly in use on at least some royal carts in the first decades of the thirteenth century. By the middle of the thirteenth century, manorial documents show the presence of metal-wheeled carts on demesnes. An inventory from the manor of Wellingborough, Northamptonshire, for example, includes four iron carts among the manor's equipment in 1259.[41]

Precisely when metal wheels came into regular use is difficult to pinpoint. No physical survivals of carts or wheels from the period have yet been unearthed, nor are illustrations in manuscripts and other artwork detailed enough to shed light on cartwheel construction. But there is some evidence to suggest that the use of metal-clad wheels did not go back much before the early thirteenth century. There is, first of all, linguistic evidence. Medieval scribes had to invent a vocabulary to describe the pieces of metal that were affixed to different parts of a cartwheel. They came up with Latin words like *cluta*, *fretta*, and *straka*; the English equivalents are clouts, frets, and strakes, words that could be commonly heard in wheelwright shops for centuries thereafter. According to the standard dictionaries of medieval Latin based on British sources, all three of these specialized technical words are first attested in the thirteenth century.[42] There is also the fact that a German source of the early fourteenth century mentions that wheels with metal banding had fairly recently come into use in Germany.[43] Neither of

---

[38] *Pipe Roll 6 John*, p. 120. For a similar entry in 1225–6, see Fred A. Cazel, Jr., ed., *Roll of Divers Accounts for the Early Years of the Reign of King Henry III*, PRS 82, n.s. 44 (London, 1982), p. 4.

[39] Doris M. Stenton, ed., *Pipe Roll 13 John*, PRS 66, n.s. 28 (London, 1953), p. 178.

[40] Emilie Amt, ed., *Pipe Roll 8 Henry III*, PRS 112, n.s. 54 (London, 2005), p. 120.

[41] Frances M. Page, ed., *Wellingborough Manorial Accounts*, A. D. 1258–1323, Northamptonshire Record Society 8 (Kettering, Northants., 1936), p. 3.

[42] R. E. Latham and D. R. Howlett, eds, *Dictionary of Medieval Latin from British Sources* (London, 1975–), s. v. 'clutum' and 'fretta'; R. E. Latham, *Revised Medieval Latin Word-List From British and Irish Sources* (London, 1965), s. v. 'straca'.

[43] Hermann Aubin and Wolfgang Zorn, eds, *Handbuch der deutschen*

these pieces of evidence is definitive, but taken alongside the very concrete references in the pipe rolls, they certainly lend weight to the suggestion that metal cartwheels were an innovation of the later twelfth or early thirteenth century.

Innovations in carting were thus part of a series of changes in transportation that were under way in the era of Magna Carta. Experiments in vehicle design effectively complemented the growing use of horses in haulage and of stone in bridge construction. None of these changes was sudden or dramatic, but collectively they facilitated a faster and more efficient transportation system. Their confluence in the later twelfth and early thirteenth centuries suggests that transportation was becoming a more substantive part of the period's economic mix. And in this respect, the chronological overlap between improvements in transportation and the developments of towns, markets, and fairs is especially noteworthy. The material that cartwheels were made from began to matter in the early thirteenth century because new demands were being placed on them. People invested in expensive metal wheels because they wanted to haul heavier loads over longer distances. They also did so because the commodities in circulation were changing. Before the commercial developments of the later twelfth and early thirteenth centuries, most commerce involved high-value items that were relatively easy to transport, things like spices, silk, furs, and unusual foods like raisins and nuts. But from the later twelfth century, English commerce expanded and diversified. It began to revolve around bulky agricultural commodities, such as wheat and wool. It came to include a growing array of manufactured items, such as cloth and metalware. And it even began to cater to the tastes of moderately well off consumers who wanted to spend money on such things as Gascon wine and fresh sea fish.

The commercial expansion of the later twelfth and early thirteenth centuries, visible in such things as the growth of towns, the development of markets and fairs, and improvements in transportation, had major repercussions for the English economy as a whole. Indeed, the economy of the later twelfth and early thirteenth centuries can scarcely be understood without positing a vibrant commercial sector. Advances in commercial infrastructure are clearly relevant, for example, to the country's involvement in foreign trade. England's success on the international cloth market is first substantively documented in a Genoese notarial register of the 1190s, although the trade itself probably originated somewhat earlier.[44] The Flemish wool trade

---

Wirtschafts– und Sozialgeschichte, Bd. 1. *Von der Frühzeit bis zum Ende des 18. Jahrhunderts* (Stuttgart, 1971), pp. 209–11.

[44] R. L. Reynolds, 'The Market for Northern Textiles in Genoa, 1179–1200', *Revue belge de philologie et d'histoire* 8 (1929), 495–533; H. Krueger, 'The Genoese Exportation of Northern Cloths to Mediterranean Ports, Twelfth Century', *Revue belge de philologie et d'histoire* 65 (1987), 722–50.

was also flourishing in the era of Magna Carta. The early development of that trade has been hotly debated, but Paul Harvey's argument for substantial expansion in the later twelfth century still makes a good deal of sense.[45] T. O. Lloyd and J. L. Bolton have both drawn attention to the fact that the wool trade was sufficiently large by the later twelfth century to make it a primary target for diplomatic wrangling between rulers in England, France, and Flanders, as it also was for John when dealing with the wavering loyalty of Flemish towns in 1208.[46] It is also worth noting that Richard and John both targeted international trade for systematic taxation. Our knowledge of the customs system at this time is based mainly on a pipe roll account of 1203–4, which, as Edward Miller and John Hatcher have noted, documents a foreign trade with an annual value equal to that of all landed estates recorded in the Domesday Book.[47] But the account of 1203–4 does not mark the beginning of systematic royal taxation of trade; according to John Gillingham, King Richard set up the first customs system at some point in the early 1190s.[48]

Substantial commercial growth in the later twelfth and early thirteenth centuries also helps to make sense of the period's agrarian development. Michael Postan's argument that manorial estates moved away from leasing and toward direct production in this period still has much to commend it.[49] Paul Harvey portrayed the advent of direct production as an attempt by lords to keep inflation at bay, but Postan's original formulation that it was a response to growing commercial opportunity actually makes much more sense. It is true that the transition to market production was not as universal as scholars once thought, but it was nonetheless still widespread. In the context of agrarian development, it is also worth noting that a market in land began to emerge at about this same time; indeed, by the time of Magna Carta, a functioning land market can be found even at the level of the peasantry.[50]

---

45 Harvey, 'English Inflation', 27.

46 T. H. Lloyd, *The English Wool Trade in the Middle Ages* (Cambridge, 1977), pp. 6–7; Bolton, 'English Economy in the Early Thirteenth Century', p. 36.

47 *Pipe Roll 6 John*, p. 218. The document is also printed in N. S. B. Gras, *The Early English Customs System* (Cambridge, MA, 1918), pp. 221–2. The analysis of its import by Edward Miller and John Hatcher can be found in *Medieval England: Towns, Commerce, and Crafts* (London, 1995), pp. 195–6.

48 John Gillingham, *Richard I* (New Haven, 1999), p. 277.

49 The argument is made most forcibly in Postan's essay 'The Chronology of Labour Services', in his *Essays on Medieval Agriculture and General Problems of the Medieval Economy* (Cambridge, 1973), pp. 89–106.

50 Paul Hyams, 'The Origins of a Peasant Land Market in England', *Economic History Review*, 2nd ser. 23 (1970), 18–31; P. D. A. Harvey, 'Introduction', in *The Peasant Land Market in Medieval England* (Oxford, 1984), pp. 21–2; Phillipp R.

Fluctuations in the money supply may well have served as a drag on growth in John's reign, as Bolton and Latimer have argued.[51] It is certainly true that John, like his father and brother, repeatedly drew on the kingdom's silver supply to finance his military expenditures, and that he did so on a large enough scale to hamper commercial development. But somehow silver kept making its way back into circulation, seemingly in ever larger amounts. The kingdom was able to finance Richard's Crusade in the early 1190s and ship 100,000 marks out of the country for his ransom in 1193–4, apparently without notable economic consequences.[52] Indeed, the drain of silver continued through the rest of Richard's reign as he fought to protect his lands in France. The chronicler Roger Howden states that extravagant quantities of silver left England again in 1196.[53] And yet England had more than twice as much silver currency in circulation in 1205 as it had had in 1180, according to the best recent estimates.[54] Where was all this silver coming from? How did the country constantly manage to replenish the supplies sent abroad for political purposes? As Nick Barratt has shown, political expenditures reached extraordinary levels in the 1210s, but the experiences of the 1190s should at least make us cautious when considering how state intervention affected the money supply between 1205 and 1215.[55]

One of the major virtues of positing a prospering economy in the early thirteenth century is that it helps to explain the connection between the economy and politics that one finds in Magna Carta. It is worth remembering that commercial matters did have a place in the document: Clause 13 of the 1215 version ensured London and other towns the right to enjoy their privileges and customs; clause 35 called for the use of a standard measure for wine, ale, cereals, and cloth; and clause 41 guaranteed the security and property of merchants and promised to end unwarranted tolls. Several other clauses dealt less directly with commercial interests but had commercial implications: Clause 23 dealt with obligations to build bridges; clause 30 forbade the commandeering of horses and carts by royal officers; clause 33 mandated the removal of fish weirs from the Thames, Medway, and other

Schofield, *Peasant and Community in Medieval England 1200–1500* (New York, 2003), pp. 54–6.

[51] Latimer, 'Early Thirteenth-Century Prices'; Latimer, 'English Inflation of 1180–1220 Reconsidered'; Bolton, 'English Economy in the Early Thirteenth Century'.

[52] For details of the financing of both, see Gillingham, *Richard I*, pp. 114–16, 238–48.

[53] *Howden*, iv, p. 13, cited in Bolton, 'English Economy in the Early Thirteenth Century', p. 33.

[54] Bolton, 'English Economy in the Early Thirteenth Century', p. 31; Martin Allen, 'The Volume of the English Currency, 1158–1470', *Economic History Review*, 2nd ser. 54 (2001), 607.

[55] Nick Barratt, 'The Revenues of John and Philip Augustus Revisited', in Church, *King John: New Interpretations*, pp. 75–99.

rivers, presumably to facilitate navigation. These clauses indicate that commercial interests had developed to the point that they could now be treated as general matters of concern rather than as matters of purely local interest.

Magna Carta is, however, first and foremost a political document, and connections between the economy and the revolt against King John are neither easy nor straightforward. The economic growth and especially the economic reorientation that characterized the era must have given growing currency to the issue of how the spoils associated with growth would be divided. It was not, however, a simple matter of winners and losers. The growth had far more winners than losers; the old adage that a rising tide lifts all ships is very nearly true of the English economy in the era of Magna Carta. But it is just possible that the tide lifted the king's ship faster and higher than it did anyone else's. Lords certainly derived benefits from the rising tide. They were well placed to engage in market production and they were very often the recipients of the rents and revenues derived from the period's new commercial venues. But kings probably benefited even more from growth and change. They generally succeeded in drawing commercial life into the orbit of royal interest. By the end of John's reign, for example, every new market or fair set up in the kingdom had to be authorized by a royal grant, and its owner had to pay a fee to the king.[56] This had not been true in his father's reign. Royal authority intersected with a wide range of commercial developments, from the rights and privileges of towns through the imposition of tolls and taxes to the provision of silver coins. Richard and John knew opportunity when they saw it, and in their reigns economic opportunity increasingly revolved around commercial activity.

Acquisitiveness defined their treatment of commerce as much as it did their treatment of widows and heirs. In the final analysis, their political power was closely associated with their ability to tap into national wealth. As that wealth went up, their power followed. This did not make a baronial revolt inevitable, but the growing discrepancy between royal access to the new wealth and everyone else's access must have been obvious to many people, and in that sense may have fuelled the resentments that led the barons to confront the king at Runnymede.

---

[56] Britnell, 'King John's Early Grants', 90–6.

The Complaint of King John against William de Briouze (*c.* September 1210)

The Black Book of the Exchequer Text

DAVID CROUCH

IN THE IMMEDIATE AFTERMATH of William de Briouze's flight to France in 1210, King John dictated this document in council to establish his side of the case in his actions against Briouze. Such documents (*querimoniae*) are not common in medieval society, but there are some other famous examples. One of the earliest is the recital *c.* 940 AD by King Æthelstan of England of the troubled relationship between himself and his murderous brother Alfred. The original was once to be seen at Malmesbury Abbey, and was copied there around 1126 by the abbey's historian, William, but is now lost. More famous is the 'Conventum' published by Hugh le Brun of Lusignan against his overlord, Count William of Poitiers, around 1030.[1] *Querimoniae* are always important documents as they give remarkable insights into medieval motivation and world view.

Naturally King John's version of the Briouze affair puts the king in a good light. From the opening address it seems it was intended to be published widely throughout England to counter any suggestion that the king had acted unjustly in his persecution of William. The fact that it was published at all indicates that the king expected criticism from the political community and wanted to head it off. The copy we have here was entered in one of the Exchequer registers in the later thirteenth century from an earlier copy which seems to have been damaged, in that the copyist believed that the opening initial was 'H' though the document could only have been issued by John. The draft has to have been drawn up not long after the king's return from his successful Irish campaign at the end of August 1210. Its last datable event is John's court at Bristol, where he was September 1210. It was clearly also drawn up before the tragic deaths of members of the Briouze family in Windsor Castle (to which they were transferred from Bristol) before the end of the year, and its most likely time of issue was in the immediate aftermath of the flight to France of William de Briouze and

---

[1] Roger A. B. Mynors, Michael Winterbottom, and Rodney M. Thomson, ed. and trans., *Gesta Regum Anglorum*, 2 vols (Oxford, 1998–9) i, pp. 221–2; George Beech, Yves Chauvin, and Georges Pon, eds, *Le Conventum (vers 1030): un précurseur aquitainien des premières épopées* (Geneva, 1995), pp. 123–53.

the imprisonment of his wife and many of his family. The document has been discussed several times by historians of John's reign, though not up till now offered in a critical edition.[2] The text taken as the basis is that in the Black Book of the Exchequer (National Archives E 164/12), the version used to date by historians.

❰ Text

Abbreviations are extended in parentheses. Capitalization has been modernized. Medieval punctuation has been retained, with a comma used to signify a punctus elevatus.

> B = Kew, TNA:PRO, E 164/12 (Little Black Book of the Exchequer), fols 82r–83r, bifoliate (s. xiii[fin])
> C = Oxford, Bodleian Library, MS Dugdale 31, fols 82r–83r, from B (s. xvii[med.]).
> D = Oxford, Bodleian Library, MS Rawlinson c. 434, unfoliated, from C (s. xvii[fin.]).

> Printed, *Liber Niger Scaccarii*, i, pp. 377–85 (from D); Rymer, *Fœdera*, i, pt I, pp. 52–3 (from B).

B

[J.][3] dei gratia rex Angl(ie) dominus Hybern(ie) dux Norm(annie) et Aquit(annie) comes Andeg(auie). vniuersis hoc presens scriptum inspecturis. salutem. Vt uniuersitati uestre notum fiat qua de causa et quo forisfacto Will(elmu)s de Braosa de terra nostra recesserit, sciatis quod idem Will(elmu)s debuit nobis in ultimo recessu nostro de Norm(annia). quinque millia marcarum argenti pro terra nostra Mononie in Hibernia quam ei dimiseramus. nec infra quinquennium aliquid nobis inde reddidit. Et cum multos inde terminos cepisset, nullum terminum tenuit. Et preterea debuit nobis firmam ciuitatis nostre de Limeric de quinquennio tunc preterito. et de toto predicto debito nichil nobis reddidit. preter .c. libras quas nobis accomodauerat apud Rotomag[um]. unde nos postea rogauit quod illas ei computatemus in firma de Limeric. et id ei concessimus. De debito autem quod nobis debuit pro Momonia, termini ei fuerant assignati. sed omnes preteriit. et de plurimis terminis quos inde postulauerat, nullum tenuit. Post quinquennium autem completum. secundum consuetudinem

---

[2] The earliest dedicated treatment is in Kate Norgate, *John Lackland* (London, 1902), pp. 287–8. The most extensive discussion to date remains Sidney Painter, *The Reign of King John* (Baltimore, 1949), pp. 242–5. A partial translation is in H. S. Sweetman, *Calendar of Documents relating to Ireland, 1171–1251* (London, 1875), pp. 65–6.

[3] The document opens with the initial H.

regni nostri. et per legem scaccarii nostri consideratum fuit quod distringeretur per catalla sua Angl(ie) ad debita nostra nobis soluenda. Sed ipse omnia catalla sua ita summouerat, quod inueniri non potuer[un]t. Et mandauimus balliuo nostro de partibus Wallie Gerard(o) de Athiis. ut ipsum distringeret per catalla sua Wallie propter eadem debita. Et tunc uenit ad nos Matill(dis) de Haia uxor sua. et W(illelmus) comes de Ferar(iis). nepos suus. et Adam de Port(u). qui sororem suam habuit in uxorem. et multi alii amici sui apud Glouorn(iam). et rogauerunt nos ut predictus [*col. b*] Will(elmu)s ad nos uenire posset ad loquendum nobiscum et nobis satisfaciendum de debitis nostris et de terminis preteritis. et id eis concessimus. Et interea accessimus Heref(ordiam). et ibi uenit ad nos predictus .W. et tradidit nobis tria castra sua Wallie. scilicet Haiam. Brechenn'. et Radenour' in tenanciam reddendi nobis predicta debita nostra. et satisfaciendi nobis de transgressione sua infra terminum quem ad petitionem suam ei posuimus. et insuper totam terram Angl(ie) et Wallie nobis in plegio posuit. incurrendam nisi terminum illum seruaret. et hoc modo ea recepimus. Et preterea ipse nobis liberauit in obsides Will(elm)i de Braosa junioris. et vnum filium Reginald(i) de Braosa. et .iiii^{or}. filios hominum suorum. Sed nec propter hoc terminum illum magis quam terminos predictos obseruare curauit. Post modicum uero temporis cum Gerardus de Athiis cui castra commiseramus illa mandasset constabulariis eorum quod uenirent ad pacationes suas recipiendas que eis fieri solebant de mense in mensem. predictus Will(elmu)s audiens quod constabularii illi absentes fuerunt, ipse et Will(elmu)s iunior et Reginaldus filii sui collegerunt magnam multitudinem gentis. et inuaserunt tria predicta castra et omnia una die obsederunt. Sed cum ibi proficere non possent, diuerterunt ad quandam villam. scilicet Limenistre que cella est abbatie de Rading' de libera elemosina nostra. et medietatem ville illius combusserunt. Et de balistariis et seruientibus nostris ibi inuentis. et de alia gente nostra quosdam interfecerunt. et quosdam uulnauerunt. Gerardus uero de Athiis hoc audiens adunauit de gente nostra quot potuit. ut subueniret partibus illis quas illa inuaserant. Will(elmu)s uero de loco ad locum se retrahens, fugit in Hyberniam [*fol. 82v*] cum predictis filiis suis. et cum uxore sua et cum familiis eorum. et ibi a comite Will(elm)o marescallo. et Walt(er)o de Laci. et Hug(one) de Laci fuit receptus. et contra nos receptatus. Et nos eis mandauimus quod de sicut ipsi homines nostri ligii fuerunt. in fide qua nobis tenebantur non receptarent inimicos nostros qui nobis forisfecerant. et propter forisfactum suum terram nostram Angl(ie) reliquerant. sed nichil propter hoc mandatum nostrum inde fecerunt. Mandauerunt inde nobis quod manuceperunt pro eodem Will(elm)o quod ueniret ad nos infra certum terminum quem in litteris suis nominauerunt. ad satisfaciendum nobis de predictis excessibus suis. et quod nisi infra terminum illum hoc faceret, ipsi eum decetero non receptarent. nec in societate sua haberent.

sed de Hybernia eiecerent. et hoc concessimus. sed nec illi nec ille terminum illum uel promissum suum seruauerunt. Nos igitur tot et tantos omnium illorum excessus amplius sustinere non potuimus. et exercitum adunauimus ad eundem in Hybern(iam). et dum preparauimus iter nostrum idem Will(elmu)s uenit ad balliuos nostros Hyb(ernie). et petiit ab eis conductum ut ad nos uenire posset ad querendum pacem nostram et assenserunt balliui nostri. et sacramentum ab eo ceperunt quod nulla parte diuerteret. sed recto tramite ad nos iret. Sed cum uenisset in Walliam dimissa in Hybern(iam) familia sua, nos non respex(it). sed attraxit ad se quos potuit de inimicis. et nobis malum querere cepit quod potuit. Et interim uenissemus usque Penbroc cum exercitu nostro super mare Hybern(icum) accessit ad nos Will(elmu)s de Ferr(ariis) nepos eius. et rogauit nos ut liceret ei ire ad ipsum Will(elmu)m ad inquirendum animum eius. et hoc ei concessimus. et misimus cum illo unum militem de domo nostra scilicet Rob(ertum) de Burgate. et ipsi reuertentes [*col. b*] rogauerunt nos ut idem Will(elmus) propius posset accedere ad loquendum nobiscum per internuncios. et hoc eis concessimus. Et cum uenisset usque ad aquam de Penbroc. optulit nobis per internuncios quadraginta milia marcarum pro habenda pace et beniuolentia nostra. et pro omnibus debitis suis predictis et castris suis et terris Angl(ie). et Wallie. et nos ei respondimus quod bene nouimus quod non erat omnino in potestate sua. sed magis in potestate uxoris sue que fuit in Hybern(iam). et manduimus ei quod ituri fuimus in Hybern(ia). et quod ueniret nobiscum in saluo conductu nostro usque in Hybern(iam). ad loquendum cum uxore sua et amicis suis de fine quem optulit. et ad firmandum ibi conuentiones que inde optulit. et ad firmandum ibi conuentiones que inde inter nos fierent. et si ibi inter nos conuenire non posset, ipsum ad eundem locum in Walliam saluo remitteremus in eodem statu quo tunc fuit. Ipse autem hoc facere refutauit. et remansit in Wallia. Et postquam transfretauimus in Hibern(iam), ipse nobis malum fecit quod potuit. et vnum molendinum. et tres bordellos combussit. Interea Matill(dis) de Haia audiens aduentum nostrum in Hibern(iam). fugit uersus Scotiam. cum Will(elm)o et Regin(aldo) filiis suis. et cum priuata familia sua per mare in societate Hugon(is) de Laci qui similiter propter aduentum nostrum fugerat. Et cum essemus apud Cracfergus. capto iam castro illo. mandauit nobis quidam amicus et consanguineus noster de Galweia. scilicet. Dunecanus de Karric. quod ceperat predictam Matill(dim). et filiam suam uxorem filii Rog(er)i de Mortemer. et predictum Will(elmu)m iuniorem. et uxorem suam. et duos filios suos. Sed Hugo de Laci. et Regin(aldus) de Braosa euaserant. Et misimus propter eos Joh(ann)em de Curci et Godefr(idum) de Craucumb cum balistariis et ser[*fol. 83r*]-uientibus et duabus galiis. Qui cum adducti essent ad nos ipsa Matill(dis) cepit loqui de fine faciendo nobiscum. et optulit nobis .xl. milia marcarum. pro uita et menbris uiri sui. et suis et suorum. Ita quod uir suus

omnia castra sua et totam terram suam nobis quietam clamaret. Et sic
conuenit tunc inter nos. Post triduum uero penituit illam finis illius. et
dixit quod finem illum tenere non potuit. Post hec cum recederemus de
Cracfergus reuersuri in Anglia, duximus illam et suos nobiscum sub
custodia. et ipsa iterim optulit nobis .xl. milia marcarum. et insuper decem
milia marcarum. quia a prima conuentione resilierat. et assensimus hoc
pacto. quod quociens ipsa a conuentione illa resiliret, decem milia marcarum
argenti fini suo adderet. pacanda in prima pacatione sua. Et hec conuentio
scripta fuit inter nos et ipsam et suos. et sacramento et sigillis eorum. et
sigillis comitum et baronum nostrorum qui aderant confirmata. et termini
pacationum in scripto illo fuerunt assignati. Et ipsa cum suis prenominatis
sub custodia teneri debuit. donec uniuersum debitum predictum nobis
esset persolutum. Preter hec quod predictus Will(elmu)s statim post
transfretationem nostram in Hybern(iam), inceperat male facere. et terram
nostram comburere ut predictum est. Vic(ecomes) Heref(ordie) in cuius
ballia hoc fecerat, demandari fecit eum in comitatu suo tanquam
malefactorem. Et cum vtlagari deberet secundum consuetudinem Angl(ie),
nos propter finem quem predicta Matill(dis) nobiscum fecerat mandauimus
eidem vicecomiti quod hoc differet donec in Angl(iam) ueniremus. Post
reuersionem uero nostram in Angl(iam) cum ipsa .M. et sui essent apud
Bristoll' in custodia. petiit quod licenciam daremus uiro suo ueniendi ad
ipsam [*col. b*] et loquendi cum ea priuatim. et concessimus ei. Et post hec
uenit ad nos idem Wil(elmu)s. et concessit finem illum quem uxor sua
nobiscum fecerat. et promisit se paratum esse libenter ad soluendum. Et
cum ire deberet ad perquirendam pecuniam illam, liberauimus ei ad
petitionem suam. vnum seruientem G(alfridi) filii Petri iustic(iarii) nostri.
qui cum eo esset et ipsum conduceret ne forte alicubi impediretur eo quod
tociens demandatus fuerat ad comitatus tanquam malefactor. Et cum dies
prime pacationis aduenisset, misimus ad predictam .M. G(alfridum) filium
Petri iustic(iarium) nostrum. et comitem Saresb(u)r(ie). fratrem nostrum.
et .S. comitem Winton(ie). et alios de magnatibus nostris. ut sciremus quid
super hoc esset factura. Et illa precise respondit quod nichil nobis solueret.
et quod non habuit plus pecunie ad finem illum. nisi .xxiiij. marcas argenti.
et .xxiiij. solidos bisantiorum. et .xv. uncias auri. Et sic nec tunc nec postea.
nec uir suus. nec ipsa. nec aliquis pro illis aliquid nobis inde soluit. Cum
igitur audissemus quod predictus Will(elmu)s ita recesserat de terra nostra.
et quod nichil nobis de pecunia nostra solueret, precepimus quod
consideratio regni nostri de eo fieret. et sic de comitatu in comitatum
demandatus et non comparens, tandem secundum legem et consuetudinem
Angl(ie) est vtlagatus. Vt igitur de ueritate huius rei certiores efficiamini,
nos et comites. et barones nostri subscripti. sigilla nostra huic scripto
apposuimus. et testimonium ueritatis. scilicet W. comes Saresb(u)r(ie). G.
filius Petri comes Essex'. S. comes Wint(onie) R. comes de Clara. comes

Alb(e)r(ici). H. comes Heref(ordie). W. comes de Ferr(ariis). Rob(ertus) filius Walt(eri). Will(elmus) Brewer'. Hug(o) de Neuill'. Will(elmus) de Albenn'. Adam de Port(u). Hug(o) de Gurnac(o). Will(elmus) de Moubray.

❡ Translation

[John] by the grace of God king of England, lord of Ireland, duke of Normandy and Aquitaine and count of Anjou, to all who may one day read this letter, greetings. Let it be known to all of you, what was the reason and what was the offence that led William de Briouze to flee from my realm. Be aware that William entered into debt to me for five thousand marks at the time I last left Normandy[4] on account of the territory of Munster in Ireland, which I released to him. He failed to pay me anything of the sum he owed over the next five years, and though there were several deadlines set, he met none of them.

In addition he owed me the rent for my city of Limerick for the same five years, but again he paid me nothing for it, except that he had lent me a hundred pounds one time at Rouen, and afterwards he asked me to set it against the rents of Limerick, which I did.[5] Terms for payment were set for the Munster debt, but he passed them by and he kept to none of the many deadlines which he had suggested for payment.

At the end of those five years[6] it was decided that, according to the custom of England and the law of the Exchequer, he should have his possessions in England seized for non-payment and I should recover my money. But William had concealed his possessions in such a way that none could

---

[4] John abandoned Normandy on 5 December 1203, taking ship at Barfleur: T. D. Hardy, 'Itinerarium Johannis regis Angliae e rotulis in turri Londinensi', *Archaeologia* 22 (1829), 124–60 at 137.

[5] The grant of Munster and Limerick occurred before August 1202: *Rot. Litt. Pat.*, p. 16. In 1206 Briouze owed £2,865 6s. 8d. for Limerick: *Pipe Roll 7 John*, PRS 57 n.s. 19 (1941), p. 107.

[6] The first direct action against Briouze seems to have come in March 1208, when he was directed to surrender a son to Walter de Lacy, lord of Meath, as hostage for his behaviour, which he duly did: *Rot. Litt. Pat.*, p. 80. Roger of Wendover believed that the crisis was precipitated by Briouze's wife's outspoken refusal to surrender her sons to John's officers because the king 'had shamefully killed his nephew Arthur, whom he should have imprisoned honourably', but this is unlikely: *Wendover*, ii, 49.

be found.[7] So then I instructed my bailiff in Wales, Gerard d'Athée,[8] to seize his possessions there to pay the debt off.[9]

After that Mathilda of Hay,[10] William's wife, William earl of Ferrers,[11] his nephew, Adam du Port,[12] who had married his sister, and many other friends of his, came to me at Gloucester[13] and asked me to let William come and talk over the payment of his debts and the failure to meet the deadlines. I agreed to this with them.

So I moved on to Hereford,[14] where William met me and surrendered

---

[7] It has been suggested that William (III) de Briouze the elder had resigned many of his lordships to his son William (IV) by this date with the king's permission, for which some evidence was to be found in the lost annals of Neath Abbey: F. R. Lewis, 'A History of the Lordship of Gower from the Missing Cartulary of Neath Abbey', *Bulletin of the Board of Celtic Studies* 11 (1937–9), 151, as suggested in I. W. Rowlands, 'William de Braose and the Lordship of Brecon', *Bulletin of the Board of Celtic Studies* 30 (1982–3), 127, and developed in B. Holden, 'King John, the Braoses and the Celtic Fringe, 1207–16', *Albion* 33 (2001), 11–15. This might account for the difficulty in finding Briouze's goods.

[8] Gerard d'Athée (Athée-sur-Cher, dep. Indre-et-Loire), one of John's Tourangeau followers, made sheriff of Gloucester on 5 January 1208, following the disgrace of William Marshal in the spring of 1207; for his origins, see Nicholas Vincent, *Peter des Roches: An Alien in English Politics, 1205–38* (Cambridge, 1996), p. 27 and note.

[9] Gerard was leading troops into the March of Wales on 18 April 1208: *Rot. Litt. Pat.*, p. 81; *Rot. Litt. Claus.* i, pp. 112–13. King John met the Briouzes on 22 April 1208 at Gloucester (see below) presumably after the expedition failed to locate the Briouze treasure.

[10] Mathilda, daughter of Bernard de St Valéry, called here Mathilda of Hay, perhaps from her customary residence at the Briouze castle there. In her husband's charter to Brecon Priory she appears as *domina Matildis de sancto Walerico uxor mea*: R. W. Banks, ed., 'Cartularium prioratus sancti Johannis evangeliste de Brecon', *Archaeologia Cambrensis*, 4th ser. 14 (1883), 155–6. The Béthune clerk extols her prudence and enterprise, 'She was a fair lady, very wise and accomplished and particularly energetic. She was never absent from any of her husband's councils. She carried on warfare against the Welsh in which she conquered a good deal': *Histoire des ducs*, p. 111.

[11] William de Ferrers II, earl of Derby († 1247), who was the son of Earl William I († 1190) and Sybil, sister of William de Briouze (III): G. F. Cokayne and others, eds, *The Complete Peerage of England, Scotland, Ireland, Great Britain and the United Kingdom*, 14 vols in 15, rev. edn (London, 1910–19), iv, pp. 193–4.

[12] Adam du Port († 1213), son of John du Port, lord of Basing, Hampshire, married the widowed Sybil, countess of Derby. He had a cousin and namesake, Adam II du Port, son of Roger de Port, lord of Mapledurwell, Hampshire, and Kington, Herefordshire, who was called Adam du Port 'of Wales' to distinguish the pair.

[13] John issued acts from Gloucester on 22–3 April 1208.

[14] John moved on from Gloucester to Hereford, 24–8 April, and on 29 April 1208 was at Tewkesbury, where he fined William de Briouze 1,000 marks for the expenses 'which we incurred on our expedition into Wales on your account': *Rot. Litt. Pat.*, p. 81.

three of his Welsh castles (Hay, Brecon and Radnor) as security that he would pay me what he owed, and make some satisfaction for his failure to meet the deadlines which I had set for him, at his own request. Besides this, William put up all his lands in England and Wales as his security to me unless he met the next deadline.[15] These were the terms on which I took them. As well as this, he handed as hostages for William de Briouze the younger,[16] both a son of Reginald de Briouze[17] and four sons of his retainers. But he did not bother to meet that deadline any more than he had met the others.

A little while later, when Gerard d'Athée (to whom I had entrusted the castles) summoned their constables to come to get their salaries, which he used to give them monthly, William (hearing that the constables were not there) with his sons William and Reginald gathered a large force of men and put all three castles under siege for a day. But since they could get no immediate result, they moved on to the town of Leominster, which is a priory of Reading Abbey under my patronage.[18] They burned down half the town, and when they encountered my crossbowmen and serjeants in the town, they killed some of them and others of my people, and wounded more.[19]

When Gerard d'Athée heard this, he gathered what he could of my supporters to reinforce those areas which the Briouzes had attacked. But William, retreating from one place to the next, fled to Ireland with his sons,

[15] The Annals of Worcester confirm that Briouze handed over five castles, hostages, and a thousand marks after King John's first expedition against him: *Annales de Wigornia* in *Annales Monastici*, iv, p. 396.

[16] William de Briouze (IV), son of William (III), who had married Mathilda, daughter of Earl Richard de Clare of Hertford.

[17] Reginald de Briouze had married Graecia, daughter of William Brewer, a prominent courtier and friend of King John.

[18] The *parrochia* of Leominster was granted to the royal foundation of Reading Abbey in 1123: B. Kemp, ed., *Reading Abbey Cartularies*, 2 vols, Camden Society, 4th ser. 31, 33 (1986–7), i, pp. 287–8.

[19] The Worcester annals mention a second expedition against Briouze after the first: *Annales Monastici*, iv, p. 396. Presumably the outbreak could not have happened until some time after Gerard d'Athée was made sheriff of Hereford, which was on 23 May 1208: *Rot. Litt. Pat.*, p. 83. The attack on the three castles and Leominster had been made by 29 September 1208, when Briouze's tenants gave pledges that they would not return to their allegiance to him: *Rot. Litt. Pat.*, p. 86. Other accounts insinuate that the king precipitated the crisis by moving troops against Briouze: *Wendover*, ii, 149; T. Jones, '"Cronica de Wallia" and other documents from Exeter Cathedral Library MS 3514', *Bulletin of the Board of Celtic Studies* 12 (1946), 33. The Marshal biography however implies that Briouze was the aggressor, though provoked by the king's relentless hostility, and explained his retreat to Ireland as a consequence of his tenants' refusal to back him: *HWM*, ii, lines 14157–64.

wife and household, and was sheltered there by Earl William Marshal, Walter de Lacy and Hugh de Lacy, despite my actions.[20] I sent to them to say that as they were my sworn men, by the faith which they had sworn to me, they had no business sheltering my enemies, who were at my mercy and had run from England as a result. But they completely ignored my message. But they did send to say that they had taken security for William de Briouze that he would come to me within a certain period of time which they set out in their letter, so as to satisfy me over his violent outbreaks, and if he did not do it within that period then they would shelter him no longer nor would they be seen with him, but throw him out of Ireland. I went along with this, but neither he nor they kept to the deadline or the promise.

I really could not put up with those people's outbreaks – so many and of such a nature – and I summoned an army to deal with him in Ireland.[21] While I was getting ready to cross over, William de Briouze sent to my officers in Ireland and asked for a safe conduct to come to me to solicit my peace. My officers agreed and took an oath from him that he would make no side trips but come direct to me. Yet when he got to Herefordshire, having left his household knights behind him in Ireland, he took no heed of me. He gathered together many of my enemies as he could and attempted to do as much damage to me as he was able.

In the meantime, when I and my army had marched to the shores of the Irish Sea at Pembroke, Earl William de Ferrers, Briouze's nephew, arrived and asked my permission to go to William to see what he had to say. I agreed to this and sent along with him one of my own household knights, namely Robert of Burgate.[22] On their return, they asked me that William might be allowed to move closer to me to negotiate with me through intermediaries. I allowed this.

When Briouze came to the coast at Pembroke he offered me 40,000 marks by intermediaries, to have my peace and goodwill over all his debts, castles and lands, in England and Wales. I told him that I knew very well that this was beyond his capacity, but more within that of his wife who

---

[20] This is confirmed by *HWM*, ii, lines 14166–87, saying that he survived a storm and put in at Wicklow, where Earl William Marshal was in residence. It also says that the crossing happened in winter (*li tens … ivernaiges*), which would imply Briouze held on in Wales till at least the end of October 1208.

[21] The Irish expedition assembled and camped at Cross, near William Marshal's castle of Pembroke between 3–16 June 1210: Thomas Duffus Hardy, ed., *Rotuli de Liberate ac de Misis et Praestitis* (Record Commission, 1844), pp. 172–8.

[22] A known knight of King John, of Burgate (Suffolk) who appears in his service from around 1204: Stephen D. Church, *The Household Knights of King John* (Cambridge, 1999), pp. 33–4. He was to marry Graecia, daughter of John's close friend William Brewer, after her divorce from Reginald de Briouze, younger son of William (III) during the crisis of 1208–10.

was in Ireland. I told him that I was going to go to Ireland and that he could come with me there with my safe conduct to speak with his wife and friends about the fine he had offered and finalize agreements there between us. If he did not want to accompany me there, he could go back safely to his Welsh refuge in the state he was then. He rejected the suggestion and stayed in Wales. After I crossed over to Ireland, he did what harm to me that he could, and burned down a mill and three houses.[23] In the meantime Mathilda de Hay, hearing I was in Ireland, fled on to Scotland by sea with her sons William and Reginald and their household, in the company of Hugh de Lacy, who had likewise run for it when I appeared.

When I was at Carrickfergus, after capturing the castle,[24] our friend and cousin of Galloway, namely Duncan of Carrick,[25] sent to tell me that he had arrested Mathilda and her daughter, the wife of Roger de Mortemer,[26] the younger William de Briouze and his wife, and their two sons, but that Hugh de Lacy and Reginald de Briouze had escaped. I sent John de Courcy[27] and Godfrey of Crowcombe[28] with crossbowmen, serjeants and two boats on

---

[23] William's period of outlawry in Wales seems pitifully unsuccessful by this account, but that he was there in alliance with the Welsh is evident from *Annales de Wigornia*, p. 399.

[24] The siege of Carrickfergus occurred 19–28 July 1210.

[25] Duncan son of Gilbert, lord of Carrick († 1250), second cousin of Roland, lord of Galloway († 1200): *Complete Peerage* ii, 55. Duncan was the grandson of Fergus of Galloway, who married an illegitimate daughter of Henry I of England, so Duncan and King John were second cousins. Duncan was known to John personally from his time as a hostage at Henry II's court in the late 1170s and 1180s, and there is some indication of his involvement in Ulster before these events. Alan, son of Roland of Galloway, was in fact with King John's army in Ireland in 1210: *Rotuli de Liberate ac de Misis et Praestitis*, p. 186; and Duncan received considerable lands in Ulster from the king following the capture of Mathilda: *Rot. Litt. Claus.*, i, p. 402. For the Galloway family and its ambitions, see G. Barrow, *Kingship and Unity: Scotland, 1000–1306* (London, 1981), pp. 113–15; R. A. McDonald, 'Rebels without a Cause? The Relations of Fergus of Galloway and Somerland of Argyll with the Scottish Kings, 1153–1164', in E. J. Cowan and R. A. McDonald, eds, *Alba: Celtic Scotland in the Medieval Era* (East Linton, 2000), pp. 170–84; R. Oram, *The Lordship of Galloway* (Edinburgh, 2000), esp. pp. 100–17 (for Duncan of Carrick).

[26] A mistake for Hugh III de Mortemer of Wigmore, Herefordshire († 1227) who married Annora, daughter of William (III) de Briouze. She survived captivity in Windsor.

[27] Probably the John de Courcy whom Hugh de Lacy had ousted from Ulster in 1207. John was brother of William III de Courcy, lord of Stogursey, Somerset. For his origins, see Seán Duffy, 'The First Ulster Plantation: John de Courcy and the men of Cumbria', in Terence B. Barry, Robin Frame and Katharine Simms, eds, *Colony and Frontier in Medieval Ireland* (London, 1995), pp. 4–5.

[28] Crowcombe, Somerset. Godfrey was in the king's household from around 1205: Church, *Household Knights of King John*, pp. 32–3.

their account. When they were brought to me, Mathilda began to negotiate the making of a fine with me, and offered me 40,000 marks for her husband's life and limbs, for her own and those of her family. Her husband was to surrender all his castles and land to me, and this was what we agreed. But after three days she changed her mind, and said she could not agree to the fine.

After this, when I had moved on from Carrickfergus to go back to England, I took Mathilda and her people with me as prisoners, and she offered me once again 40,000 marks and a further 10,000 more to reactivate the original agreement. I agreed to this, that should she wish to reactivate the agreement, she should pay an additional 10,000 marks, payable with her first down payment.[29] The agreement between me, Mathilda and her family, was written down and confirmed by our oaths and seals, and the seals of my earls and barons who were there present. The deadlines for payments were fixed in the agreement and she, with her family, had to stay in custody until every bit of the debt had been paid me.

Besides this, since William – as soon as I had crossed to Ireland – began to attack and burn across my lands, as I said before, the sheriff of Hereford, in whose province he had done it, had him proclaimed a public enemy in the shire court. But since he would be outlawed, as the law of England demanded, I wrote to the sheriff to tell him to hold back on it until I returned to England, because of the agreement that I had with Mathilda.

After I had returned to England, with Mathilda and her family being under arrest in Bristol,[30] she asked my permission to go to her husband and talk to him privately. I agreed. Afterwards, William came to me and agreed to the fine which his wife had negotiated with me and stated that he would willingly pay it. Since he had to go to raise the money, I assigned him, at his request, a servant of my justiciar, Geoffrey fitz Peter, who would accompany and escort him, not to prevent his going any place, but because he had been denounced so often in the shire court as a public enemy. But when the day of the first payment was approaching, William gave his escort the slip and secretly fled my land of England.[31] He paid me nothing of my money.

On the day of the first payment, I sent to Mathilda Geoffrey fitz Peter my justiciar, my brother the earl of Salisbury, Saher, earl of Winchester, and others of my magnates to tell her what had happened. She told me curtly

---

[29] The sum of 50,000 marks owed by the Briouzes is also mentioned by *Annales de Margan* in *Annales Monastici*, i, p. 30.

[30] The king landed at Fishguard on 26 August 1210, and was at Bristol by 1 September: *Wendover*, ii, p. 57.

[31] William would die near Paris in 1211.

that she would pay me nothing and she had no more money to pay towards the fine than twenty-four marks of silver, twenty-four gold coins and fifteen ounces of gold. So neither then nor subsequently did she, her husband, or anyone else on their behalf, pay me anything of the debt.

When I had heard that William de Briouze had left my realm in this way, paying me nothing, I ordered that there should be a national enquiry about him. So in his absence he was outlawed from shire to shire according to the laws and custom of England.

So that there should be an authoritative statement of the truth of all this, I and my earls and barons whose names are appended have set our seals to this document as witness to the truth, namely:

William, earl of Salisbury, my brother
Geoffrey fitz Peter, earl of Essex
Saher, earl of Winchester
Richard, earl of Clare
Earl Aubrey (of Oxford)
Henry, earl of Hereford
William, earl of Ferrers

Robert fitz Walter
William Brewer
Hugh de Nevill
William d'Aubigné
Adam du Port
Hugh de Gournay and
William de Mowbray, and others

Index

Modern names are inverted – surname, forename;
medieval names are shown with forename first.

Printed and bound by CPI Group (UK) Ltd, Croydon, CR0 4YY

13/04/2025

14656516-0004